United Road, Take Me Home

A Manchester United Collection, 1997-2003

Tony Smith

Printed in Victoria, Canada

Contact the author: red.devil@virgin.net
Contact Red News: www.rednews.co.uk

Cover design by Paul Windridge
Cover photographs by Paul Windridge and Tony Smith

National Library of Canada Cataloguing in Publication Data

Smith, Tony, 1958-
    United road : take me home / Tony Smith.
Includes bibliographical references.
ISBN 1-4120-0700-3
    I. Title.
GV943.6.M3S54 2003   796.334'63'0942733   C2003-904058-5

TRAFFORD

This book was published *on-demand* in cooperation with Trafford Publishing.
On-demand publishing is a unique process and service of making a book available for retail sale to the public taking advantage of on-demand manufacturing and Internet marketing. **On-demand publishing** includes promotions, retail sales, manufacturing, order fulfilment, accounting and collecting royalties on behalf of the author.

Suite 6E, 2333 Government St., Victoria, B.C. V8T 4P4, CANADA

Phone	250-383-6864	Toll-free	1-888-232-4444 (Canada & US)
Fax	250-383-6804	E-mail	sales@trafford.com
Web site	www.trafford.com	TRAFFORD PUBLISHING IS A DIVISION OF TRAFFORD HOLDINGS LTD.	
Trafford Catalogue #03-1070		www.trafford.com/robots/03-1070.html	

10   9   8   7   6   5   4   3   2   1

Contents

Foreword 3
The Bearded One 5
Standing Up for the Champions 8
Dennis Viollet – One of the Best, One of Our Own 11
From the Red Corner: A View of the Blue 13
The Game of the Name 17
Past and Pleasant? 20
Feeling the Benefit 24
Lack of Hunger? A Review of the 1997/98 League Campaign 28
Becks, Oh-La-La! 33
If the Cap Fits 36
The Passing Game 39
Riches from Rags 42
The Greatest Dane 45
Musings from the North Stand 48
The Cup Overflows 50
Neville With A Cause 52
Team Changes 56
Leagues Apart: A Review of the 1998/99 League Campaign 59
Barcelona 1999 – The Time of Our Lives 62
Denis the King – Part 1 67
Denis the King – Part 2 72
The Govan-or 76
Wheel of Fortune 80
Stand Up for the Champions' League 83
Worldly Matters 86
Public Image plc 89
Painting the World Red 93
Just Champions: A Review of 1999/2000 96
Resting Assured 99
Style and the Council Pitches 102
Recalling Scarlet Ribbons in the Merry Month of May 105
The Luck of the Draw 110
Jingle Bells 113
Yankee Doodles 116
Teams that Matter, Games that Don't 120
Three in a Row – Enjoy: A Review of 2000/2001 123
The Gaffer, the Wizard 127
Days of Awe? 132
The Super-Coach 135
Nobody Does It Better 138
Keep the Red Flag Flying High 141
Goals for Life 145
Banana Kicks and Scary Beards 148
Eric and the Universe – Discuss 151

On Our Toes – A Review of 2001/2002 154
Who Do You Support? 158
Time Wasting 161
Siege Mentality.. 164
A Hero – And Some Villains.. 167
Fergie for England... 171
After Being Famous 174
On Juventus and Socks 177
Red Barrels and Chianti Reds... 180
Rising from the Dead: A Review of 2002/2003 183
United Road, Take Me Home.. 187

Foreword

United Road, take me home
To the place where I belong
To Old Trafford
To see United
Take me home, United Road

- Terrace Song

Manchester United began the 1997/1998 season as English champions, having enjoyed sustained success throughout the 1990s. A frustrating season was to follow, but the best was yet to come.

Red News was the first Manchester United fanzine, having started up during the dark days of 1987, and it happened to be my favourite. For some reason that is now obscure, I contributed my first article to *Red News* in September 1997, and for reasons even more unclear it concerned a footballer that most United fans had spent years trying to forget. The article was intended as a one-off, but somehow I ended up contributing to each and every *Red News* in the following six seasons. This book is a compilation of most of those articles.

My own ups and downs as a United fan go back to the glories of the mid-1960s. I have walked down United Road many hundreds of times. In a metaphorical sense it's been a lifelong journey.

These articles reflect the highs and lows of a remarkable period through the eyes of a very ordinary fan. Never losing sight of United's great but often turbulent history, this is my view from the North Stand.

Tony Smith
Manchester, June 2003

The Bearded One

September 1997. New signing Teddy Sheringham was trying to make an impression in place of the recently retired legend, Eric Cantona. Although Sheringham would leave Old Trafford four years later having earned his own special place in United's history, his early struggles brought to mind a player who never overcame a tricky start.

Teddy Sheringham's settling in period was another opportunity for the critics to apply pressure onto a new United striker, while some of the less thoughtful United 'supporters' had begun to get on his back just three and a half games into his United career. The old chestnut about Old Trafford being a strikers' graveyard was heard again, and you began to realise that these people were actually wanting Sheringham to struggle in order to justify their own pontifications.

The fact that Sheringham once played for Nottingham Forest enabled the know-alls to point to the relative failures of Garry Birtles and Peter Davenport to fulfil their potential as United forwards – presumably Keano's midfield position negates the effect of the Forest-factor?

Hearing again the perennial references to Garry Birtles in particular, I began to recall the bearded-one's spell at Old Trafford, and was startled to realise that it is fifteen years since he returned to Forest after his two year sojourn at Old Trafford. Fifteen years. This means that nobody much under the age of 28 will be able to recall his career with real accuracy.

Of those who do remember, I suspect that very few would have a decent word to say about Birtles. Maybe they're right, at least about his United spell, though he went on to have a long and respectable career without hitting the heights that earned him his million pound chance to wear the United shirt. But that tells only half the story, because he was a great hope when he came, and most of us hung in there with him as he battled to make his mark. I'd say that he left with no hard feelings at the end. In other words, we mostly stood by him as the United-haters revelled in his travails – much as we did with Andy Cole as critics sharpened their knives.

Were you at Stoke when Birtles made his debut? It was October 1980, a Wednesday night, and the chant 'One Garry Birtles ... ' was sung loud and long. If he'd tucked away a chance to go round the keeper his whole career might have been different, but the games passed by and our expectations turned to hopes, until we began to hope against hope. He scored at Brighton in an FA Cup replay in January 1981, but it proved to be a false dawn. In the end we longed for him to score a league goal because we shared his embarrassment. I recall that April 1981 saw us play Crystal Palace in a game won through a rare Mike Duxbury goal, but not before Birtles had a goal disallowed for an offside against a colleague; Old Trafford had heaved with relief, but the referee had ice in his heart, and ruled out the goal. The season ended with Birtles still goalless and the music hall comedians in seventh-heaven. Then Atkinson replaced Sexton as manager, and Joe Jordan was replaced by Frank Stapleton as Birtles' partner up front.

In the pre-season build-up, United held an 'Open Day' at Old Trafford. It was pretty dull fare and featured a mock training session during which the first team practised one-on-one situations against the goalkeeper. Poor Garry was even under pressure in this context, and several thousand hearts were in mouths fearing that he would still be unable to hit the net at Old Trafford. Whether goalkeeper Gary Bailey was feeling generous, I do not know, but Birtles tucked away his meaningless shot and we all felt pleased for him. That's how bad it had become, and how much we wanted his fortune to change.

The agony was not to end until September 1981, eleven months after the million pound striker's signing. He scored the winner against Swansea and appeared on television the following day, humble enough to repeat some of the tiresome jokes. If anything showed that Garry was probably too nice, it was this. Needless to say, with the boil lanced, Birtles scored again in his next match, away at Middlesbrough. He ended the season with eleven league goals (just two fewer than top-scorer Stapleton), which though no great shakes is on a par with many a United striker's return over the last twenty-five years.

It was to be his last season for us, though, and I'd seen the writing on the wall at a training session at the Cliff. It was in the days when you could stroll round the training pitch without attracting any attention, and when the place wasn't full of fenced-off supporters every day. (If there's one thing I miss about the old days, it's the access to the players at the Cliff.) I wandered down with my camera to watch the seven-a-side game, and was a little surprised to see Birtles playing in defence – I wasn't to know that he'd make the switch late in his career. It was awful. Maybe he didn't have the confidence to play as a striker, even in training, but he seemed really depressed, and generally out on a limb. He wasn't playing well, and after one mis-placed pass I was shocked at the reaction of the United coach (whom I shan't name). The player needed a lift, but was simply told he was useless.

I was glad that he picked up his career on leaving United because Garry Birtles was a nice bloke who would pass the time of day with you. And today when I sense his name has become synonymous with failure, and is quoted with a shake of the head when a new striker is settling in, I remember that we were on his side once, and that we suffered a bit with him.

It would have been too easy to write a smart little article about Birtles the failure, when things were not so simple. But then maybe I'm a bit too nice – just like Garry Birtles?

Standing Up for the Champions

November 1997. United rode the crest of a wave throughout the 1990s, but the team's fine football did nothing to endear it to an often bitter nation. From time to time we Reds feel a little 'got at', and it's nothing new.

I suppose we should feel a bit sorry for the sensitive soul who felt compelled to report Teddy Sheringham to the police for the inciting act of kissing the badge on his shirt at Highbury. No doubt the fan's sensitivities were less tested by exposure to the abuse directed at Teddy and the boys during the game. So yet another match ends with one of our players said to be under a possible official investigation, and this just days after Alex's anger at a potential career-ending assault on Denis Irwin led the press to speculate on a UEFA inquiry into the great man's fury.

Thankfully, UEFA seems unlikely to take Alex to task, though it is doubtful whether the dubious behaviour of the Feyenoord players will take up much of UEFA's time. Ever since United were (temporarily) thrown out of the Cup Winners Cup in 1977, when the St. Etienne supporters were, by most accounts, at least equally responsible for any disturbances at the first leg, we have tended not to expect too many favours from the powers that be.

The most likely reason for United's continual brushes with authority is the pressure cooker within which our team is forced to operate. I heard it suggested recently that it is hard for a London team to win the league because of the number of derby matches they have to play. The fact that United have to play 38 derbies in the league alone makes our club's recent achievements virtually unparalleled. The modern fad for anti-United-ism lends an ironic twist: while these people can recite every United defeat in the last five years (OK, there haven't been many), and revel in every reverse, they cry 'Paranoia' whenever Alex states the obvious truth that all opponents raise their game against his champions.

The daft thing about the banner headlines that accompany every alleged indiscretion involving United is that most of these investigations tend to fizzle out after a while. Examples include the calls for Roy Keane's head after the Palace semi-final in 1995 (when the sending-off alone would have been deemed sufficient for most other players), and the Schmeichel/Wright affair, where no official action ensued. That being the case, it would be better if the authorities simply knocked the speculation of sanctions on the head, rather than drawing out the investigative process, and fuelling the belief that United are always facing some charge or other. Two exceptions in recent times include the extension to Eric's ban, when the mob was given its pound of flesh, and the deducted point following the Arsenal fracas some years ago, a punishment that did not set a precedent for similar flare-ups which followed.

The expectation of some bad publicity each weekend surfaced when we were several goals up against Barnsley recently, with a back four comprising the Nevilles, Curtis and Wallwork. A weak attempt at humour, caused me to speculate that there would be calls for the deduction of three points for fielding a weakened team. This idea of clobbering United for blooding young players seems to arise annually, though I now laugh at the perennial criticism that accompanies Fergie's progressive team selection policy in the League Cup. The papers have constantly raised the possibility of sanctions against United, while the Football League often seems slow to rule it out – until the crunch comes, and the issue fades away. Again, I would ask why, if they are not going to act against United's selection policy, such speculation is not instantly killed off. It would have been amusing with hindsight if they'd thrown United out of the competition in 1994/95 for the heinous crime of playing Neville, Scholes, Butt, Beckham, and company against Port Vale. The fact is that they are now England players, and their progress has benefited from Alex Ferguson's policy of nurturing them correctly.

As is often the case, United have taken the flak for paving the way, with others following in our wake. This year Arsenal have used the League Cup to utilise their squad, and the competition has been slightly reformed to abolish replays and the involvement of the European competitors from the two-legged round.

Possibly the best example of United standing up to the authorities, and being proved right was the insistence of Sir Matt Busby that United should play in the European Cup. Chelsea had bowed to pressure from the small-minded Football League, and did not compete in the inaugural competition in 1955/56. Sir Matt and United incurred the wrath of the authorities by going ahead the following season, and time has proved the good sense of the club's stance. You can imagine the abuse United would have received had modern attitudes been in full flow at that time, encouraged by today's radio phone-in programmes.

For me, United's least pleasant encounter with the English football authorities followed the Munich disaster. UEFA showed its appreciation of United, and its sympathy with our loss, by inviting the club to play in the 1958/59 European Cup despite having lost the previous season's semi-final, and despite having failed to win the English championship following the crash. It was a decent, gracious and honourable offer, which United had been proud to accept. Our own loveable authorities, however, took the opportunity to kick the club at its darkest moment, thus gaining some kind of revenge for their failure to prevent United from entering the European Cup in 1956. Geoffrey Green in his centenary history *There's Only One United*, reproduces the curt letter from Stanley Rous, then FA Secretary, to Les Olive at United. The essential paragraphs state:

> *The Consultative Committee of the FA has considered an*
> *application by Manchester United FC under FA Rule 18(b) for*

consent to take part in the European Champion Clubs' Cup Competition during season 1958/59.

The Committee is of the opinion that, as by its name this is a competition of Champion Clubs, Manchester United FC does not qualify to take part in this season's competition. Consent is therefore refused.

Nice eh? Geoffrey Green explains that the club had originally had the backing of the FA, but not the Football League, and that these two bodies switched positions before the final refusal. If you ever thought that official attitudes to United were a recent phenomenon then this will be an eye-opener. Interestingly, there were no official objections to the second club appearing in this year's so-called Champions' League.

Equally heartless was that United were forced to play both legs of the 1958 European Cup semi-final defeat against AC Milan without Bobby Charlton. With the club struggling to field a competitive team just weeks after the human tragedy of Munich, Charlton was ordered to play in friendlies for England. So no club versus country argument permitted in those days; and no problems about United fielding an understrength team, either.

As football gets bigger, with its progression into the lifestyle and fashion magazines, the microscope grows ever more intense, and the world's greatest football club is a handy subject for selling newspapers. Personally I wouldn't care if I never saw United in the papers or magazines ever again, beyond the essential reports of the football they play. But that's a dream. Let's be grateful that we've at least got the best, and toughest, football manager of his generation to stand up for the champions, and recalling 1958 we know that he is following in the footsteps of the greatest of them all.

Dennis Viollet – One of the Best, One of Our Own

December 1997. United fans were sad to hear of the illness of former striker Dennis Viollet. This is an edited version of a short article, written as a tribute. Dennis died in March 1999.

The red shirt of Manchester United, as befits one of the world's truly great football clubs, has been graced by some of the greatest forwards ever to play the game. To those of us brought up to appreciate and value the heritage of which we are a part, the names trip easily from the tongue, whether or not we are personally old enough to have seen these men play: Rowley and Stan Pearson, Taylor and Charlton, Law and Best, Greenhoff and Stuart Pearson, and, of course, Eric Cantona. There have been, and will be, many more.

Imagine then being able to claim a goalscoring achievement of which any of the above would be proud. One man able to do so is Dennis Viollet, whose 32 league goals (from just 36 games) in 1959/60 give him the club record for goals in a season. It is a record which may never be equalled, and on its own would give Dennis a special place on our roll of honour.

In fact those goals tell only part of the story of Dennis Viollet's contribution to United's cause. A Manchester boy, he joined the club at the age of 16, and served the club for 13 years. His league debut came against Newcastle in April 1953 and his last match for United saw him sign off with a goal against Leicester in November 1961. In all, he played 259 league games and scored 159 goals; and his amazing record of 13 goals in 12 European appearances included United's first ever European Cup goal, away to Anderlecht in September 1956.

During 1957/58 he partnered Tommy Taylor until the devastation of Munich. He had scored 16 league goals before the February disaster, including a goal in what may have been United's greatest ever league game: the 5-4 win at Highbury, the last game played by the Babes in this country. He was also on target in the chill of Belgrade four days later. He was in that team, probably (certainly potentially) United's greatest, for the simple reason that he was good enough. He was a league champion twice.

After Munich, Dennis was vital in keeping alive the flame, and his scoring exploits were resumed the following season. In January 1962, he signed for Stoke City in a 25,000 pounds deal. He helped them to the second division title in 1963, and scored 59 league goals in his spell at the Victoria Ground. His later career saw him play in the USA, and in non-league football, and included some late glory as he won an Irish cup winner's medal with Linfield. Eventually he settled in Florida, where he has enjoyed a successful coaching career.

United's survivors from the Munich disaster were the guests of UEFA at last year's European Cup final. Although United had fallen at the semi-final stage, Dennis and his colleagues enjoyed their rightful place of honour at the match. Dennis Viollet is still a true Red.

From the Red Corner: A View of the Blue

January 1998. Every club regards United as an enemy these days. It wasn't always so, and I still like to reserve feelings of rivalry for the old foe.

One of my favourite football books of recent years is *Football Against the Enemy* in which Simon Kuper explores some of the world's fiercest rivalries. The cover picture, showing the clash between Holland's Rijkaard and Germany's Voller was worth a thousand words. The only British rivalry included in the book was that between Celtic and Rangers, and United's rivalries with various English clubs tended to pale in comparison with many described. To some extent, United have become the whole nation's rivals in recent years, so much so that it is difficult for United supporters to return the feeling to everyone with any great passion. Sorry, Nick Hancock, but however much you hate 'Man U' (as our club is not called), I just couldn't give a stuff about Stoke City.

Many United supporters now put Liverpool at the top of their list of rivals, and Liverpool's crowd would probably return the compliment. It's like Spain (without the political undertones), where Real Madrid and Barcelona treat their neighbours Atletico Madrid and Espanol with some disdain, preferring to focus their hatred on one another. For Atletico and Espanol, read Everton and Manchester City. But it wasn't always quite like that.

It occurred to me recently, when some away fans were singing You'll Never Walk Alone, and were rapidly condemned as 'Scouse Bastards' by the United fans, that the Stretford End often sung that song in the 1970s, whilst holding scarves aloft in the accustomed fashion. The words may have been sharpened, but at that time Liverpool weren't quite the devil they are now. Who remembers the end of the 1977 FA Cup final? I can't be the only one old enough to recall the defeated Liverpool team trudging round on a lap of honour and applauding the United supporters as we magnanimously chanted 'Liverpool, Liverpool … ' in tribute to their efforts. I can imagine half of you having a fit reading this, but believe me, it happened, and almost all Reds joined in. I agree that if we had lost we'd have abused them mercilessly, but that isn't the point. The point is that the rivalry has escalated now to the stage when even shallow magnanimity is not possible; in 1996 they didn't bother looking for it. Likewise, in 1977 we mingled pretty well outside Wembley (though I grant it wouldn't have been so peaceful on any other occasion); in 1996 I was glad to escape the threatening air and get inside the ground.

The Liverpool thing really grew up in the 1980s, when we were head to head for the honours for several years. United did OK in the Cup, but continued to blow it for the big one. We really hated that, and they really hated the fact that for all their trophies we remained the glamour outfit. The concentration on Liverpool as rivals was also increased by the decline of a team in light blue as a serious force.

Once, when I was very small, I saw two football scarves in a shop window. I didn't need to ask about the red and white one (there was no black on our scarves in the mid-1960s), but had to ask what the blue and white was for. It was in front of that window that I was told of the existence of another football team. Actually, I'll never forget my mother's words: she said 'Manchester City – they're not very good'. So succinct, and such truth. It was a terrible revelation in many ways – not quite as bad as the moment when it first dawns on you that you are going to die one day, I admit, but it meant that life wasn't so simple after all, and as the years went by I began to wish I'd never asked. At first I felt a bit sorry for this other team; I was curious about them, and I used to check the league table to see how they were doing. I found out that their captain was a bloke called Johnny Crossan and that their manager, Joe Mercer, seemed a pretty decent man.

He was decent at his job too, and a couple of years later, in 1968, his side won the championship, pipping United on the final day. I was at Old Trafford that afternoon as we slipped up against Sunderland, but to my young senses there seemed to be no real feeling of despair. All thoughts were on the forthcoming European Cup final, and all that it entailed. Thus United managed to totally out-trump our blue neighbours by putting their only post-war championship firmly in the shade.

For the next few seasons the boot was on the other foot, and it was during this period that the existence of this other lot became something of a problem. One notable FA Cup tie apart, we just couldn't seem to beat them. Mind you, we couldn't beat anyone else half-decent either. It really hurt on a bleak November afternoon in 1972 when we were thumped 3-0 on their ground. We'd lost heavily to them before, but this was a grim day. For me this was much worse than the famous 5-1 seventeen years later; that was a bit of a freak score, a one-off, and I think they realised it amid their jollity. But the 1972 game was no fluke; it was merely confirmation of a process that had gone on for four years. Quite simply they had it over us, and they knew it. There is something about the roar of a crowd when a goal is scored by the opposition on an away ground: there is this sickening (to me) roar, which is almost a shriek. It is pointed like a dagger, and on that day it found its mark. It was dark and horrible towards the end; United couldn't wait to get off the pitch, and in a bitter encounter the enemy took the piss.

The final match of 1973/74 does not need to be recounted. Suffice to say that there was glee etched on the faces of the visiting players, and the view was expressed from within their club that they were about to assume the position of the undisputed number one club in Manchester. For me it was the final straw, and I vowed that if ever they were to be relegated, I would be there to say cheerio. It is interesting with hindsight that they felt United's relegation would improve their status. Beating us consistently for five years had failed to see them hailed as the town's top dogs, and it was never to be as the Reds stormed back with a vengeance. The crowds still flocked to Old Trafford, and we knocked them out of the League Cup as we returned to the big time.

The following season, 1975/76, marked the end of blue pretensions. They won the League Cup, while we lost the FA Cup final, and plans to parade both cups at the end of season derby were shelved. We won the match, and sang 'Oh we'd rather win the derby than the Cup', but we didn't really mean it. Although their last trophy to date seems a bit second-rate these days I'd have given a lot for it, as United had won precisely nothing for eight of the formative years of my life. But we haven't lost to them at Old Trafford in all the years since, and though they inevitably won the odd derby at their place, they were heading for a serious fall. And so it was that on the day of David Pleat's famous hush-puppy shuffle, I sat in their main stand quietly smiling. The buggers were going down. Let's see how they like it. I'd kept my promise by being there. A week later we had another giggle when their chairman Peter Swales arrived at Wembley to see the United in the Cup Final. I'll give him credit for the way he kept smiling as we sang 'Going Down, Going Down ...', because I know how he felt inside. If only he'd shown some sympathy for us nine years earlier.

As our old rivals have endured a series of promotions and relegations United have become firmly established as one of Europe's top clubs. Our famous 5-1 defeat in 1989 (still Fergie's only derby loss) was a low point for me, no question, but it didn't carry with it the underlying malaise of the 1972 game I mentioned earlier. In fact the 5-1 winners in 1989 were history within months, whereas United lifted the FA Cup that season to begin an unimaginable period of glory. Just for good measure we later chalked up a nice five-nil to call time on the 5-1 jibes.

During their last relegation season the old foe were no longer regarded as serious rivals. I even heard United supporters expressing the hope that they would stay up – it seemed that they had become so bad that sympathy had begun to set in – and Alex's programme notes also included hopes for their survival. Thinking back to 1974 I couldn't recall similar sentiments in the opposite direction, but one of my blue chums said that this attitude tended to bug him even more. Once he explained that it is really insulting when your former deadly rivals actually feel sorry for you, I began to feign a similar attitude. In fairness to him, though, I said little when the axe finally fell. Over the years I have gained some respect for people who go out and support their team – whatever the team, and I did not rub it in. For me the extreme disappointment of relegation in 1974 and the cruel way the opposing players seemed to enjoy it meant that I could not gloat as they had appeared to do. I was able to empathise with the plight of their fans, if not their chairman, who had rubbed our noses in it on many an occasion.

I think my feelings are probably unique to those who grew up in that late 1960s/early 1970s period when Messrs. Allison and Doyle were in their prime. Earlier generations still talk about going to our ground and theirs on alternate weekends, and they often express some feeling for both clubs. Later generations tended to pick up on the intensifying rivalry with Liverpool. For me, then, there will only be one real enemy. Unlike some of the feuds described in Kuper's book, though, I think that a keen, yet healthy, local rivalry is a welcome thing. One thing is for sure: if the old foe ever rise from the ashes, it will put the Liverpool enmity firmly in the shade.

The Game of the Name

January 1998. Some say that great players are born and not made. Maybe they are christened?

It should have been me: Red shirt, adoring crowd, Old Trafford legend. Instead I'm 39 years old, and the nearest I've been to the big time was taking a pee in the old United dressing room toilets (don't ask – it's a long story). So where did it all go wrong? Sadly I never had a chance from leaving the baptismal font – you just don't get United strikers called Anthony, do you? Knights of the theatre, yes; hairdressers, certainly; but centre forwards, never. "On my head, Anthony old son, far post", just doesn't have the right ring somehow.

Having thought about this for many years, I've developed an uncanny knack of judging a footballer simply from his name. I could save Alex and Kiddo a fortune in scouting trips, and save them studying lengthy videos of the latest Chilean sensation. Just give me the player's name and I'll tell you his worth.

I'm not the first expert in this field, the Brazilians having cottoned on to the science many years ago. Whereas Ajax have eight year old kids training for ten hours a day, the Brazilians just call some nipper out of the *favelas*, or off the beach, and give him a cool name. "Who are you, son? Edson Arantes do Nascimento? ... OK, make that Pele." And there you go. It's more a statement than a name; the guy just couldn't fail. The list is virtually endless: Garincha, Rivelino, Jairzinho, Zico, Socrates, Romario, ... Some say that Brazil were unsuccessful in 1974 and 1978 because they tried to play a European style game, but I think it was because they'd lost all their flash names. If they'd had eleven Anthonys they probably wouldn't even have qualified.

In this country we have mimicked the habit to some extent: thus we add '-ie' or '-o' to inject an element of flare into a footballer's name. Successful examples include 'Hughsie' and 'Keano', of course. Maybe I should have gone the whole hog like that player from Stevenage, Guiliano Grazioli, who hit the news recently; I bet his real name is Amos Postlethwaite or something.

In United's history the greatest players have had the best names. If anyone ever doubted that somehow there is order in the universe, let him explain to me why the finest of them all just happened to be called George Best. There's no equivocation in that surname is there? And the first name was both macho and smooth. Great name, great player.

My all time hero remains Denis Law, not least because he was my first ever hero. His name added to his appeal for 1960s kids. Law: the Lawman, sharp shooter, in on the action, firing the bullets. Brilliant, but also so accurate. And didn't 'Denis' suit the cheeky Menace persona, so accessible to a young generation of Beano readers? Denis Law was a huge star in his day; in the over-hyped 1990s he would be in a galaxy all of his own.

Then there's Eric, the only man to give Denis a serious run in the hero stakes. He so valued his name that he tried to copyright it. He's one of those people that can be referred to by their first name only (in fact I've just done it). Talk about 'Eric', and the whole of Europe will know you don't mean Hattie Jaques's co-star. Interesting then that he signed autographs simply as 'Cantona', though that was equally cool.

I'd put Bobby Charlton, Tommy Taylor, Jack 'Gunner' Rowley and others in the category of *Boys' Own* hero names. They are the real life equivalents of Roy Race, which makes me wonder how successful *he* would have been if he'd been called 'Anthony of the Rovers'! The Busby Babes all had great names, come to think of it 'Busby Babes' is a great name in its own right. Duncan Edwards, a solid, uncompromising and unique name. Roger Byrne, suave and mature.

One of the best from the history books is Frank Barson, the United defender from the 1920s. Have you ever heard of him? If not, then pause a moment to guess his style before reading on. It will come as no surprise to hear that the rough, tough Barson was one of the most feared players of his era, and that he is alleged to have pulled a gun on one of his former managers in the dressing room. I may try putting a picture of Frank Barson on the mantelpiece to keep the kids away from the fire.

Sometimes the name, like the player, can flatter to deceive. A good example is Albert Quixall, whose surname was so intriguing, semi-exotic even, and whose appearance with the slick haircut and short-shorts had him cast as some sort of glamour boy. Unfortunately, the chubby-cheeked Albert in his character meant that his play, like his name, didn't quite make him top-notch.

Others, without the benefit of Quixall's surname never really had a chance of greatness. Ralph and Clayton spring to mind here. Ashley Grimes was christened 'Augustine Ashley', which is a little unfair even by *my* mother's standards. And Garry Birtles just sounds too nice. But perhaps the biggest shame was the case of Arnold Sidebottom. Now I don't wish to offend anyone here, but Sidebottom is just a funny name, isn't it. It may be a junior-school sort of funniness, but it is funny all the same. What he needed was a cool first name, though I can't readily think how this surname could best be offset. Even 'Eric' wouldn't work in this context. We tried to help by calling him Arnie, but it wasn't to be. This was unfortunate because we were crying out for a decent centre-half at the time. It was great that he had a good cricket career (even playing for England), but to do that he had to go back to Yorkshire where the name Sidebottom isn't funny at all.

So if there are any young mums-to-be reading this, please hear my plea. If you have a lad, give him a chance. Before you name the child try chanting it out loud, and ask yourself if it sounds good. Name him right and he may be a Red Devil one day.

Past and Pleasant?

March 1998. Who said nostalgia is not what it used to be?

I first suspected that middle age was creeping up on me when I set the video to record an episode of Gardeners' World, and I suppose the confirmation is the fact that I don't particularly mind admitting it. To maintain a degree of Red credibility, though, I should add that one advantage of the programme is its total lack of ABU-inspired jibes: an increasingly rare thing on the box these days. Another haven of peace and tranquillity that I can recommend is BBC Radio 3. I thanked heaven for this radio station in that woeful fortnight in May 1995, when not a single reference to United's Double disappointment was to be heard. You may find that tuning into Radio 3 at six minutes past six on Saturday evenings can do wonders for your blood pressure, and it can come in handy to learn that Joaquin Rodrigo and Manuel de Falla are not Atletico Madrid's wing backs.

One of the worst things about this time of life (which on the whole is pretty damn good) is the eventual disappearance of so many things that have formed the backcloth to your whole existence; things that you took for granted. These days they are even demolishing the hallowed football grounds, though thankfully not ours. As life's certainties disappear you feel that you are approaching the frontline of mortality yourself. I realise this is a perception more than anything else, and that things are constantly changing, but events like the recent retirement of Peter O'Sullevan suggest that we are all sensitive to the loss of some of life's fixtures.

Following United certainly isn't what it used to be, and those of us who went right through the lean years have our feelings of relish at the current on-field riches slightly tinged by the loss of old comforts (of the familiar, not the physical, form). There has arisen a degree of sensitivity among sections of the crowd, as the loyal faithful question the motivation of the new breed; it seems important to recognise the difference between them and us, and to make it clear that you are indeed one of us.

We all have our own acid tests. My benchmark is an end of season game in May 1989 when just 23,368 turned out for a dire evening encounter with Wimbledon. Frustration that season had led to some pretty poor (for United) attendances, and I often wonder where the recipients of today's precious away match tickets were that night. If you travelled up from somewhere like Hastings or Torbay, then I salute you. It is certainly hard to imagine a similarly grim atmosphere in the near future (hopefully never), and thinking of that match caused me to reflect on other lamented aspects of the past, things that at the time were taken for granted:

1. 1960s European Away Matches. My abiding memories of the glorious 1968 campaign concern United's trips to play Sarajevo and Gornick Zabrze, especially the latter.   Unlike today, the team flew off to mysterious places behind the scary-sounding Iron Curtain, to play 'crack outfits' (as very good foreign teams were always called) in front of 'partizan' crowds. You knew the opposition would get every break going, and you feared for United's chances.   The backs-to-the-wall effort in overcoming Gornick in the snow was a quintessential occasion. There would be little travelling support, and no live TV. The team was alone. But it seemed a dashing sort of venture, unsullied by the brutalities of Galatasary and Porto in recent years.

2. Classic TV. Television coverage of the modern Euro-away makes the game seem comfortingly close to home; we wouldn't be without it, but the mystique has gone. The last vestiges of remoteness were lost with the introduction of satellite communications, so that the commentators no longer sound as though they are speaking down crackling telephone lines from a distant war zone. If I were a producer I'd restore the muffled phone lines as a special effect, and while at it I'd bring back the Horizontal Lines. You must remember those? If not, put on the video of Georgie scoring his brilliant solo goal against Chelsea in the League Cup in 1970, where Chopper Harris just couldn't nobble him. And what happens when the ball hits the net? The TV set gets as excited as you, and a series of horizontal lines appears on screen as the electrically-charged atmosphere leaps out and grabs you. I never did find out why that used to happen, but it happened all the time until those television engineers managed to cure (ie ruin) it.

3. Coleman and Meek.   Georgie's most memorable goals were often accompanied by the commentary of the legendary David Coleman. Although he hasn't done the football for many years, and although his name has (unfairly) become associated with the commentator's cock-up (Colemanballs), he remains my favourite. I don't know for sure, but I always thought he was a Red, as he seemed to genuinely enjoy describing United's goals. At least he's still doing the athletics, and it will be sad when he finally calls it a day. The retirement of David Meek as the Manchester Evening News United correspondent was one of life's watersheds.   This guy had always been the United reporter, and I'd grown up reading his reports and stories almost every day of my life. Meek was never a cult figure like Coleman, however; it was more a question of admiring his professionalism and longevity. The story of how he almost accidentally became the United correspondent on the death of his predecessor at Munich is well known, and it seems that David Meek had, up to that time, no strong affection for United. To that extent he was different from those of us with United in our veins, and I suppose it is to his great credit that he became so accepted as one of us.

4. The last minute away match. For as long as I can remember there has never been an option as to how I would spend my time when United were playing at home. Nobody ever asks me if I'm going to the match, because if United are at home, I'll be there. Away games were a little different, because they required parental permission, or a lift. Time was when you could wait until Saturday morning to see how you were fixed, then make the decision to drive down to the Midlands (or wherever) to see the lads. Once you got there you could pay to stand behind the goal or, if you were early enough and felt extravagant, get yourself a seat. These days it requires a dedicated administrative exercise, listening out for the announcement of ticket sales, and ensuring that the application includes more forms and vouchers than you'd need for an Albanian visa. Applications are invariably unsuccessful, and I reckon that the small dividend I receive on my United shares is spent on wasted stamps for ticket applications.

5. The walk to the ground. I wish I had a quid for each time I'd traipsed up Trafford Road and across the swing bridge; a fiver for the rainy Tuesday nights when I turned up for a token at a youth match. The area has changed constantly over the last 30 years, as demolition and rebuilding have occurred, and as the docks declined and died. But lately they've even ripped up the roads. The new junction of Sir Matt Busby Way and Trafford Park Road is really disorienting: if you'd been away for a couple of years, and were beamed down at this spot, you wouldn't have a clue where you were. At least the pitch is still in the same place, though I understand that it is to be ripped up and relaid this summer. In a few years I'll be reminiscing about the camber which currently means that from the front row of the North or South stands you can't see the feet of players on the opposite wing, nor the ball if it's on the deck.

6. The Cliff. I used to love going down to the Cliff during the school holidays, and taking the appearances of Best and Law a little bit for granted. It was always pretty relaxed, and many is the time I've stood on the touchline of the pitch or sneaked into the indoor area to watch from close up. There was no need for stewards, and it never seemed to get too crowded. I don't blame Alex for closing the place to visitors on pre-match days now, as it is pretty chaotic. I actually stopped going down there when I noticed that lots of the playing staff were younger than me, and were walking round with a cocky swagger. Total jealously was my reaction, of course, and it all seemed like fate's way of mocking my inability to share their dream. To retain a grip on my shattered dignity, I promised myself that I'd never ask someone younger than me for an autograph, and I went off and sulked for about 15 years. It took Eric (a mere youngster) to make me break the vow, and I returned to the Cliff one day just to get his signature. When Bryan Robson left the club I was older than all the remaining players, which was another shock to the system. No wonder I was sorry to see him go.

7. Policemen inside Old Trafford. A bit of an odd reminiscence, I admit, but events in recent months made me hanker after the comfort factor of the constabulary in control of the crowd. Thinking back, I recalled the weekly routine of the Stretford End whistling the Laurel and Hardy tune as a long line of policemen marched from the old tunnel to take up their positions around the ground near the end of the game. I don't know whether it annoyed them, or whether they saw the funny side, but it all seems nice cosy stuff with hindsight.

8. Stretford End. At the plc AGM a few years ago someone complained about the Stretford End being renamed the West Stand, and said that match tickets for that end should have the words 'Stretford End' printed on the front. He was dismissed as a bit paranoid, and was told that the name change was only for safety and emergency reasons, and that even the Board still referred to the Stretford End by its old name. Why, didn't the map of the ground on the back of the ticket still say 'West Stand / Stretford End'? But in the intervening period, even the supporters have started referring to 'West Lower', and so forth; hardly anyone says 'Stretford End' any more. If there ever was a considered plan to rid the ground of its old image, then it seems to have worked. Nevertheless I was a bit sad to see the flashy new ticket design for the 5th Round FA Cup: on the back the old map was replaced by a 3-D drawing of the ground. Lo and behold, instead of 'West Stand / Stretford End' we now have 'West Stand / Megastore'. An unwelcome sign of the changing times.

One thing I don't miss, though, is the frustration of supporting an under-achieving club. If the brave new world includes the championship every year, then I'll be pretty content. But there is a serious point behind this rose-tinted reminiscence, and it is the fact that thousands of us have grown up with United in our hearts. We haven't simply bought into the new vogue, and we won't make a penny out of our devotion (on the contrary). If it wasn't for us there would be no club, and it is important that the things were care about are respected. Because if the glory days disappear, or the financial bubble ever bursts, we'll still be there. Just as we were, all 23,000 of us, in May 1989.

Feeling the Benefit

April 1998. Testimonial matches for very rich players have become a frequent debating point, all the more when compared with the most deserving of good causes.

United's pre-season friendly against Real Sociedad in August 1986 was a bit of a watershed for me. On a fine Sunday afternoon I sat watching a very dull football match in a sparsely populated Old Trafford thinking that there must have been something better to do. That day I hadn't considered any alternatives to the football because a United team was playing at Old Trafford, and for nearly 20 years the rule had been that if the team was appearing then I would be there. I think the boredom I suffered was particularly felt because only 11 days earlier United had played out a goalless, and lifeless, draw against the Brazilian side Fluminense, an occasion not enlivened by the meaningless penalty shoot-out that followed. And so it was that I decided that something had to give: I could not justify religious attendance at every meaningless friendly played at Old Trafford. I had to stop being a mug-punter.

The final straw came on a freezing January night in 1987 when United played a nothing-match against Red Star Belgrade. I have long forgotten the excuse for this fixture, but Red Star have a special place in our history, and I felt that I should support the game. Not many others felt the same, however, and the fact that the United Road stand was closed because of a burst water pipe was of no consequence. Just 10,000 hardy (or daft) souls watched a tedious 0-1 defeat, the main significance of which was that Manchester United had lost at home to a foreign team for the first time since 1960. Never again, I vowed, as I thawed out at home.

I was as good as my word, though I was tested by the visit of the great AC Milan side the following year, when my irrational pangs of guilt were quite tangible. For once, ironically, it was a decent game, though missing it made avoiding subsequent friendlies against less interesting opposition relatively painless. Now I don't even consider paying the silly prices for the pre-season games against the likes of Inter Milan and Slavia Prague. Watching United costs me well into four figures each season, and I cannot justify these little extras, especially considering that the motivation for some of these matches seems to be to ask the fans to top up a transfer fee.

The 1980s provided a couple of classic examinations of fan sanity, when two utterly meaningless competitions were staged. In 1985/86 the Screen Sports Super Cup, for those excluded from Europe because of the post-Heysel ban, was such a non-event that it was not until the following season that Everton and Liverpool could be bothered playing the final. I hated this competition, and the fact that my loyalty (or stupidity) was being tested in this way. I'd missed our home tie with Everton because I'd been on holiday, and was thus spared from deciding whether to turn up, but I attended United's group match against Norwich (which we drew, to nobody's concern). I was pleased when we were finally eliminated. I'd come a long way from our 1970s Anglo-Italian Cup days, when my enthusiasm was based on the delusion that it was a prestigious European competition – at least it was until we were knocked out.

Then in 1988/89 we were treated to the Football League's centenary celebrations, which included a competition for the Mercantile Credit Football League Centenary Trophy. By no means as grand as its name, this was a competition for the previous season's top eight clubs, and United found themselves playing Everton then Newcastle at Old Trafford. There was talk of this becoming a regular competition if interest was high, and that ensured my non-attendance. It seemed to me important that the fans said 'No' to this nonsense. Crowds of around 15,000 (appalling by Old Trafford standards) showed that I was not alone. We lost the final to Arsenal at Villa Park in early October; despite Clayton's diving header, by Christmas the competition had probably been forgotten by most that turned up.

The reason for these games is often the most off-putting feature, but the issue becomes more complicated where testimonial matches are concerned. The only redeeming aspect of the Real Sociedad game mentioned earlier was that it was the testimonial for Steve Coppell, a huge favourite at Old Trafford, whose injury-induced retirement had upset us all. For Coppell, I didn't begrudge the ticket, nor even the lousy football match. I'd been to every testimonial for years, and it had become a thing of habit. When I was a kid I didn't really understand what these games were for. It took me many years to question the justification for boosting the coffers of an international footballer, who had been driving a nice car all the years that my dad had been catching the bus to work. Players in the 1960s and 1970s were not in today's millionaire league, but they were relatively wealthy, and lucky, young men. There are only two testimonial games that I recall as good football matches. The first was the visit of Celtic for Bobby Charlton, when a 0-0 draw summed up the genuine contest; the second was United's 1-0 win over the great Ajax in Denis Law's game. Other than those, it was the cause, rather than the entertainment that justified the ticket.

These days routine testimonials are also off my agenda. I don't go along with the view that they should be abolished, because it is the right of Brian McClair (for example) to have a game organised on his behalf, and it is the fans' right to support the player if they so wish. But I've been loyal to United for over 30 years, I'm not well-off, and I think the players do well enough out of me and my kind. It doesn't detract from my commitment if I choose to say 'No, but good luck to you anyway'. There will always be a special case, however. Steve Coppell is one example, and more recently David Busst, for whom I'm glad I made the trip to Coventry.

The ultimate good cause, a game for which I purchased an expensive ticket without a moment's hesitation, was the forthcoming benefit match for the Munich survivors and dependants. To be honest I don't care if the game is never played – I am happy to have contributed to the fund. But there are aspects of this match that have caused unease, and a feeling that the ordinary supporter is again bearing the brunt. It's not as bad as subsidising a transfer fee, because this is one cause that we support whole-heartedly, but the onus seems to be on the supporters, and we wonder why it has taken so long to organise a benefit of this scale.

We understand that immediately post-Munich things may not have been clear-cut. Some of the survivors were able to resume their careers, and so may not have been seen as victims in that sense; some survived never to play again; others lost husbands, fathers and sons. The suffering was not shared equally, and subsequent misfortunes may not have been attributable to the disaster. It is also true that the club was not the wealthy institution it is today. And of course the likes of me do not know the details of the compensation arrangements that were made at that time. It's just that forty years is half a lifetime. If the cause is just today, then wasn't it was just many years ago? Or has the issue become clearer over time?

In a recent United Review the club addressed some of the criticisms that had been aired. It was suggested that now was a good time for the game because (and I quote) "many of the people involved approach the age when they must think about their pensions!" I don't think this was sensitively expressed. I'm sure that the widows, and the players whose careers were terminated, must have been worrying about their daily lives, not just their pensions, for many years.

The United Review article added "Manchester United are naturally giving their services free and [are] passing on all profits from catering and programme sales."   This confused me a bit, as I wondered to whom United were giving their services free of charge. I assumed they meant the club is not charging the Munich Memorial Committee for playing the game and staging it at Old Trafford, which made me wonder about the distinction between the club and the committee. As for the catering and programme sales, well those revenues are again coming from the supporters.   The United Review article did not say that the club was contributing to the memorial fund other than those monies described which will be generated by the event itself.

The Review article is the main public statement I have seen from the club, the programme being the main organ of communication between the club and the fans. It may well be that the club is making its own private contribution to the fund for these most deserving and dignified people, without whom United would not be the legend it is. I hope so. I also hope that there will be no free seats in the ground on the night, and that everyone present (even the press) chips in at least the price of a ticket. The only free seats should be for the beneficiaries: the people whose sacrifice put United on the map.

Would it have been possible to have looked after these people in a better way? The present board is not responsible for the last forty years, but the contrast between the share options available to modern executives and the sight of Busby Babes selling medals or fighting serious illness against financial insecurity is quite stark. As an insignificant shareholder, I would be delighted to donate my tiny dividend this year to the Munich fund. Wouldn't it be great if some of the serious shareholders were to divert some of their returns into this fund also? And wouldn't it be great to be told that the money from the advance ticket sales had already begun to make its way to the Munich survivors and dependants, after all these years?

Lack of Hunger? A Review of the 1997/98 League Campaign

April 1998. Oh dear. A third successive championship seemed assured as winter gave way to spring, but United went to pieces as the season drew to a close, and we finished empty-handed as Arsenal won the Double. What on earth went wrong?

As I write these words Manchester United are the champions of England. For someone who suffered the full 26 years of under-achievement, the pleasure it gives me to write that statement is hard to describe. But for how long will it remain true? A few short weeks ago another title seemed all but won, and the season's question mark appeared to surround our prospects of lifting the European Cup. After a storming autumn and the blitzing of Chelsea in the 3rd Round of the FA Cup, United were being talked-up by most commentators, though I suspect that many were secretly hoping to apply the kiss of death to our prospects. Personally, I never bought that line, and I remained unconvinced about our prospects of silverware. I accept that pessimism comes easy to me, and I advised caution to all who would listen, but the main response seemed to be that however many points United threw away, our rivals would prove equally inconsistent.

I write after the home game against Newcastle which leaves us praying for a drastic change in form by both United and Arsenal. The destination of the title is yet to be confirmed, but what is not in doubt is that United went from being certain champions (witness the generosity of Manchester bookie, Fred Done, who paid out after our league win at Chelsea) to being second-favourites as we entered the final furlong. The team had begun to resemble a racing driver running out of fuel just short of the chequered flag. Something went wrong.

It was hardly an auspicious start to the campaign, not helped by the injuries which kept Cole and Solskjaer out of the side. There was a flowing away win at Everton (a performance later put into perspective as Everton lost many times at Goodison), but it was not until five games later that United won away for a second time: even then we threw away a two goal lead before getting a second wind. Arguably the only other wholly-convincing away performance of the season was at Anfield in early December.

Meanwhile the Reds ran into some impressive home form, with 13 goals fired past Barnsley and Sheffield Wednesday on successive Saturdays. Whatever the quality of the opposition (and those teams were also well-thumped on their own grounds by Chelsea, among others) we could ask no more than what was produced. Perhaps the most significant aspect of these games was the final emergence of Andy Cole as an undoubted class act. The best performance of that awesome autumn was the destruction of 2nd

place Blackburn Rovers, a victory which sent shivers through the Premiership.

But we did not realise at the time just how significant our 3-2 defeat at Highbury in November would prove to be. Coming on the back of a fine European win, we were forgiving, but the second half of the game was characterised by United constantly surrendering possession, and consequently doing a lot of chasing. I argued at the time that if you give a pub team 45 minutes' possession, and even if they just hump the ball into your box, there is a chance that a goal will result – even if it goes in off the referee's backside. For me, Platt's winner from a nothing header following a corner was in that category: it was hardly special but, as they say, it had been coming.

Many is the time I have heard professionals declare that supporters (or journalists) know nothing about the finer points of football, because they have "never played the game" at top level; you'll hear this on radio phone-ins when some caller disagrees with the expert. As a mere fan, how do I know how true this is? What I do know is that I must have seen United play almost 800 times, and I reckon that entitles me to an opinion. My opinion before Christmas was that for several seasons United's swift counter-attacking style had been based on brisk, accurate passing, plus width and pace, but that lately all accuracy in passing had been lost, and that we had begun to rely too much on Ryan Giggs for the last two qualities.

I put my fears down to pessimism until the awful defeat at Coventry just after Christmas. If this wasn't what I'd been banging on about, nothing was, and for that reason I took that loss pretty badly on the day. There appeared to be no urgency, an inability to retain possession, and no ruthlessness. To concede two goals in the last five minutes was tough, but was about what we deserved – by 'we' I mean the team, not the fantastic travelling support.

I wonder how helpful the FA Cup thrashing of Chelsea proved to be in the end. It was so enjoyable at the time that I wouldn't change a thing, but it seemed to convince the media (and the players?) that the championship was a formality – especially given the inconsistency of everyone else. But that result was followed by a wretched sequence of performances, especially at home. Basically we haven't hammered anyone since, and rightly or wrongly the impression was gained that United had taken their eye off the ball and were looking ahead to Europe. Take a look at the following table, which shows games played after 21 December and up to 18 April; as well as Arsenal and United (who were top at the start of the period), it shows Barnsley, who were bottom of the league leading up to Christmas.

	P	W	D	L	F	A	Pts	GD
Arsenal	15	12	3	0	29	7	39	+22
United	16	7	4	5	20	13	25	+7
Barnsley	16	6	3	7	20	27	21	-7

If the title is not to be ours this table explains why: for four months we have performed little better than Barnsley. Home games became stressful tests of endurance, as United faced packed defences (often a goal behind), with the main tactic being to loft one into the box, rather than break down a defence or get in round the back. We have been banging on the door, rather than putting a key in the lock. Ominously, the slump began when the European Cup was on the back-burner, and in a run of games against second-rate opposition. In my undoubted ignorance, I saw four problems here.

First, the team was affected by injuries, and some allowances have to be made. But hadn't we been conditioned to believe in the squad's strength in depth? In reality this meant that we had four good central defenders and five good full backs: any problems in midfield meant that Johnsen and Phil Neville were pushed forward, and during the crucial defeat by Arsenal John Curtis also spent a period in the middle of the park. We resorted to playing Ole wide (doing nothing for his self-confidence, nor for results), and it even began to seem as though the sale of Poborsky had been premature.

Secondly, we desperately needed leadership. In the moments after Overmars struck his blow, as we lost 0-1 at home to Arsenal, the players needed someone to turn to for inspiration, and it became clear that we had finally begun to miss Roy Keane. Results had gone so well after Keano's injury that it seemed we would get by, but when things got tough we could have done with him there. There have been times this season when I've wondered if a temperamental Roy would have lasted the 90 minutes (the niggly first half of the home game against Liverpool springs to mind), but if our man returns stronger in mind he will be as good as a £20 million signing for next season.

Thirdly, how much of an eye did the players have on Europe? It's impossible to know, I suppose, maybe even for them, especially with the poorest form coinciding with the Euro-break. But I'm in little doubt that Arsenal twice caught us at just the right time, certainly for the Old Trafford game just four days before the Monaco return. Less easy to understand was the inept display at Hillsborough a week earlier, and impossible to accept was the fact that this non-performance did not set alarm bells ringing out loud. Many seemed to concur with Sheffield Wednesday manager Ron Atkinson's crafty pre-match assessment that it didn't matter if his side won because the title was already United's.

Fourthly, despite an impressive personnel list a problem in defence was becoming clear. For a team that has won so many titles in recent years we have always given other teams chances to score. This season Pallister played every league game until his back went at Chelsea, but he has lacked a strong and consistent partner (Johnsen has been superb, but has suffered his own injuries, and has played in midfield on many occasions). If I were a visiting manager I would tell my team to attack United at Old Trafford in the knowledge that chances would fall our way. Leicester and Bolton were two of the more ordinary sides to chance their arm, score a goal, and gleefully harm our title prospects by packing their defences and heading away the succession of hopeful crosses that United pumped in.

And so we come to the home straight. United looking ragged, nervy and uncertain; the fans feeling the strain; and Arsenal playing without a care in the world. There seems no danger of our rivals giving away stupid goals, and no danger of them failing to score themselves – with or without Bergkamp. Their win at Blackburn was reminiscent of United's destruction of Norwich towards the end of the 1993 season: assured, deadly and mighty impressive. A shock to the system after United's torrid first half against the same opponents just seven days earlier. United remained top of the league, but not for much longer. It was beginning to look as though our six months in first place had, after all, been due to the inconsistencies of the others, rather than our own qualities. Arsenal had stopped reading the script – weren't they supposed to drop points with the same regularity as ourselves? But what else did we expect – hadn't United in 1993/94 and Newcastle in 1995/96 seen significant leads eroded away as the final games approached?

In the gloom following our slip into second place, a ray of hope, albeit for our longer-term prospects, appeared. A revealing interview with Alex Ferguson in the Times showed that the manager felt as hurt as the supporters, and he asked himself how big a part complacency (on and off the pitch) had played in the season's outcome. I was reminded of the anticlimactic title presentation at the end of 1996/97, which was partly due to an over-stage-managed ceremony, and partly due to the (now understandable) demeanour of our captain – Eric knew he was about to retire. But I remarked at the time that something else seemed wrong. For a start, I had heard supporters argue that the season had been disappointing because we hadn't reached the European Cup final, with the implication being that winning the Premiership was no longer a big enough deal. Then, on the lap of honour, I detected a true sense of jubilation on the face of just one man: Fergie himself. I wonder if the hunger (to which he so often refers) was beginning to fade for some? Alex Ferguson's reported comments in the Times suggest that significant changes are inevitable over the summer months, and that this may need a reappraisal of transfer market policy.

With Alex Ferguson and Brian Kidd at the helm I believe we can look forward with some optimism. I see parallels with 1994/95, when we ended the season trophy-less, much to the glee of the rest of the country. That season marked a watershed, signified by the departure of a number of key players and the introduction of the kids, an initiative that represented a bold experiment. Could a club as massive as United compete at the very highest level on the basis of a youth policy, supplemented by occasional signings? In the event, the title was regained and retained, and we dreamed of our home-grown young team conquering Europe.

Now 1997/98 could prove to be another watershed. It has become clear that our squad is nowhere near as strong across all positions as is necessary to cover a season's injuries, and the flow of genius from the junior ranks seems to have returned to a normal level after the extraordinary crop of 1992. Furthermore, there is a growing belief that even at our strongest we are some way from seriously worrying Juventus. The seemingly imminent acquisition of Jaap Stam (a man whose desire to wear the Red shirt has already endeared him to the fans) may be the first sign that the problems have been recognised and will be acted upon. United will emerge far stronger from the disappointment of 1998 than if we had gone on the take the title in comfort.

The plc half-year report to 31 January 1998 recorded a £1.5 million increase in players' wages, and I only hope that the arrival of more top quality players does not lead to a significant (and unaffordable) hike in season ticket prices over the next few years. I have often wondered whether the financial expectations of the game's top performers could be met through initiatives such a royalties on personalised merchandise (allegedly claimed by Eric) or through executive-style share option schemes. Merchandise royalties for players would allow their remuneration to be related to their performances, indicated by their popularity. Even though the fans would ultimately pay the price, the element of consumer choice would be preferable to the season ticket price rises reported from other clubs, and dreaded by those of us with United-supporting families.

So we need a miracle to win the league this year, but as long as we heed the lesson, strengthen the side and continue to be the team to beat, we should not be too downhearted. To be the whole nation's rivals simply means that United matter. I was greatly amused by the Liverpool supporters' banner declaring that they were 'Monaco Supporters – Liverpool Branch'; they were about to win nothing again, but were delighted because United faced a race to the wire. Can you imagine United supporters declaring themselves to be followers of any other team, and can you remember which mighty club knocked Liverpool out of Europe way before Christmas?

I'm already looking forward to 1998/99, in the anticipation of what Fergie will serve up, and I'm hoping that our first match is Arsenal, away.

Becks, Oh-La-La!

August 1998. The World Cup was played in France this summer, and England lost their quarter-final against Argentina on penalties. Manchester United's David Beckham was sent off in the match and thus became the nation's scapegoat. But United fans stood by their man amid the unseemly hysteria.

Before the 1994 FA Cup final there were a few young lads wearing United blazers outside Wembley Stadium. They were unfamiliar to most of the crowd, and went by unnoticed, but I recognised one as a promising reserve player called David Beckham. For a moment I watched him wind his way through the throng, and I wondered if the day would come when he would be starring in the Cup final, rather than looking on. Thinking about the superb side that was about to clinch the Double that afternoon, I confess that I couldn't see when Beckham's chance would arrive. In my ignorance of his abilities I didn't think he was knocking on the door to quite the same extent as, say, Gary Neville or Paul Scholes. Even further from my mind was the idea that Beckham would one day replace the hero of that rainy afternoon – the great Eric Cantona – as the *enfant terrible* of English football.

Towards the end of the following season, with Kanchelskis on his way out of Old Trafford, Beckham was recalled from a loan spell at Preston (where he had shown signs of quality) to appear in United's FA Cup semi-final against Crystal Palace. He performed reasonably well, but was still finding his feet; superstardom did not seem imminent. But United reached the final, and on the big day Beckham was no longer an unknown face in the crowd.

As Ince and Hughes followed Kanchelskis through the exit door, Fergie threw in the kids. The first match of 1995/96 is more often remembered for the flawed analysis of Alan Hansen than for David Beckham's spectacular consolation goal at Villa Park, but Beckham was in the side to stay. By the season's end his progress had been remarkable; with his young mates he was a league champion, and there was no doubt that he possessed a very special talent.

It was during the following season that David Beckham began attracting the wrong sort of publicity. His once-in-a-generation goal against Wimbledon (interestingly not the BBC's Goal of the Season) marked his transition to footballing celebrity, but as the Reds won the league yet again, anti-United hysteria reached the proportions of a national obsession. If United's continued success was getting up the nation's collective nose, it was Beckham who personified all that the United-haters liked to focus on. He was young and flash, immensely talented; he displayed what was referred to as 'arrogance' when combined with a United shirt. His game had become more combative, and he increasingly nagged at referees; no different to hundreds of other players, but in a United jersey this becomes 'whinging'. As an east-ender with a passion for Manchester United he also represented the mythical 'You Don't Come From Manchester' jibe.

As Beckham's high profile romance attracted the tabloid treatment he, with his young United mates, would be abused by the England crowd at Wembley. If they'd been Dutch they'd have stuck up two fingers and walked off the pitch. Nor did he find peace when he returned to his home.

It was claimed by the cognoscenti that Beckham was becoming 'affected' by his pop star lifestyle. It was also suggested that when he was left out of United's team at the start of 1997/98 that this was a sure sign of his manager's wrath. Beckham would be on his way out of Old Trafford, to the delight of his girlfriend, who was said to prefer the shopping malls of Milan and Turin. Such talk was fuelled by United's decision to give new signing Sheringham the number 10 shirt, previously worn by Beckham. But within weeks Beckham was back, and shining as United made the running in the first half of the season.

Beckham had been handed the number 7 jersey vacated by Cantona, and previously worn by another all time great, Bryan Robson. Perhaps it was coincidental, but by Christmas, with Keane out injured, Beckham had also assumed the mantel of United's most talked about – and most abused – player. As unoriginal, unimaginative and uncouth Posh Spice chants greeted him everywhere he did little to persuade his tormentors that they were wasting their time; his inability to remain aloof encouraging them to redouble their efforts. When he hit back in the most effective way – by scoring a goal for United – his initial reaction was inevitably a metaphorical two fingers, which confirmed that the taunts had hit home.

As United's title challenge hit the buffers Beckham was not playing well. He was recognised as a deadly free kick expert and as a superb crosser of the ball, but the free kicks were missing the mark and the crosses were being hoofed in from 35 yards out, rather than whipped back from behind the defence. But he was running his socks off for United, and the crowd recognised that Beckham – still young, however talented – could not be expected to hold the fort alone as an injury crisis took its toll on the team.

And so to the World Cup. Perhaps enough has been written about the decision of Hoddle to omit Beckham (an ever-present during qualification) from the opening match against Tunisia. But if the coach argued that this was because of the player's lack of focus (whatever that meant), it seemed that the result was for Beckham to be placed in the focus of the whole nation. Had he played against Tunisia he would not have become a debating point. When he appeared briefly against Romania, then against Colombia, he did so with a point to prove. Did this cause him to be too hyped-up in the next match against Argentina?

When he was dismissed for an act of petulance my immediate thoughts were for United, and on how the club had been let down. I was disappointed in him for that reason alone. Again there is the Cantona parallel, as Eric's greatest indiscretion hurt United in the main. The media fuelled the hysteria (nicely filling the front and back pages). An objective criticism of Beckham would conclude that he had been stupid; to argue that he had cost England the game is debatable; to demonise the player is solely due to the fact that he plays for Manchester United. But the vilification that followed England's elimination (like that heaped on Cantona) had the effect of rallying United supporters behind their man. Was his crime worse than the foul by Owen which ended Ronny Johnsen's campaign last season? Was it worse than the shove on referee Ellery that earned Batty a suspension? Was it worse than Shearer's attempt to release his foot from the presence of Neil Lennon? Whereas those three 'lions' returned to sympathy, our man cleared off to join his girlfriend in New York. Accosted at both ends of his journey he looked a picture of misery as he fled the cameras and reporters. How can you be so young, so talented and so rich, yet be so unhappy?

It has been suggested that he will make a public apology to the English people! I hope he follows Cantona's example and refuses to be so manipulated. His pop at Argentina's Simeone, though silly, was nothing in comparison to the maliciousness and vindictiveness (even criminality) of some of his accusers. It is a disgrace that his parents have required protection, and a bitter irony that those responsible see fit to adopt a high tone. Such types would ignore any apology anyway. The fact is that they abuse David Beckham simply because they want to. His main crime has been to be foolish enough to give them an excuse.

The solution, we were told, was for him to leave United and the Premiership. He must go to Italy for rehabilitation. The English crowds would never allow him to settle again. But we have heard that before, haven't we? And didn't Eric sort out his head and return triumphant? Can the abuse in store for David Beckham be any worse than that he has endured already? With the support of the United crowd, the guiding hand of Alex Ferguson, and maybe even a word of encouragement from Eric himself, David Beckham will overcome. Maybe the United fans will even come up with a decent song about him some time soon.

If the Cap Fits

September 1998. Getting a few things off my chest …

It was United's greatest night, and will probably ever so remain. But whenever you look back at the moment of triumph, in a yellowing old annual or on a zippy new video, there is one figure that keeps getting in the way. God knows what thoughts and emotions were going through the mind and body of Sir Matt as he ran onto the Wembley turf to hug Charlton, Best, and the rest of the team of '68. What was sure was that he wasn't going to be allowed to savour the moment as he chose. You'd expect the cameras to be under their noses (how else could the images be saved for the books and the videos), but on most of the pictures Busby and the players are not alone. Maybe you too have noticed him? Like me, have you been bugged for thirty years by that bespectacled old bloke in the security uniform with the words Wembley Stadium on the front of his jobsworth-cap? "Excuse me, Mr Busby," he seems to be trying to say, "you may have reached your Holy Grail, your mind may be trying to deal with a bewildering array of emotions, from the joy of this victory to the heartbreaking recollection of the team you lost, but allow me to grapple with yourself and Mr Foulkes, thus ensuring my face is on almost every photo of your finest hour. Can you please calm down, form a line and go and collect that big trophy, because I need to lock up at eleven o'clock."

Aaaargh! I just hate him. There, I've finally got it off my chest. Maybe it is just his all pervading and eternal presence that is the source of my annoyance, because as irritants go he was innocent in intent. These days the effort of ignoring the ubiquitous ABUse is akin to wafting a forlorn palm when picnicing under a wasps' nest.

For example, I had the misfortune recently to catch a few minutes of a dire game show hosted by Clive Anderson. He asked Jeremy Hardy where Manchester United supporters live, and Hardy replied "In easy street". I suppose it was a moderately amusing answer off the top of his head, and it was certainly light years ahead of Anderson's scripted punchline: "No, the answer is 'Anywhere except Manchester'", quipped the balding barrister. In the few seconds before I switched off the set I wondered whether the comic genius had managed to write this joke all by himself, or whether he had needed the help of a team of scriptwriters.

There was nothing unique, of course, about the experience of switching on a random TV show and hearing anti-United jibes. It would help if they were original or even funny, but that may be asking a little too much. Serious Reds now find that football considerations can affect all manner of other interests, and I often boycott television presenters or pop stars who have declared themselves to be United-haters. Stick to Beethoven, I say: he may have been a German, but he never slagged off United. Mind you, I also avoid some of those purporting to be United supporters – especially the bandwagon jumpers who leapt aboard about four years ago.

I wouldn't include Mick Hucknell in the latter category, but you can imagine my surprise (make that horror) when he told the United Video Magazine that in the 1970s he'd gone watching City because United were so bad and had lost George Best. He was lounging round a hotel room with Giggs and Ince prior to the defeat in Barcelona when he gave that interview. Respect due? Well, you pays your money, as they say, but having stuck by United throughout the 26 year misery, I hope I can be forgiven for being less than impressed. Still, he gets to be mates with Eric, so why should he care?

I had to get round to Eric, didn't I? What a great night the Munich testimonial was, with the right balance, I feel, being struck between commemoration and celebration. The minute's silence and the words of Gordon Taylor ensured that those lost in 1958 were at the forefront of our minds, but the joy of the football was also a fitting tribute to the Babes. Let us hope that the money raised by the supporters (put in perspective by the transfer fee for Dwight Yorke which Villa squeezed out of United) is not too little, too late. Meanwhile, Cantona showed that he is still good enough, and he looked in better shape than Paul Gasgoigne to me. But although he may still be better than most, he cannot be as great as he once was, which is why a return is impossible. As he made that final lap of honour to universal acclaim, I wonder if Gasgoine was watching on, and was thinking 'If only I'd signed for United'?

The only disappointment on the night was provided by the linesman who clearly felt that 55,000 had gathered to celebrate his semaphore skills. I bet he watched the video of himself disallowing Eric's header over and over again. Then popped down to his local and recounted his greatest moment, "Oh, it was wonderful, I just waved my little flag and 50-odd thousand all went quiet. I'm sure they appreciated that a Red shirt had been in an offside position at the precise moment the ball was played forward". I wonder if his grandfather was a security man at Wembley in 1968? Perhaps it was fitting that Cantona wasn't even offside, as a little injustice has always been his companion.

It was neat in a way that the man who so piously pronounced the judgement and sentence following Eric's worst moment became embroiled in a little local difficulty of his own last month. David Davies, said to be a Red, and often seen around Old Trafford during his BBC North days, is now the public voice of the Football Association. He dismissed suggestions that his role as Glenn Hoddle's ghostwriter was in any way inappropriate. Personally I have little interest in Hoddle's little book, and I've no desire to read another word about his chum, the faith healer. Like many other United supporters I'm still amazed that ITV was able to set up the Hoddle versus Ferguson 'confrontation' on their panel. The two predictably, and correctly, played down the whole thing, but how could a disagreement between a manager who has won virtually everything and a manager who has won virtually nothing be presented as a conflict of equals? In any case, Alex isn't quite panel material in the same way that the likes of Venables and Hansen are. He's more impressive when snarling at post-match interviewers or waving his stopwatch at referees, than tamed and dispassionate in a studio.

I wonder if David Davies (who'd make a good linesman, come to think of it) scripted Teddy Sheringham's grovelling apology to his coach, his son, his cat and his hamster for the dreadful embarrassment he had caused them by having a night on the town? OK, the town was in Portugal and it was early morning, rather than night-time, but they had poor old Teddy over a barrel, didn't they, with the axe hanging over his one and only chance of playing in a World Cup? Although I don't generally feel able to empathise with people who can take a private plane to Portugal (when I can't afford to take a taxi to Tescos), Hoddle, Davies and the FA Sunday School made it possible this time.

They'd never have made Eric read it out.

The Passing Game

October 1998. Manchester United were at a crossroads with the proposed takeover of the club by the television company BSkyB. A highly organised campaign against the sale of the club was undertaken by fans' groups, and some months later the deal was blocked by the powers that be. This article appeared soon after the proposals became public, and unashamedly put the emotional case for independence.

This Murdoch business has made me come over all profound. It's all this talk of 'buying' Manchester United. How do you buy Manchester United? What is Manchester United, anyway? The answer to the first question seems to be that you offer lots of money to people who possess little pieces of paper called share certificates. And because most of these people will care little, if at all, for a certain football club, anyone who offers enough dosh will have a reasonable good chance of owning more of these shares than anyone else. That makes him the majority shareholder, as they say, and it gives him power to decide what to do with the company that controls a football team. He also gets a nifty car parking space and lots of people keen to make his acquaintance. It must be rather nice for him. But it doesn't mean he has bought Manchester United, does it? He hasn't even bought all its shares – at least not if enough of the little people tell him to get lost. So what does he own exactly? Just the ability to generate some profits and reap a decent dividend, maybe.

Proper writers like to use a metaphor, so think of Manchester United as a tree. A really big one; the biggest in football's jungle. It was a sapling once, but its roots grew strong, and it's now a pretty complicated organism. It lives and breathes. It blossoms and it sleeps. A multitude of living things turn to it for nourishment, for support, for a place to be, for a home even. But who owns it – the man who bought the forest, the kids whose swing hangs from its branches or the squirrels on its bark? Does it belong to the world that provides its oxygen or to the lumberman with the chainsaw? Does control equate to ownership?

There's more to a tree than wood, and there's more to Manchester United than share certificates. Manchester United is in the hearts of its supporters: from Alex in the dug-out to Joe Bloggs in Row Z to the exile in Timbuktu with a short wave radio. Manchester United-R-Us.

It feels like one of those defining moments in history. There haven't been many: the railwaymen of Newton Heath start up a football club; Davies saves it from oblivion and United is born; Gibson keeps the Red flag flying in the 1930s; Busby arrives; Munich; and now. For over 100 years Manchester United existed for the glory of being. Glory at football was everything, and financial soundness was the foundation for better football. The flotation of the club changed that: some of the money went outside the family, but the tills were ringing and co-existence became the norm. There remained mutual interest in Manchester United achieving glory, even if the joy of the supporters in Rotterdam and the glow of the fund managers after a rainy night in 1991 were for different reasons.

Now we're not so sure. And even if the new 'owners' give every assurance in the world one thing seems clear: United won't be a standalone glory-and-profit machine anymore; it will be a cog in a corporate wheel, with its own part to play in a grander design. United won't exist simply to be United; simply to win at football. You've heard all the arguments, the talk of big business and the lexicon of finance. To me some things just don't feel right, and I think that is enough.

The trouble is that this is a runaway train, and if it's not to be BSkyB it is likely to be someone else – or rather something else, another corporation. United are going to get swallowed up it seems. The Big Five days are a long way off, a quaint station we passed through as the train got up some steam. Spurs and Everton were derailed, Liverpool have chugged along; Arsenal are like the guard's van trying to hang on to the locomotive from Newton Heath.

I'm not arguing for an eternal status quo, because a body can change its clothes without losing its heart. We talk about tradition, and about 100 years of football history, as if this were a long time. Maybe we should recognise that organised soccer is a recent human phenomenon, a product of the latter stages of industrialisation. Back then the trip to an away game at Arsenal was a serious journey, certainly more of a trek than a flight to Barcelona would be now. So why the fuss about the Euro-league as a next step? One hundred years ago the southern amateurs were up in arms when northern industrial towns started taking the game seriously, and began recruiting professional players, often Scots. Now those same clubs are unhappy about United, Juventus, etc going one step further. It's now about globalisation, and our concern that things are getting out of hand is natural. We can envisage a Rollerball future when a contrived global pseudo-sport is presented for the benefit of multimedia conglomerations. It's scary and it's confusing.

Perhaps we just fall into the trap of believing in the importance of our own existence at this point in history. It wouldn't matter a jot to us now what happened to the Roman 'sport' of gladiator fighting, but at the time there's no doubt that people got quite hot under the collar about it. There are, for example, recorded instances of amphitheatres being closed for periods in response to crowd trouble. And those events took place over a much longer period than football's short century. No doubt after the first 100 years of gladiatorial contests people thought the pastime was with us forever. Will football also be ancient history one day, will the sands of time literally blow over Old Trafford, and will future generations wonder what all the fuss was about? To misquote King Eric, we are all just passing through.

If that reality is startling, then it does not mean we should not care here and now. When I see the fuzzy photos of United returning to Manchester with the Cup in 1909 I look into the faces of the crowd around the team coach. They were as proud and as pleased back then as we were in Albert Square in our own time, in the days before gathering in Albert Square became too 'dangerous' to be permitted. Those crowds didn't care about balance sheets; as long as the club was on a secure footing the only thing that mattered was the glory. I wonder how proud those people would be of what their club became, just as I wonder how proud today's supporters are of Meredith and Turnbull, and of Roberts and Barson. We should be proud of them because they were Reds, and they did their bit. Future generations will have the celluloid to convince them of Eric's genius, but we would hope that whatever becomes of Manchester United after our time, that future generations would be proud of him. And we hope they'd be proud of us, 'mere' supporters, for how we played our part. One day we will be faces in an old photo, a crowd on a fuzzy, pre-digital film, but we'd hope to be recognisable as supporters, just as we see our own equivalents in 1909. Our hope is that United will still be recognisable as the club we followed. Perhaps the crowd scenes over the generations provide the common thread: as players come and go, as fashions change and as sponsors grab the spotlight, the fans are the beating heart.

Manchester United is its supporters, and I don't think we are for sale. We just need a driver we trust at the head of this train.

Riches from Rags

November 1998. Some thoughts on United's defensive talents, and how times had changed.

United's brilliant early '90s youth teams possessed more than great talent. They were blessed with impeccable timing, maturing into potential first team players just as the side required their fresh natural talents. From early on it was clear that half of them would make their mark, and long Old Trafford careers seemed assured.

The result is that we now have a brilliant young first team squad, supplemented by big signings with time also on their side. But it represents a problem for the latest crop of players – how do they make the breakthrough? It is right that only the very best should graduate into the sacred Red jersey, and it is unavoidable that those not up to the standard will be released, but I hope that fine prospects don't end up giving good service to other clubs simply because we have too many good players. The choices in defence are mind-boggling: Berg and May seem to have slipped behind Stam and Johnsen, but what is Gary Neville's best position? Will Phil Neville play regularly when Irwin is fit? How do we ensure that Clegg and Curtis continue to progress? If Brown becomes the star we expect, who makes way? And how must all that sound to Danny Higginbotham, a debutant at the close of last season having impressed at junior levels?

You only have to look at Brian McClair to see how reserve football can take the edge off a good player. So what does the future hold for John Curtis, deemed good enough to play for England under-21s, but scrapping for a chance at Old Trafford? How patient can Curtis afford to be? I held my breath when a loan switch to Manchester City was mooted last season, dreading the idea that one of our lads would be helping to save City's first division skin. I suppose we can only hope that if any of these boys do move on they will achieve long and successful careers, though not at the expense of United, nor on behalf of any club we are, how shall I put it, not too fond of.

This wealth of defensive talent is almost unreal for those who recall the bleak early '70s, when United had a perennial problem in recruiting or nurturing decent back four players. Apart from the immaculate Martin Buchan, few of the players from that period would have got a game in the present reserve team. Far worse defenders than Chris Casper (a good player, unlucky to be at United at a time of intense competition for opportunities) were given a decent run in the team, and those with long memories will be able to reel off a series of lads who didn't last the course: O'Neill, Donald, Edwards, Watson, Griffiths, Sidebottom, Young and James. To those who were there, that is a pretty evocative list, and United's reluctance to splash out for a top notch set of defenders (and a number of the period's star performers were up for grabs) heralded the spiral towards relegation.

It was against this backdrop that Jim Holton became a serious folk-hero, for at last we had someone to get a grip, someone with an edge; we were sick of being soft touches. He was also a good footballer, one deserving of his international place, but he occasionally lived up to his fearsome reputation, not least when he was sent off for butting the back of Malcolm MacDonald's head in front of the Old Trafford dug-outs. Younger readers may be able to relate to the hero's departing ovation when it is pointed out that 'SuperMac' was a cocky Newcastle number 9 with a talent for not actually winning many medals.

Strange to realise that those days, which seem so vivid, were well before today's rising stars were even born. Wes Brown, born 16 March 1979 – makes you think; at least it makes me think. Here we have a lad playing for United who was born as I was preparing to take my final exams, who was a baby when I bumped into Phil Lynott on Wembley Way before the 1979 Cup final, and who is presumably oblivious to so many of the trials and tribulations suffered by growing United supporters in the decade before his birth.

My first visit to Old Trafford was well before the suffering '70s, with European Cup triumph still on the horizon. The full-backs that day were the progressive Tony Dunne and Bobby Noble, a player of unbridled promise for whom a career-ending car crash just a few months later was sadly only the beginning of a catalogue of personal tragedy. Noble was never effectively replaced, though United were also unlucky to lose the young and tenacious John Fitzpatrick (who did a stint at full-back) due to a troublesome knee. Injury also curtailed the United career of Nobby Stiles, and with time catching up on Bill Foulkes, and with David Sadler failing to reach the heights, the second division began to beckon. The drying up of the youth system and an unwillingness to wave the cheque-book in anger led to the antithesis of today's defensive riches.

As a growing lad smitten by all things United I, like many others, took this in my stride. Before these dark days, say at the age of nine or ten my appetite for football had largely been fed by a now-forgotten publication called *Jimmy Hill's Football Weekly*, the initial attraction being George Best's column. George's articles became of a chronicle of United's decline, with an ever-optimistic suggestion that good times were just around the corner; I wanted so much to believe him. I also became captivated by a football clinic feature called *Your Soccer in Depth* by Jim Clarkson: I took to studying this closely at that beautiful age when it has not dawned on a young boy that perhaps he will never play for Manchester United. I was probably a bit young to be devouring all this stuff, which may explain why I never met anyone else who read this magazine, but I recall it fondly, and still have the odd copy.

So it was that I grew to be besotted with United. In the playground I would defend Ian Ure's reputation at risk of my own, and I thought the world of all those players who – with the benefit of hindsight and the opportunity to watch some decent United teams – weren't really of United calibre. Worst of all I remember being smiled at in a patronising sort of way by 'grown-ups' who had a more realistic appreciation of the limitations of my heroes.

Nonetheless I remember them all with some affection: they were my life as I entered my teens, and thoughts of watching them play as I stared out of a classroom window on many a grey Wednesday sustained me through the baffling tedium of chemistry and physics. When all is said and done, those lads played for United. They did what we all wanted to do, and however briefly their stars shone they can open an old programme, see their names, and feel content that they played on that pitch and wore that shirt.

The lucky devils.

The Greatest Dane

December 1998. Peter Schmeichel wasn't enjoying his best spell of form, but it was time to support the great Danish goalkeeper. One more crucial penalty save was to follow, and by the end of the season Schmeichel would experience the ultimate triumph, as the last sentence of this article almost predicts.

The gleaming, sporty motor car looked rather undignified with an up-turned paper cup sitting on its rooftop aerial. The owner was none-too-pleased as he emerged from the pavilion at the Cliff, fresh from the post-training showers. This particular United striker was more intent on identifying the culprit than on signing autographs. "Who done that?" he growled, and looked accusingly around the knot of fans that had been drawn towards him. "It was Big Peter," replied one of the supporters, whereupon the player tossed the cup on the floor and took out his annoyance on his tyres as he screeched away. I bet he never did have a word with the giant goalie.

That minor incident has probably been forgotten by most who were there, but it stuck in my mind because it said something about the stature of Peter Schmeichel, at that time approaching the peak of his powers. Schmeichel has since achieved a level of performance unrivalled in the memories of United supporters. It is not simply the number of miraculous saves that he has pulled off, but the dominance of his terrain, and his pivotal role in the United psyche.

Goalkeepers are never any good if they are nice. They must have an edge to their character, whether it is the obsession of a Shilton, the robotic iciness of a Jennings or the arrogance and intolerance of a Schmeichel. United have had too many nice guys in goal, and only the lovable-loony Sealey seemed to have the requisite missing screw. The personal offence that Schmeichel takes when conceding a goal is probably his most endearing quality. He may snap and snarl, glower and glare, but the fact is that we in the crowd feel just the same way. It is good for us to see that it is hurting one of our players too; good to see that he cares as much as we do – even if we've only conceded a sloppy 90th minute consolation.

You get the feeling that it's more than petulance (though that's how his detractors may like to present it). Peter Schmeichel really is a tough man – probably the only bloke in south London capable of grabbing Eric's collar on a certain night in January 1995. If Schmeichel had been on the left wing that evening, he may have prevented the whole thing. I recall one of the United staff discussing players' nicknames, and saying that Schmeichel wouldn't have one – not *didn't* have one, but *wouldn't*. He wasn't having it, and no one seemed to be arguing.

Scheimchel and Cantona were eighty percent of the reason that United won a second Double in 1996: take away one or the other and the whole thing would never have happened. It sounds tough on the rest of a very good team, but the contribution of the pair was quite disproportionate. The team lacked the all-round experience and quality of the 1994 Double winners, but the Schmeichel/Cantona combination, supported by the emerging young stars repeated the feat. Newcastle, away, was the quintessential display, and the feeling remains that without Big Peter we'd have needed a thirty goal striker to make up the deficit.

Maybe he could have scored a few more himself, given the chance. You get the feeling that he enjoyed the *Schmeichel up front* chant, and that he was disappointed never to have been let off the leash. The Busst testimonial (when Coventry goalkeeper Ogrizovic played as a striker in the second half) would have been perfect, although he was a virtual striker for the last five minutes of the 1995 FA Cup final. At one late point he stood hands on hips in the centre circle while Roy Keane dealt with an Everton counter attack on the edge of his own penalty area. Unfortunately his forays up front were always in pursuit of precious equalisers, rather than occasions to enjoy, but as the years have erased the disappointment of being dumped out of Europe by Rotor Volgograd, Peter Schmeichel's late goal warms the heart and augments his legend.

Schmeichel has also been the first line of United's attack. His swift and accurate distribution has been fundamental to the deadly counter-attacking style that United have employed to thrilling effect, especially in 1993/94: feeding Cantona; releasing Kanchelskis or Giggs; finding Hughes to supply the runner; milking the applause of the crowd behind his goal as United hit the net. I've never seen a ball thrown so well, nor so far, by anyone. Hell, I didn't know a ball could be thrown that far. Which all made it so odd that his kicking could be so erratic – how many times have we seen him lump it into the stand when seemingly under no pressure, then deliver a quizzical look at Andy Cole, who was somehow to blame?

It's hard to recall now how we felt on hearing of Schmeichel's signing. It seemed to drag on for a few weeks during the summer of '91, and it's fair to say that few of us would have worried if the deal had fallen through. We hadn't after all had a lot of luck with foreign imports up to that time, and our previous Danes, Olsen and Sivebaek, hadn't made the desired difference. Come to think of it, who had heard of Schmeichel? But fans standing behind his net in that first season soon saw what this man had to offer: he was bloody enormous, built like a house. A keeper to inspire fear in the opposition – that would do for us. Within twelve months he was a household name, as a first season in which he learned very quickly to stamp his authority on the English game was followed by his enormous contribution to Denmark's European Championship win. His heroics in the semi-final penalty shoot-out against Holland, coupled with the crew-cut he sported around that time, made him one of the tournament's most recognisable stars.

Despite the Euro '92 shoot-out and a couple of Charity Shield deciders, Schmeichel has an unremarkable record when facing penalties for United. There was a save against Everton in the League Cup in 1993, and Spurs missed one against him a year later, but by my reckoning he conceded all the other penalties he faced, without ever looking like saving any of them. Not being a brilliant penalty-stopper, but the man you'd want on your side when one-on-one with a striker is only one paradox – there is also the music. Peter Schmeichel has a reputation for being a brilliant pianist, and he certainly has the hands to rival Rachmaninov, but he's never allowed us a glimpse of that particular talent (unlike Lee Sharpe fooling around to no great effect on his drum-kit). The reason seemed to be that he regarded it as more than a gimmick, and that he wanted to retain his privacy and gravitas. And that is fair enough. All the more bizarre then to see his appearance in that embarrassing Danish bacon advert – it's to be hoped he was well paid for that.

As a proud man and a proud goalkeeper Schmeichel feels bad enough when he concedes a goal, but appears humiliated when it is down to him. Every striker misses a chance, every midfielder misplaces a pass, but a keeper's error makes him a fall-guy, and when that keeper is Manchester United's prowling Dane the antis have a field day. He's made a few mistakes over the years, all redeemed by his miracles, but there have been a few this season (notably in Munich and at Sheffield Wednesday). Perhaps this has influenced his decision to retire at the end of the season. Like Eric before him he will not tolerate declining standards under the glare of Old Trafford's floodlights. He has spoken of the difficulties of maintaining his fitness, but he has appeared to rush his returns from injury: towards the end of last season when he played on with the hamstring injury he sustained in the opposition's half; then earlier this season when he returned to the side but was unable to take the goal-kicks. Maybe a decent break was all he required.

As it is we are witnessing the end of a great era. Each week until the end of this season we will be able to observe United's greatest ever goalkeeper with an ever closer eye, securing to memory the enormity of his presence, and ready to tell the next generations tales of the giant we once knew. And there is this thought to lift our hopes this final winter: in the autumn of 1996 United had a dire spell, losing three times in a week, and conceding 13 goals in the process. How they laughed at Peter Schmeichel, yet how they ground their teeth six months later when Schmeichel, back to his best, became a champion yet again.

Musings from the North Stand

December 1998. A few gentle ruminations ...

On 20 October 1973 Alex Stepney scored a penalty to give United a 1-0 win over Birmingham City. The match was notable too for being one of Georgie's numerous come-back games, and he was greeted by a young lad who bowed down in reverence before him on the pitch. It is often remarked that Stepney's goal made the United keeper the team's top scorer, since he had netted another penalty in a defeat by Leicester in the previous month. In fact things were not quite so dire: Stepney was in fact only the joint-highest scorer, as McIlroy and Kidd were also basking in the glow of two league goals at the time. If memory serves me right, Stepney missed the chance to notch a third spot-kick in the 0-0 with Wolves at the end of February that same season, but by the end of term with the club down and out he was still only four goals short of top scorer McIlroy, who had six.

This little sequence of woe was brought to mind three times recently. First, by one of those television programmes about Manchester City – you know the sort, all about how City are the salt of the earth and how wonderful their long-suffering supporters are. Nothing like the glory-seekers at Old Trafford who have taken the soft option of following a winning team. As if it's always been this way. Secondly there was the recent 'crisis' at Liverpool, with their fans filling the airwaves in anguish. Liverpool may be mediocre (and that's quite an insult to their pride), but the phrase 'some crisis' sprang to mind.

Then there was the full-time whistle at the end of the Newcastle match a few weeks ago, when the nil-nil result was greeted with rapture by our friends from the north. Twenty-five years ago visiting sides were turning up, turning us over and turning away with their expected points. Mind you, we did beat Newcastle even on the way to relegation. I suppose it's better to suffer the ecstatic cheers of inferiors achieving a draw than for home defeats to be the norm. But sometimes I feel we should put a podium in the middle of the pitch and present these sides with a 'we-got-a-draw-trophy', before they undertake a lap of honour.

* * *

The departure of Brian Kidd brought to mind another name from the golden era: Jimmy Murphy. Towards the end of his life Murphy, one of United's greatest ever servants, could walk unrecognised through many a crowd. The iron Welshman turned down vast riches in order to serve United, and he guided the club through the grim days after Munich.

In his autobiography Jimmy Murphy revealed he'd turned down an offer of £30,000 a year to coach in Brazil; this when he was managing the Wales team at the 1958 World Cup. Some time earlier he had been offered the Juventus job on a £20,000 salary. While Matt Busby was still in hospital one of United's 'biggest rivals' offered to double Murphy's money, but the man of principle declared that the offer had 'sickened' him, and that he had hung up on the caller. In all he said he was offered the management of more than a dozen top English sides, with an opportunity to join Arsenal making him stop and think. In the end he stayed, saying: "How can you state in terms of hard cash that where your heart belongs is worth more than all the money in Fort Knox ... My heart is at Old Trafford, so I went back to help Matt pick up the pieces and start all over again."

Being the great man that he was he probably had no regrets, but he never achieved riches, nor personal glory. It's true that no one at United made a real financial killing in Murphy's day, least of all non-football men behind the scenes, but many Reds feel that Murphy received scant official recognition for his service and loyalty.

I wonder whether the example of Jimmy Murphy was an influence on Brian Kidd's decision to leave United and have a crack at making a mark of his very own. Kidd is probably all too aware of how short memories can be, and may feel he deserves more than relative anonymity. There's a whisper that Kiddo's departure will prove temporary and that he is earmarked to succeed Alex Ferguson one day. But there's no reason why Fergie cannot carry on for at least five more years (what else would he do?), by which time Kidd will, remarkably, be nearly 55. A lot can happen in that time.

We'll never know (at least not for a long time) just how badly United tried to hang onto Brian. Most Reds will feel that the club should have moved heaven and earth to keep him, but at least we didn't get involved in an undignified tug-of-war with Jack (Shearer to United over my dead body) Walker. I'm not sure how to wish Kiddo good luck – we are talking about Blackburn Rovers here, after all – but I hope he finds what he's looking for.

Meanwhile, it was nice to see Harry McShane stride onto the pitch to make the half-time draw during a recent game. Harry is remembered fondly for his gentle style as pre-match DJ some thirty years ago. It was never easy to understand a word he said because the loudspeaker system was so awful, but he didn't annoy, nor patronize, in the manner of certain successors. He regularly played fifteen minutes of the commentary from extra time of the 1968 European Cup final, I recall. Come to think of it, I don't think I'd ever seen Harry before (his fifty-odd appearances for United being many years before I appeared on the scene), but it was a shame that his name was greeted with bewilderment, and the merest ripple of applause. Bizarre too to watch his muted greeting while Fred the Red was prancing round signing autographs on the touchline – why does anyone want Fred the Red's autograph? Harry McShane was playing the Calypso before every match once upon a time; I'm sure he appreciates the manner in which it has been adopted as a fans' anthem in the last year or two.

The Cup Overflows

February 1999. United's season was building up to a fantastic climax. In the FA Cup the team scored two very late goals to beat Liverpool at Old Trafford – it wouldn't be the last such heroic effort of the season.

"Four times!" they cried, over and over again. It's a history lesson that they seem to enjoy delivering. I recalled on hearing it the days when they didn't have to live in the past, when I had genuinely welcomed their European success. Rampant United hatred was a thing of the future, and in the late '70s/early '80s it was still possible to take pride in English success abroad, whilst wishing that United could also get in on the act. I particularly remember that horrific night when, sitting in a hotel room on the eve of a trip to France, I sat back in the hope that I'd see them win it for a fifth time. It wasn't to be, but no one cared, and the following day I was asked by bemused French friends to explain the events of the night before, as an Englishman with a passion for *le foot*. It seemed beyond analysis, and still does; it also seemed like the end of football as the sport I'd grown up with. But 14 years on, and it seems not so much forgotten, as obliterated from the nation's consciousness.

If fate had not dealt another cruel blow, maybe Matt's young boys would have gone on to win the European Cup – who knows how many times? There isn't a United fan who thinks that the 1968 team was a patch on the Babes, so "four times" was a possibility. We'll never know, but our pride in the Busby Babes goes beyond the counting game; we wouldn't trade our proud history for any number of European Cups.

Every few years you see a game that you know will live forever in the memory, and Ole's last gasp FA Cup winner against Liverpool led to an explosion of euphoria among Reds in the ground that has few parallels. Watching the goal celebrations on a TV re-run, it occurred to me that I'd witnessed none of it in the ground as emotions poured forth. Later I tried to explain the feeling, and sought a comparison, but struggled to come up with more than a handful of examples. Over the decades United have scored many late and dramatic winners – we did it again at Charlton – but it takes something extra special for a match to achieve legendary status.

For personal highlights of skull-expanding euphoria I suspect that few Reds would exclude Barcelona in '84, the mass jubilation of Sheffield Wednesday in '93 and the last-gasp roof-raising, courtesy of Eric's *coup de grace*, at Wembley in '96. Now a certain FA Cup tie from 1999 is sure to rank equally highly. For hysterical joy to be experienced in the context of the FA Cup 4th Round says much about the rivalry with the defeated side, and they might even take it as a compliment.

Whilst not wishing to sympathise with them in the slightest (after all, they weren't exactly paragons of magnanimity with five minutes to go), I tried to think of an occasion when we were similarly shattered in spirit. The agonising end of the 1995 season is probably the most recent example; far, far worse than losing in the 4th Round of the FA Cup, but not accompanied by fans blubbering for the TV cameras. We took that one on the chin, all right.

The 1979 Cup Final was perhaps unique in giving us both extremes, and an emotional somersault that I've no wish to experience again. At 2-0 down with time running out we were resigned to defeat; moments later, two goals had prompted scenes of uncontrollable joy and relief (I never did see my bowler hat again); only to throw it away from the restart, within seconds of the final whistle. What the hell, it was a crap hat anyway.

A final thought on the recent Cup tie concerns the way tickets are allocated to visitors. Not for the first time, 10,000 away fans gathered at the Scoreboard End (East Stand, if you must) have been able to out-roar the United crowd for long periods. Three years ago Sunderland did the same thing. It's clear that K-Stand / East Lower has become 'the End' for the most vocal United support, largely because of the gentrification of the Stretford End. Not exactly 'All Quiet on the West Stand Front', but difficult for the dispersed Reds to compete in the decibel stakes.

The upshot is that United must be the only team in the country whose fans do not have an 'End' to claim as their own. I suspect visitors are given the Scoreboard End for reasons of security – easy to get them in and out, for one thing – but can you imagine away fans being given the Kop, or the North Bank, or the Holte End? It simply couldn't happen could it? The United Review for the recent West Ham game contained two pleas for greater vocal support, one from the manager, and the other from the club on page 5; but it takes two to tango, and the fans will need the support of the board on this one.

Neville With A Cause

February 1999. Gary and Phil Neville had published a diary of their life at Old Trafford. Gary's Red credentials came over loud and clear.

It must be something to do with being a full back. He is one of United's most consistent players, a home-grown local boy, and a regular international. He's so passionate a Red that at times it's like looking in a mirror to watch his antics. But despite always being the last player to leave the field after applauding the supporters, you'll search long and hard to see the name 'G. Neville' and the number '2' on a shirt in the crowd. And he must lie in bed at night wondering what he's got to do to get his name sung out loud. It's not that the fans don't respect and admire him totally – maybe he just seems a little too much like the fan in the next seat, lacking the outrageous charisma of a Keane, a Yorke or a Stam. But with Gary Neville things are not always quite as they seem.

Reading the Neville brothers' diary* recently, a couple of contrasts became apparent. For a start, the ordinary boy next door is nothing of the kind. After all, few of us have neighbours with three England internationals in the family (sister Tracey being a netball star, of course), and with mum and dad being on the staff of Bury FC, Gary and Phil always had a foot across the threshold of the professional game.

Once Gary Neville had played half a dozen matches for the first eleven, his destiny seemingly fulfilled, we knew immediately that Paul Parker's days were numbered. But Gary hadn't quite been born to greatness, despite his rapid transition from cool United youth team captain to regular first teamer and automatic choice for England. It seems that Gary's graduation had never been a certain thing, indeed it was young Phil who had generated the expectations. While Phil played for England schoolboys at football and cricket, breaking most of the batting records in Lancashire, Gary wasn't even picked for the county football team. Forsaking his education (his dad reminding him that 'A' levels can be taken when you're 75!) Gary Neville got his head down, and set about becoming a United player. It is possibly the need to apply himself, and to focus on succeeding, that has left Gary with the mature demeanour that made him an obvious captain; lacking the God-given talents of his pal David Beckham, Gary Neville couldn't afford the luxury of acting flash. Interestingly, another non-international contemporary, Paul Scholes, also rose above the cream with graft and a level head.

In the diary Gary pays tribute to coach Eric Harrison for nurturing his talent, saying "I didn't have a clue – I hated tackling!" He's surely being modest, but the result is that we have a player in whom we can be proud; a representative of the fans out there on the pitch. He gets well paid, for sure, but accepts that he can't command the contracts of some of his more

---

glamorous team-mates. You might take the view that he should hold out for parity, but his stance strikes a chord for those of us who would pay to play for United. No big ego when it comes to team selection either – he missed out on 88 minutes of the 1996 Cup Final because he was unable to reclaim his place in the side following a suspension incurred helping United to the title. He'd played so well before his ban that at any other club he'd have stepped straight back in, but he knuckled down and was on the field as the Double was won. And who can forget his lap of honour, singing "Cheer up Kevin Keegan" with Andy Cole? It was the act of a true Red.

That side of Gary Neville, perhaps most passionately evident following Ole's unforgettable FA Cup strike against Liverpool, is evident after each and every match he plays for United. As most of the team offer a cursory wave before heading off to the showers, the Reds with Heart – Gary Neville and David Beckham in particular – show their appreciation of our loyalty. It doesn't take much to do it, but most don't bother. Neville and Beckham know how much it matters, because if they were not so blessed they'd be on our side of that fence. You can't imagine many other United players echoing these sentiments: "If United signed Roberto Carlos and he was playing better than me, or if Phil or Denis Irwin were playing better than me, I wouldn't complain about not making the team. I've supported Manchester United all my life and they should always have the best players available. If that means me, good; but if it doesn't, hard luck."

As a fan with qualms about the newer breed of passive spectator, Gary recalls being one of the loyal 30,000 who stuck by United in the bleak years when Alex Ferguson was beginning the revitalisation of Manchester United. You know he means it when he says, "We have got to make sure it never goes back to that".

Gary Neville has acquired the endearing knack of sounding like a biased United fan in his public pronouncements; a bit of a trainee Paddy Crerand. Perhaps his classic so far followed defeat by Juventus in 1996, when United seemed scared to play, and were outclassed by a greater margin that the single goal suggested. Although the team was slightly more relaxed in the second half, Gary's claim that we "played them off the park" was stretching it a bit. His policy of saying what he thinks, and rejecting the straight-bat blandness of an Alan Shearer, even had him banned by Fergie from speaking to the press last season. "Every time I pick up a paper, you're in it!" the boss is quoted as saying. But this outspoken approach makes the Gary-half of the Neville brothers' diary a compulsive read.

Teddy Sheringham, in his autobiography, referred to Ole Solskjaer's professional foul on Rob Lee which possibly saved United a point against Newcastle towards the end of last season. Sheringham says that while the team appreciated Ole's actions, Alex Ferguson "weighed into him", and told him never to do it again. Here Gary Neville echoes the Sheringham standpoint, but with reference to the supporters: "He did it for his team-mates and the club. He saved us a point and the fans were right to give him a standing ovation as he walked off the pitch". Perhaps Alex Ferguson was simply applying some wise discretion, but if Gary Neville ever becomes United's manager the press will have a field day with the quotes.

Probably the most moving expression in recent years of the meaning of Manchester United was the 40th anniversary tribute to the Munich victims before the Bolton match. During the minute's silence the young United team on the pitch stood with heads bowed, arms around each other's shoulders, at one with their predecessors. It was simple yet powerful, a perfect gesture that could only have been conceived by one who understands: "It was something I'd suggested to Peter Schmeichel in the players' lounge before the game. I wanted us to show everyone that we were together and that we cared. Every player was happy to do it". Gary Neville deserves our thanks for that.

Gary is fan-like too in his views on some of our rivals, where even Pat Crerand occasionally applies some even-handedness. Anfield is said to be "the best place in the world to win a game of football". Of Leeds he comments: "When Becks scored all the lads ran over to the Leeds fans; we don't particularly like their style of abuse." And elsewhere Munich taunts are dismissed as "Sick, absolutely sick". Some of his most Red-eyed remarks are reserved for Chelsea: "Their Chairman has been quoted as saying that we are just a club from the slum side of Manchester. To me, Chelsea could move their stadium to the middle of Harrods and win fifteen championships on the trot, and even if you moved Old Trafford to the middle of Beirut they still wouldn't be as big as us". Mark Hughes remains a true United great, but even he found it in him to go and play for Chelsea with a United contract seemingly in the offing – it's not easy to see Gary Neville following such a route (though I wouldn't rule out a swansong with Bury in a dozen years' time). And those of us who won't allow our kids to wear Kappa gear will relate easily to Gary Neville's quandary when considering prospective boot deals: "Kappa have told us not to sign with anyone until we speak to them, but I can't get past the fact that they sponsor Manchester City!" Marvellous.

As with the other United lads who wish to play on the international stage (and despite our certainty that United are bigger than England, we can hardly blame them), Gary has to suffer the anti-United baggage that comes with the England crowd. He has little choice but to play through the abuse, but unlike his mate Becks, it seems that Gary had a bit of good fortune on the night England went out of the World Cup. England's lack of preparation for a penalty shoot-out has become common knowledge, and Gary Neville noticed that only three decent penalty-takers were on the field at the end of the Argentina game. Hoddle was clearly struggling at this point because as the penalties were about to commence he invited Gary Neville to take number six. Despite his qualities, not even his biggest fan would trust Gary Neville with a shot on goal from any more than 12 inches out, never mind 12 yards with a goalie to beat as well. Neville described his own finishing as "unacceptable" and even "disgraceful", but in the heat of the action Hoddle proceeded to give our man a few tips about concentrating and not changing his mind. Poor old Gary as Batty walked up to take England's fifth: "I have never been so nervous. I started thinking how I would take my penalty. I decided to just put my head down and whack it". I think we can all imagine the likely outcome, with the ball being ballooned to Boulogne, but fortunately Batty missed, and Gary didn't have to take up advertising pizzas, as brother Phil had feared.

In recent months Gary Neville has re-emerged from an inconsistent spell which probably owed much to the devastating end to last season and the rigours of France'98. It bodes well for the challenges ahead that this classy young defender is rediscovering his best form. So at the age of 24, having won virtually the lot, where does he go from here? Fortunately the possibilities are plentiful.

Assuming England don't win the World Cup in the next seven years (hardly an outrageous presumption), the aim is to win it all again and again for United, hopefully adding the Holy Grail of the European Cup to the honours. With the potential to be a future United captain, Gary Neville can be pre-eminent in the glories to come, probably as a full-back rather (than as once seemed possible) a modern Martin Buchan. The problem is that full-backs these days must be seen to do more than defend, so he must seek to emulate a Maldini rather than a Baresi. But if he takes on that challenge in his accustomed fashion, adding to his repertoire on the other side of the half-way line, his reputation could extend Europe-wide. Go and do it, Gary, for your fellows on this side of the fence.

For Club and Country: the hunt for European and World Cup glory, by Gary and Phil Neville, Manchester United Books, 1998.

Team Changes

March 1999. We are football fans, but what is it that we actually support? Players – heroes and villains – come and go, and the game itself changes endlessly.

I heard one of those Jerry Seinfeld monologues recently, the sort where he makes observations in a quizzical what-the-hell's-going-on-here sort of way (a standard comic device, I know). He was talking about American sports franchises, and how the concept of a team or a club increasingly lacks any concrete basis. They move the clubs, he said, from city to city; they change their names; they change the owners; the players come and go with rapidity, heroes becoming villains, and vice versa. He reckoned the only thing that remained stable was the colour of the kit, and that barracking a former player on his return as an opponent was tantamount to sitting there yelling "Boo! Boo! Wrong clothes – he's wearing the wrong clothes!" It's stretching the point, but I got his drift.

There's an argument, of course, that this is not quite as preposterous as Seinfeld made it seem. When you analyse it, supporters of a club like Manchester United may adopt the occasional super-hero such as Law or Cantona, but the true focus of the passion is seldom any individual. I believe that the essence of Manchester United is in the hearts of the supporters, for without them the whole thing ceases to matter. This may seem a childishly romantic point of view, but while centre-forwards or share certificates are for sale, there is no price on a fan's loyalty – it simply isn't for transfer, no matter what.

Football clubs are aware of this of course. They know that if we have a bad experience in Sainsbury's then we will do our shopping at Tesco. They also know that no matter how bad things seem at a fan's club, that supporter isn't going to switch his allegiance to another team. At worst, the fan will take a sabbatical. The true fan remains loyal to the badge, even when the badge is altered to further promote corporate identity in a commercial world.

Thus there is little intrinsic about being a hero or a villain. It's all about fortune; about whether or not someone gets to wear the hallowed badge. It may be a lucky break or a manager's whim; or a chairman's fear of signing a cheque. Cantona became a hero because Wilkinson couldn't or wouldn't embrace him. It was a chance in a million, with United struggling, Fergie having the courage to take him on and Leeds being daft enough to let him go. And so we had the hero of our generation, soon to forget his Yorkshire past and the fact that we'd not appreciated his efforts there.

On the other hand Dalglish is a bit of a villain, the personification of Liverpool in the days when they were formidable, when he was the crosser of swords with Fergie. A villain who returned to wound us again in his Ewood incarnation; one who, thankfully, failed to repeat the trick with the Geordies. But there's a fine line between heroes and villains, and for Dalglish it was a close run thing. When he replaced Keegan at Anfield in 1977 there had been talk of him moving to Old Trafford: what course would the history of English football have taken in the 1980s had that happened, and had his striking talents been harnessed along with those of Robson and co? He'd be our hero now, and the Cantona phenomenon may never have come to pass.

Keegan himself is illustrative of the whimsical nature of heroism and villainy. Returning to football when we'd given him up, he became the devil incarnate to United supporters during the latter stages of 1995/96, and his blowing a fuse in Fergie's direction showed how personal these things can become. 'Cheer Up Kevin Keegan' was sung with some venom in reply, and Reds would hiss at this pantomime baddy each time he appeared on TV. But what a difference a couple of years can make. Keegan slips into the lower leagues with Fulham, no longer represents a threat to United, comes on ITV praising Ferguson and cheers us along in the European Cup. Then as manager of England he gives Andy Cole some over-due recognition. And that's fine, because we hiss no longer – there are other bogey men around to occupy us these days.

Wasn't Roy Keane, before his transformation into Red-icon, a Damien-with-three-sixes-on-his-head character? A good example of 'he may be a dirty buggar, but he's our dirty buggar now'. And what good fortune for our latest cult figure, Jaap Stam, that the Brazilian Celio Silva was denied a work permit and that Barcelona blocked the switch of Miguel Nadal. It's the badge that matters to us, and we'll only worship those who wear it.

Returning to the Seinfeld theme, English football may not yet (operative word there) have taken on the less desirable characteristics of professional sport across the pond, but it's a worrying fact of life that globalisation often involves Americanisation. No wonder there was concern when, prior to the USA '94 World Cup, there was serious talk of dividing games into four quarters to accommodate TV commercials, widening the goals, and so on. If we had a narrow escape there, we've had to settle for the Americanisation of the football kit (names on shirts, squad numbers front and back, competition logos on the sleeves), and the previously all-American sight of half a squad on the subs' bench.

The recent innovation that I find most troubling is this business of having footballs all round the ground, with ball-boys throwing on a new one every time the ball goes more than a few yards out of play. I'll not blame the Americans for this, as in rugby they have been doing it for some time – mind you, the rugby league lot have started marking their pitch to resemble a grid-iron field, and renaming proud old clubs in the most crass fashion. But I digress.

There are two problems with this multiple ball business. This first is that the old English custom of the crowd annoying the hell out of the players (especially the losing side) by keeping hold of the ball, only to return it as soon as a replacement appears, has been lost to the higher echelons of the game. I know that this was the idea, but the practice will enter the realms of nostalgia in the not too-distant future. The second problem I have is more troubling: if a player scores a hat-trick, which ball does he take home? You can be sure that no one will have a clue which ball was used to score any of his goals, so he'll have to grab any old ball and tell his grand-children that it was somewhere in the ground when he scored a match-winning hat-trick with three other balls! On the positive side, a few more balls in the 1966 World Cup final would have meant that Helmut Haller and the Germans could all have had one each.

It is rule changes that traditionalists fear above all else, and I suspect that most dedicated supporters of football are traditionalists, in the sense that no one likes to see the object of their devotion change too much, or grow away from them. Having grown up in the era when goalkeepers had to bounce the ball every four steps while they were walking round with it (youngsters take a look at the 1966 World Cup final to see what I'm on about), rule changes seem to have arrived thick and fast in recent years, and I suspect many of us would like to see a moratorium for a few seasons to let things settle down. There's little chance of this, with experiments such as kick-ins instead of thow-ins being tried out in less senior leagues all the time.

Any self-respecting traditionalist would have a fit if the governing bodies suggested certain rule changes. How about goalkeepers allowed to handle the ball anywhere on the field; no direct free kicks; defending sides not having to withdraw ten yards at free-kicks and corners; the six-yard box to be replaced by two half-circles around each post; the penalty area extended the width of the pitch to the touch-lines ... but these were all features of football in the Victorian and Edwardian eras. I suppose it means that tradition can only be taken so far, or maybe that there is no such thing as tradition where a constantly evolving sport like football is concerned. While the Edwardians were concerned with defining legal charging, today's talk is of outlawing tackling altogether. And France '98 demonstrated that while some of the outrageous violence of previous World Cups is a thing of the past, sneaky cheating and crafty gamesmanship are alive and well.

If the game of football changes as much in the next hundred years as it has done in the last, then it will become a very strange game indeed. But as long as Manchester United are still playing in Red Shirts and White Shorts at Old Trafford, supported by the people and winning a few cups, then we will be able to look on from the clouds, and play a happy tune on our harps.

Que Sera Sera, perhaps.

Leagues Apart: A Review of the 1998/99 League Campaign

April 1999. Manchester United were on the brink of the incredible. A Treble of Premiership, FA Cup and European Cup would be won in the space of eleven days in May. The tension was growing as this article was written, before the league was won. Would we win everything, or nothing?

This time last year I pulled myself out of a feeling of depression long enough to write a review of the 1997/98 Premiership campaign. It was a painful, if therapeutic, task, and it made gloomy reading. Although there were a handful of games still to be played, United were heading for second place; we knew it and the world knew it too. And didn't the world rejoice! Most of all there was a sense of utter frustration that the title had been within our grasp, and that complacency had been as significant a factor as the springtime injury epidemic. Still, we looked ahead with hope that the lesson had been learned and that a new season would fulfil fresh hopes.

I write this immediately after our 1-1 draw at Leeds, the day after Middlesbrough conspired to wipe out our handy goal difference advantage; Chelsea have drawn at Hillsborough, and seem to have run out of steam; it's going to be close between ourselves and Arsenal once again. I pray that we'll prevail – I'm as biased as hell, but I happen to think that we deserve it. To have come so far whilst achieving glory in Europe, through the qualifiers and into the toughest group; and reaching Wembley once again despite the stiffest draw imaginable. No other club comes close. And so you have to say that whatever happens in the few remaining matches, we are so proud of our team this year; we could have asked for nothing more.

The season's opening was a time of anxiety. Would the players be suffering from the rigours of the World Cup? Was Stam as over-priced as his critics believed (or hoped)? Would Keane return fully healed? Could Beckham cope with the promised torrent of ill-will? And having found his goal-touch would Andy Cole depart for the Villa if United signed Dwight Yorke?

Not surprisingly it was an inauspicious start, United snatching a 2-2 draw at home to Leicester, having seemed well beaten. Sheringham, a late substitute, brought United back into the game; Stam had departed injured to taunts of 'what a waste of money' from our visitors. Then we were told that Solskjaer had been sold to Tottenham, only to see him on the bus bound for West Ham, having declared his intention to stay. Yorke was clearly in the manager's sights, and it now seemed that Cole would be making way, much to our annoyance. Andy Cole had earned his shirt, and many Reds would have preferred the collapse of the Yorke transfer to the loss of our top-scorer, but we got lucky in the end. I don't know whether John Gregory refused Cole in part-exchange, but (if so) thank heaven he did, and while he didn't accept Yorke's departure with the best of grace he was able to use the windfall to steal a couple of other clubs' top strikers while his team was flashing in the pan.

The worst performance of United's season came soon after Yorke's bright arrival, with a tame and characterless display at Highbury. The lost points could yet prove crucial, but we bounced back against Liverpool at Old Trafford. Andy Cole appeared as a late substitute in that game, looked lively, and kept his place. The Yorke/Cole partnership was invented, and during October United were on fire again; even Jordi joined in for a while. Blomqvist was a quality option that had been lacking when the title was lost, and the new Roy Keane was playing with his head as well as his heart. Beckham had risen above the abuse, the booing seeming so laboured already; like Cantona before him, Beckham just played his football.

November and December brought a mixture of grafted wins and hard-fought draws, but there was disappointment in a non-display at Sheffield Wednesday and a home defeat to Middlesbrough, when the team simply woke up too late. Peter Schmeichel was struggling for form and the defence seemed jittery, with Stam unable to benefit from a steady partnership at the back. In mitigation, the Champions' League was in full flow, making huge demands on reserves of physical and mental strength, and we hadn't managed to get ourselves knocked out of the League Cup until we'd played three ties. Add in the departure of Brian Kidd and the announcement of the retirement of Peter Schmeichel, and it's a wonder we came through relatively unscathed.

The team was still nicely placed near the top of the league, however, close to Arsenal and Chelsea, who would remain contenders, and just a little behind Aston Villa, a bubble floating high, yet certain to burst. It appears that strong words were spoken in the dressing room after the Boro defeat, and the players resolved to dig in and make things happen. From then on they have been a driven team, focusing on each match in turn, and able to commit fully on three fronts. In this we have been grateful for the re-emergence of Henning Berg as a defender of international class, and it is to his great credit that he forced his way up the pecking order to establish himself as a solid partner for Jaap Stam as the Dutch giant's level of performance became immense. Unbeaten since that miserable afternoon in December, the title would already be ours in many another year, but Arsenal have refused to lose as well.

This season has been a triumph of the genius of Alex Ferguson. If we supporters feel the stress, how does this man cope? With the loss of Brian Kidd the prophets of doom predicted that United would fall apart; it was even suggested that Kidd was the real mastermind, but with all due respect to Kiddo's massive contribution that was an insult to the talents of Alex Ferguson – as he was to demonstrate. The day-to-day running of the team must have been severely altered, but from the stands the transition has been seamless and it is probably no coincidence that we were mugged by Bryan Robson's Middlesbrough men on a day when Alex was absent for family reasons. The manager continued to prove his greatness, and his new assistant Steve McClaren must have wondered why he was needed on the evidence of his first day at the office: 8-1 on a drizzly day in Nottingham when £25 did not seem too much for an uncovered seat three rows behind a goal.

You can never overestimate quality. Ferguson has it, and so do the men who made the difference from last season's grim finale: Stam is simply a Colossus; Keane, every inch the leader, is fit again and more discerning in the challenge; and Yorke not only showed why the manager was right to pursue his signature relentlessly, but also exorcised the remaining demons of self-doubt in Andy Cole. The new men may have cost £20 million, but the likes of Chelsea, Newcastle and Blackburn have spent as much for less return.

And so we enter the final furlong – one more month and we'll know the outcome. What's for sure is that for the eighth consecutive season United will be in the top two, and we'll have achieved that despite every team in the land being 'up for' our encounters. I think we can be proud of that, and grateful to the manager who has delivered it.

On 11 May 1968 I was at Old Trafford watching United lose to Sunderland in the last game of the season. With that defeat we lost the championship, but we won the European Cup a couple of weeks later. Wouldn't it be great to go one better this time around?

Barcelona 1999 – The Time of Our Lives

June 1999. On 26 May 1999 Manchester United won the European Cup in the most dramatic of circumstances against Bayern Munich in Barcelona's Nou Camp stadium. A few weeks later it was time to reflect on a night that would surely never be equalled.

At the time, I didn't think that United winning the European Cup was such a big deal. I took it in my stride, always sure that we would win. I know that the nation was buzzing, and that the match was taking up more TV air-time than normal, but the way I looked at it, United were a great side, accustomed to winning championships. I knew how important it was, and I understood that it had become a Holy Grail, but I felt it was only natural that we should become European champions. I expected nothing less, and the morning after a late flurry of goals had given us the crown I skipped along the street singing 'Champions of Europe' as if it were the most natural thing in the world.

But that was in 1968, and I was only nine years old.

Well, perhaps even then I did understand the significance of the achievement, because somehow the European thing had found its way into my blood, and I was to grow up craving the essence of it all. I don't think there has been a day in the last thirty years when I haven't thought about Manchester United, and there have been many, many days when United have consumed my attention and devoured my nerves. I know it's only a game, and that to be so engaged is illogical, but how can an obsession ever stand up to dispassionate examination? I don't want this to get out of perspective, football isn't as important as life itself or the health of our families, but the fact is that United matter to me; always have done and always will.

Having spent my formative years knowing nothing other than glory, and becoming attuned to United's divine right to attain that glory, the next few years were a nightmare. You often hear it said these days that supporting United is an easy option for gloryhunters, and that followers of a team in blue are the real devotees, having suffered for so long. But all I know is that it was hell supporting United in Manchester during the first half of the 1970s, when the enemy not only won things, but took serious delight in our failure. And don't believe the suggestion that the nation's oft-expressed dislike of our team is a function of recent success: in United's darkest days of the 1970s the whole of football lapped it up.

It reached the point when I wondered if we would ever play European football again, and I recall the strange Anglo-Italian Cup matches in 1973, when we were pretending that we still occupied the European stage – just as second division play-off finals are staged to make the participants feel like they are in a proper cup final. Eventually United did play in Europe again, but with little success. It was 1984, an age since I was a young boy taking European triumph for granted, before we reached a semi-final; and we had to wait nine more years to play in the European Cup.

I could never work out why United were so unsuccessful in Europe during the late '70s and early '80s, an era when English sides – and not necessarily auspicious ones – were amassing European trophies. Although United fans were aching for a first league title since 1967, the need (for it was a need) to re-establish ourselves on the continent was intense. I used to wonder if Benfica and Real Madrid remembered us. So when we won the Cup Winners' Cup on a soggy night in Rotterdam in 1991 I walked out of the ground telling anyone who would listen that this was the greatest night ever. And so it was in a way, though it isn't any more.

Rotterdam proved to be a false dawn over the continent, and I reached the point of refusing to anticipate victory in any European Cup tie for fear of the disappointment that would follow. Thus I was sadly resigned as Eric Cantona strode from the field, seemingly devastated, after the defeat by Dortmund in 1997. Having failed to meet the supposed destiny of a Munich final in that year I was doubtful about the good omens that were talked of prior to the final in Barcelona in 1999. Instead my genuine hopes of victory in the Nou Camp were founded on the best evidence there is: the proven quality of the team. Already Double winners, United were possessors of an indefatigable spirit and a refusal ever to bow to seemingly inevitable defeat. But no one could have foreseen how the dramatic FA Cup victories over Liverpool and Arsenal, and the quality combined with guts that overcame Juventus in the European Cup semi-final, would pale in comparison with what was to follow.

Bayern Munich were not short of self-belief either, and their physical and mental toughness gave confidence to their supporters. At my Girona hotel the night before the final I asked a Bayern fan how he thought it might go, and with an expression devoid of humour and emotion he told me straight: "Ve vill vin … two-von." End of conversation. For a little time I wondered how I could counter such certainty, but over the next twenty-fours hours I reminded myself of United's class (even without suspended captain Roy Keane), and by the time I was in the ground I began to believe that we could win, then that we would win.

Having heard in the weeks that followed of many fans with genuine tickets being denied access to the Nou Camp because the barcodes would not scan, I'm just glad I got inside the ground. How admission to a match that represents a lifetime's ambition can be dependent on such technology is beyond me. When the barcode scanner fails on a tin of peas in Tesco you go and get another tin, or the checkout operator enters the numeric code. At the European Cup final, you are expected simply to smile and say, "Ah well, just my bad luck. Not to worry." Then be happy to watch the game in a bar.

Admission procedures apart, the Nou Camp stadium is probably the best football ground in the world, and it was something special to watch it filling up in the hour before kick-off, knowing that the cameras trained on every aspect of the proceedings would transmit their images across the globe. No one on the planet with an interest in football (and that's billions of people – a mind-boggling concept) would fail to be aware of what was about to take place. And it made me feel proud that my football team was the reason for all this. My team that was born in the grime of north Manchester, then laboured to little effect amid the sweat and smoke of Trafford Park for more than half of this century, suddenly to find itself, because of the genius of a man called Busby, the most famous football team in the world. The team whose ground I would walk to as a child, the team that became, I don't know how, a part of me; a team that thanks to a latter-day Busby called Ferguson had once again become pre-eminent. That team would be playing before the eyes of the world, on that perfect pitch, for me and for thousands like me: boys from Salford; anonymous people; blurred faces in every crowd in every picture of every match for over three decades. There were those in the high, steep stands that dwarfed the pitch who had bought into the experience, but this was not their night. Because for all the wealth of the young players, and no matter how detached their lives had become from our own, Manchester United would play tonight because of the common people who had breathed air into its lungs for over 120 years, and as the Nou Camp reached capacity it was as a culmination of the passion of millions throughout the club's history.

United fell behind to a free-kick that seems less just every time I watch the replay (I think the expression is 'played for and won'). This was despite the fact that my stare almost burned through the scorer, Basler, as I willed him to fluff it: "Miss! Miss! Miss! ... Oh you bastard!" There was no panic in the stands at this point because we seemed to expect the initial set-back – it's the way United tend to go about things. But the next 85 minutes were a torment, with the Bayern defence seemingly impenetrable. Then, as we prayed for a miracle, two came along at once.

In the split-second after the first, as pandemonium erupted around me I looked at the referee and linesman – it's something I automatically do, always fearing the worst. Later, on the videos, I noticed that Teddy Sheringham looked over his shoulder at the linesman too. Normally you know it's all right when the officials are running back to half-way, but this time they didn't. The linesman, I seem to remember, stood his ground; something wasn't quite right. Perhaps he was simply as stunned as the rest of us, for there came no flag, no whistle. All this was in the time it takes to blink, but I recall the memory and the feeling vividly. The second miracle, surely the reason why a man called Solskjaer was born on this Earth, sent all normality out of the window. From high up behind the goal I saw the ball in the net and exploded from within. Nothing had prepared any of us for this. The words 'Champions of Europe' flashed across my brain, and I knew we'd won when I saw half of the Bayern team prostrate on the grass, the referee urging them to restart the game in order that he could end it. And when he did the emotional volcano erupted for a third time.

Why did it happen? What made us win like that? We've heard all the spooky theories about fate and about Sir Matt's birthday, and when the improbable happens to such stunning effect it's tempting to put it down to benevolent forces. It's a nice thought in a way, and I'm loath to reject it, but the kind omens didn't work out in 1997 when we were supposed to win the final in Munich. The fact is that this was not a one-off for this team: apart from the heroics in Turin and in the FA Cup, we'd pinched several injury-time goals in the league, which were ultimately crucial to the title success. This team simply does not give up, and that is why many felt an equaliser was still a possibility when the game moved into injury time. So I'd prefer to give credit to the team, and credit to the fans who never gave up, whilst acknowledging of course that the spirits of the past were a major part of our refusal to lose.

The long on-pitch celebrations that followed underlined the strength of this Manchester United. The players shared the euphoria with the fans; there was an understanding that neither could have experienced this without the other. The spirit of the team, the togetherness, was manifest. That half-hour as they larked about in the penalty area below us was a perfect way to savour the success, and to wash the tensions away. Thirty-odd years of supporting United had been about preparing for those moments.

As the team reluctantly left the scene of their finest hour, an arena to which all our thoughts would return for the rest of our lives, my eyes were on Peter Schemichel until he finally disappeared from view. The best goalkeeper I have ever seen would not be playing for us again. I thought back to the early part of the season when his form had dipped, and when a blunder had given Bayern Munich a last minute equaliser in the Champions' League. Some had written him off around that time (though not most United fans), and I had expressed the hope that he would confound them all by retiring from United as a champion. Some champion!

For a fortnight after the euphoria of Barcelona I dreamed about the place, the journey and the match. It lay just beneath my consciousness, coming to mind on occasions throughout each day then taking over completely as I slept. I can still close my eyes, see it all again, and relive the feeling. It's made me wonder just how awful it would have been had we lost, how deep would have been the emptiness and frustration. Like the FA Cup defeat in 1976, perhaps, when at the age of 17 I was still waiting to see United lift a trophy in my presence. Or the anguish of the summer of 1992, following the loss of the title race when a long chapter of failure had seemed sure to end. Losing to Bayern would have been like both of those occasions, but multiplied a thousand times given the seemingly near-impossibility of even reaching a European Cup final. And the drive back to Manchester would have been lousy too. It may seem odd to dwell on a defeat that didn't happen, but in some way the contemplation of that horror scenario serves to make me appreciate the success all the more. It was simply so important.

Perhaps the most common conclusion that I have heard since the match is that football, supporting United, will never be this good again. It's something I've said myself, and in all probability it is true. Another Treble is as unlikely as the first – so not exactly impossible – but surely it would be impossible to win a Treble in such a fashion again. And could a repeat performance generate the emotion of the first? The thing about football, though, is that you can never be satisfied, for the moment you stop caring you may as well just give up. A new season will bring a new hunger for the fans, and a desire to go back and do it again. After all, the alternative would be a reprise of the early-'70s decline, and one of those was enough for me. Who wants to watch others having all the fun? Not the great Sir Alex Ferguson, I'm sure, and with this man in charge Manchester United is in good hands. We've had our moments in recent years, but not all of them yet I hope.

Sitting in the afternoon heat of the Placa de Catalunya a few hours before the European Cup final, the nerves were beginning to jangle as the game drew nearer; the chanting fans around the square were sounding boozier by the minute. But Barcelona is a great city, the sky was blue and the sun was burning down. An older United supporter sat down next to me on the bench; he looked around, sighed, and said, "This is better than working."

I looked up and replied, "If United win tonight it will be better than anything."

And it was.

Denis the King – Part 1

August 1999. We all have our heroes, and Denis Law was my first and most enduring. We had met just before United's European Cup triumph in Barcelona.

My first ever United kit was the classic round-collar 1960s version. It came in a box with a picture of Denis Law on the lid. I was still in primary school (it was around 1968) and I felt pretty pleased with myself – back then replica kits were not at all common. Although it has become a cliché to claim such things, I really did used to run around holding the cuffs of my United shirt in my fists, shoulders hunched, saluting with a single up-raised arm whenever I managed to score between the huddles of sweaters that were our goalposts. And I really did get a home-made number 8 sewn on the back of my shirt, just to emphasise that I was Denis Law.

Heroes come and go, but as you grow older you know deep-down that these people are just flesh and blood, flawed humans, and are not true heroes at all. The thing about Denis Law is that he captured my imagination when I was a child, and because it's nice to stay in touch with the kid you once were, he's remained my only real hero into middle-age.

And so it was that on a warm and hazy late afternoon in May, the best sort of day that Manchester can offer, I felt a tinge of anticipation as I made my way to meet Denis the King. I was relishing the opportunity, but wondered whether the Denis Law I was to meet would be the swashbuckling hero that I'd admired for most of my life. Of course, this being Denis Law, any fears were unfounded – there cannot be a more unaffected, down-to-earth superstar. The next hour flew memorably by.

The meeting was occasioned by the publication of Denis Law's new autobiography, *The Lawman**, which comes some twenty years after a previous version of his life story. There's much in the new book that was recounted in the previous volume – the facts of his career are the same, after all – but it's startling to realise that few fans under the age of 30 will recall Law the player with any clarity, and that anyone under 25 today was born after Denis retired. The new book therefore represents an opportunity for those generations to become acquainted with the legend, and for the rest of us to relive our past.

I decided before our meeting that I would not ask Denis about 'that goal' in 1974. There were two reasons for this. First, I suspect he's sick of the question, and secondly because the question 'How did you feel?' is already answered in the most compelling section of the new book. If you read the description of his feelings on the night United were relegated you will understand why Denis Law remains the King to those of us who witnessed the deed.

We met the day after United had reclaimed the Premiership, just five days before we won the FA Cup; the miracles of Barcelona were just around the corner. Heady days indeed, and Denis was enjoying it as much as any of us:

"This present team is excellent. They are playing attractive football, attacking football, it's enjoyable. Beckham is a terrific crosser of the ball, and Cole and Yorke are on the end of it. They're sharp; Yorke is not a big lad, yet he's a good header of the ball. At the time we all wondered about his transfer fee, but you could probably say that about Cantona, who also slotted in straight away. It wasn't a matter of a few games, it was the first game. And the nice thing about Yorke is that he smiles. He looks as though he's enjoying the game even though the pressure on today's players in enormous. It's nice to see."

Denis Law's own devilish humour became a trademark, and the love he retains for football, is a recurring theme as we speak. He doesn't have a bad word to say about anyone; he is generous in praising United's rivals; and he continually emphasises the need to enjoy: "It's only a game," he says. And he means it. He pays tribute, for example, to Wenger's Arsenal:

"They've played some attractive football in the last couple of years, they have good midfield players, good forwards. Certainly this last couple of years they've been excellent. The league has been interesting. It's no use winning it with 10 games to go ..."

I begged to disagree here, my nerves still shredded from the tensions of the last week of the league season, but Denis, the sportsman, took the positive view, suggesting that, "For the neutral, it can't be better than what happened on Sunday, when United beat Spurs."

Denis enthused about the 'character' of the present United side, little knowing that the following week on a barmy, balmy night in Barcelona the team would re-write all definitions of the word. "The character of the team these last few months has been enormous: to go to Inter Milan and get a result, and beat Arsenal when down to 10 men and conceding a penalty in the last seconds of the game. Then to go to Juventus and be two goals down in ten minutes, and to come back and win! United could have scored 5 or 6 – we hit the post a couple of times and should have had a penalty. But then you got a wee bit of luck with the penalty in Milan ..."

And was it a penalty? "Well you look and you think ... but apart from anything, in Milan! You can't believe that the referee's not given it – in Milan, of all places, you think it's a guaranteed certainty. You just had a feeling then – it could be United's night tonight, it could be United's year." And of course it was.

Denis was not planning to go to the game in Barcelona, being busy with the book launch. It would be the second European Cup final he'd missed. In 1968, of course, Denis Law was the captain of Manchester United, celebrating in hospital while Bobby Charlton lifted the Cup in his absence. 'That goal' apart, I suspect that his reaction to missing the 1968 final is the question he's most often asked. But having passed on the most predictable question, I had to raise the second: how big a blow was it?

"Well, had I been injured on the Saturday prior to the game I would have been devastated, but I was injured before the second leg of the semi-final, and I knew then that I would not be playing in the final. By the time of the game the idea of playing was not there, so it wasn't the same as for Roy Keane this year. Unlike Roy I couldn't play because I wasn't fit – he's fit, and can't play because he's been suspended. So it's a different sort of feeling towards it. But I did feel at the time that if we won it we could go on and win it again, and to be fair we should have won it the following year."

In that year, 1969, United lost the semi-final 1-2 on aggregate to AC Milan. Two down after the away leg, Charlton pulled a goal back at Old Trafford, and United were denied parity when a Law effort, seemingly having crossed the line, was hooked back into play to the satisfaction of the referee. Had United gone on to win they would have had a great chance in the final against a still-emerging Ajax, who were thumped 4-1 by Milan. Denis believes we would have won.

"It was disappointing. I really did feel that we'd get another chance after 1968. In fact we should have won it before we did. We probably played the best football of any United team in 1966 when we beat Benfica in Lisbon – that was the best performance of any team in my time at United. And we should have murdered Partizan Belgrade in the semi-final that followed. They were the poorest team we played. I can't believe that they beat us. Our team had some injuries, including George, and they beat us 2-0. I missed a goal that I can't believe I missed from two yards."

The frustrations of the experience are still fresh today as Denis recalls, "They were nothing. They were absolutely nothing. We should have won it then. And then you have a feeling that you're never going to win it. But then Celtic won it, they broke the stronghold of European clubs ... that was a line for us as well."

As for 1968, "The fact that we played at Wembley gave us a little bit of a home feeling. It's a bit unfair, because I feel a European Cup shouldn't be played in a particular country if one of the finalists is from that country. It's happened on other occasions. But we were quite happy. Happy, happy, very happy."

It's been claimed so often that it is now becoming an accepted fact, that Manchester United lost ambition and direction after the European Cup win.

George Best, and others, have suggested that there arose a feeling of having done it all, while the aspirations of the younger generation such as Best himself were neglected. I put this to Denis, and wondered if he also felt that the team of 1969 was past its best. Interestingly, he completely rejected the received wisdom, arguing that there were more young players coming into the side, while he himself was still only 28 years old when the European Cup was won. "I think Bestie was mistaken, sort of grabbing at words, when he said that. I don't think he really thought the situation through. And we really should have won it the following season, so you can't say that United had given up. I disagree with Bestie – I've told him anyway that he's talking a load of garbage." And he grins the grin that once disarmed all but the most humourless of referees.

In an era when football could be brutal, Denis Law was always able to take care of himself. It led to several brushes with referees and disciplinary commissions, and the old joke was that he liked to get a nice suspension over the Christmas holiday. But this 'attitude' was essential to his appeal; like Cantona in more recent times he played for United in a style that we admired and envied in equal measure. How would he have fared under modern conditions, where defenders can only take so many liberties, but also where the all-seeing eye of the TV camera spots the slightest act of revenge?

"Did we get away with murder? Well absolutely, oh yeah. For and against us, by the way. The point today is you know that you can't retaliate. You get pulled up. When I played every team did it [misbehaved] somewhere along the line, but now with 10, 12, 16 cameras, or whatever, you can't do anything. And of course it makes life difficult for everybody – and referees more than anybody. For referees it's a nightmare. Television has improved so vastly that it's a hard job for them. You could never prove whether they were wrong in the past. Now, when you're at a game, you shout 'Penalty!', but later you see the replay on the box and you see the guy was a yard from him."

So would Denis have scored more goals today?

"It must be nice to play today, there's certainly more protection. They still kick you from behind, but the point is they get booked and they can go. And today's pitches are absolutely beautiful – at the end of the season most grounds are as they were at the beginning of the season in our day – so you feel that if you can't play in those conditions you won't be able to play anywhere. You feel that if you had the players of the calibre of George Best and Bobby Charlton, Nobby Stiles and Pat Crerand that the opportunity to score goals might be greater."

Goalkeepers permitting, of course. Denis ought to know a thing or two about goalkeepers, and in his book he speaks with admiration for Bert Trautmann. But who is the best?

"Trautmann at that time, yes. But the best goalkeeper I ever saw was Gordon Banks. He would be the best." Better than Schmeichel? "Well, to me, yes. But that's only personal opinion, and Schmeichel would come into that category – there haven't been many better than him." And he recalls some more: "Dino Zoff, Yashin; Pat Jennings was an excellent goalkeeper as well."

Few of us can enter the mind of a world class footballer at the height of his powers, so I wondered whether a striker of such quality ever took account of the goalkeeper he was facing. Denis Law's style was based on lightening-quick feet and reactions, but in front of goal did he ever think 'Hang on this is Banks'? Did it creep into the mind? The notion is quickly dismissed.

"No, no. No. Never, never. It didn't come into it." But he agrees he was an instinctive player, and he is modest enough to add, "I wish I was good enough to think I could beat the goalkeeper this way or that way."

It brought to mind the way Eric Cantona was able to psyche out goalkeepers at penalties, seemingly dictating the outcome. But Denis – who didn't take too many – suggests that penalties are a slightly different matter, and that the taker will often think things through:

"Maybe you know the goalkeeper is better this way, or he's better that way. If a guy's right-handed or maybe not too clever on his left, or whatever. It depends where he's standing as well. You've got to make your mind up where you're going to put it, or try to put it. As the years have gone on it's become more difficult – the goalkeeper can move about, and of course there is the pressure of the media as well. It's not easy."

We'll never know how many goals he would have scored under modern conditions, but there is no doubt that if Denis Law was a huge star in the 1960s, he would be in a galaxy all of his own today. If Christian Vieri can fetch £28 million, and if Anelka can be valued at over £20 million, then Denis's value would be immeasurable. For panache alone you'd pay £30 million, then you'd have to put a price on his genius. He had the lot. And he's a Red.

The Lawman: An Autobiography, by Denis Law with Bernard Bale, Andre Deutsch, 1999.

Denis the King – Part 2

September 1999. The second part of my interview with the legendary Denis Law.

It was in 1926 that Huddersfield Town won their third successive championship, a source of pride that they would justifiably cling onto in leaner times. As the century draws to a close, that achievement seems to belong to ancient history, its dim historic setting underlined by the archaic nature of the film footage. But when a young Denis Law made his league debut for Huddersfield on Christmas Eve in 1956 that triple title feat was a mere 30 years distant. In other words it was more recent than the mid-1960s, when Denis was at his pomp for Manchester United, are to us today. How time's concertina plays tricks, for how it seems like only yesterday that Denis Law was, in the words of journalist David Miller, "at the very peak of his powers, holding the Old Trafford crowds in the palm of his hand with the dramatic bravura of a matador".

After Huddersfield, Denis played for Manchester City and Torino before joining United, but fate always seemed to draw him to Old Trafford. A thread runs through his new autobiography, *The Lawman*, connecting him to Manchester United, from the time that Huddersfield turned down a £10,000 offer from United for the teenage Law (possibly saving him from the Munich disaster in the process). In October 1958 Matt Busby, in charge of Scotland at that time, gave the 18 year old Law his international debut at Cardiff; he became Scotland's youngest cap, and naturally marked the occasion with a goal. Amazingly, during his stint with Torino, Denis even played for the Italian League against the Football League at Old Trafford. I suggested to Denis that he seemed destined to play for Manchester United, and asked about his escape from Munich.

"I think you do think of that. I think we all know where we were when the crash happened. If the crash hadn't happened I might not have played for Manchester United, because the team was so young with many years to go. I thought before I went to City that Matt might come in for me, but they had Dennis Viollet and Bobby, and they were a striking partnership, so he didn't need me. It wasn't until later ..."

The circumstances became right during Denis's spell in Turin. Disappointed by the negative mentality that prevailed in Italian football at that time, he became desperate to return to the English game, and made his feelings known to Matt Busby. Were United always Law's first choice, or would any top English side have done at that time, just to get out of Italy?

"No, it would be Manchester United. They would be top of the list, yes. For a number of reasons: I'd been in Manchester for the year before, I knew the place reasonably well, I liked the people, I knew Sir Matt from Scotland –

he'd been Scotland manager – so I knew that I was coming back to somewhere that I knew. Don't forget I was only young then, just 22. In those days 22 was young; today at that age people have seen the world. Yeah, they think they have, but they're much older than we were in those days. So I was coming back to a place I knew."

He probably could not have foreseen that almost 40 years later he would remain an idol to a couple of generations of Mancunians. And, fittingly, he retains his affection for the United supporters.

"As soon as you step on the field then you've got a job to do and you've got the backing of the fans. There aren't many better fans. The fans are extremely important, oh yes. You know when you're at home there's no a problem, but away from home the fans give you a boost, without a doubt. At Old Trafford the noise must frighten teams ..."

I ask if he feels Old Trafford has become a little too quiet on occasions in recent years, but Denis, the diplomat, isn't so sure. "Well, we probably had that in our day as well. You just tend not to remember. I'm sure there were always some games that were quiet."

It was the negative nature, and more than occasional brutality, of Italian football in the 1960s that drove Denis Law back home. His Torino team-mates played the game in the same manner as their opponents, and I asked if they ever tried to justify their approach to Denis. Was there any sympathy for a suffering Scottish striker in his own dressing room?

"No, because my team played exactly the same way. Don't forget that it was the normal way they played. They didn't feel they were doing anything unjust. That's why within a short time I thought, I've got to get out of here. Everything was lovely there – the people were nice, I loved it, I loved the place as well, but the football was just awful."

Denis remains a fan of the good things in Italian football, and enjoys the modern Serie A. He agrees that the all-seeing eye of television has helped banish some of the more surreptitious indiscretions from the Italian game.

"Once, you played against an Italian team and it was awful. They were kicking you when the ball wasn't there and were doing all sorts. Now they can't do it can they? Before it was just a nightmare to play against – cynical, awful to watch. It would be 0-0, and if they got a goal that was it. You could guarantee that the game would be 1-0. They were rolling about in agony if it was a bit of a tackle. Well now you can see on television that the guy hasn't touched him. They have cleaned up the act completely. I must admit I enjoy watching Italian football on the box on a Sunday – they don't play defensively, there's always goals in the game, it's changed drastically. I've got a lot of Italian friends over here. They like their football, don't they? For many Italian people football is their life. And the same in Spain really I suppose. In those two countries football is everything."

But one thing the Italians did get right during Law's career was the physical well-being of the players.

"Yes, they knew that the players were the most important people in the club, because they were the ones that were going out on the Saturday, or whenever, for the fortunes of the club. Therefore they had to be looked after. So even in those days there was good diet, or whatever, which eventually came into British football. We hadn't even heard of it. Training as well – it was all so different"

This led us on to the topic of injuries. Denis had various knee problems throughout his career, and his later seasons were blighted by a long-standing cartilage injury in his right knee. The problem became serious after an international match against Poland in October 1965, and it eventually led to United's captain missing the 1968 European Cup final.

"I'd had a cartilage injury at Huddersfield, and the surgeon had left a piece of cartilage in the knee that had floated about for a few years. I think it was in the Poland game that it lodged somewhere. And that's when I started to get into pain."

It is impossible to think back to Denis's lengthy struggle with that knee without reflecting on the modern techniques of treatment and rehabilitation that have saved the careers of so many players – not least Roy Keane. I suggested that today Denis's injury would have been treated successfully in a matter of weeks, and that he may have gone on to score many more goals.

"Oh my knee injury would have been no problem at all. The problem in those days was that when they did operate, as soon as the knife touched your leg that was the muscles gone, and the chances of you recovering from a cartilage were fifty-fifty. When I was at Huddersfield there were three of us with the injury at more or less the same time, and the others never played again because their legs just blew up every time. Now you can play in a fortnight, ten days. The medical side of football has changed drastically. For us it wasn't like in Italy, where even in those early days it was geared up to look after players – massage, treatment. It wasn't quite the sponge in cold water but it wasn't very far short."

There's much talk these days about the effect of youngsters playing too much football, and the FA has recently introduced small-sided soccer for young children to increase the emphasis on learning skills. As a schoolboy Denis Law had the classic football upbringing for such a talent: playing for several teams every weekend. In his book he describes an injury at Huddersfield caused by overwork, so did he feel that the amount of football he played as a boy contributed towards the injury problems he suffered during his professional career?

"Oh, I don't think so, no. The injuries I got weren't due to schoolboy football. Anyone could injure a cartilage – you get kicked. I can't think of anyone whose injury problem has stemmed from playing too much schoolboy football. Now in schoolboy football you hear about a hamstring, a groin strain … the only thing we knew was a broken leg!" And he grins. "I can't remember missing a [schoolboy] game through injury."

Our conversation turned to international football. Denis's passion for Scotland is legendary, of course, and his autobiography recounts the well-known tale of his afternoon on the golf course, unable to bring himself to watch England win the World Cup. Amusing too is his recollection of being unhappy at the start of the 1966/67 season, having to join a United guard of honour for Charlton, Stiles and Connelly, all members of England's World Cup winning squad. His greatest non-United moment was Scotland's win over England at Wembley in 1967, therefore "becoming World champions!"

There was a situation in Denis's first spell at Manchester City when he didn't want to play in a match for City, preferring to appear for Scotland against England. The incident is an unusual angle on the club-versus-country issue, so prevalent today, with the clubs increasingly predominant. Suppose Denis were playing for United now, how would he feel in Ryan Giggs's position where he seldom seems able to play for Wales? Denis's pride in Scotland is emphatic:

"Yes, I'd prefer to play for my country, yes." Even more than playing for United? "I would say so, yes. Yeah. Although they are your bread and butter, the fact that you're being selected to represent your country – no, that would come first."

He recalls one experience from the other side of the fence: playing for the Italian League against the Scottish League. As a passionate Scot, how did that feel? "They were all Scots lads, yeah. It was different anyway. It was nice."

His delight in the memory is clear. To him football remains a game, it is there to be enjoyed. He has no time for the nastiness displayed by some on the field or in the stands. He has faith in the capacity of the majority of players and fans to share mutual respect. He knows that football is not, in the words of his former Huddersfield manager, more important than life or death. For not only was Denis Law a truly great player, and a continuing legend; he is a hell of a nice bloke. It is hard to believe he is in his sixtieth year now, for he seems to have changed so little. He still cuts quite a dash. Long may the spirit of the matador reside within him.

The Govan-or

September 1999. Sir Alex Ferguson's autobiography had recently been published, and included some interesting aspects of his relationship with his United employers. This book review was also a tribute to the great man.

"When you are successful it is fine for a time and then they maybe think you are too successful and that the success wasn't down to you at all." These were the words of Jock Stein to Alex Ferguson, when asked how he felt about his removal from the manager's job at Celtic. Ferguson goes on to reflect: "It made me realise how much he loved that club and I found a deep sadness in the contrast between his devotion and the treatment he received. They say something similar happened to Bill Shankly and Don Revie and there have even been mutterings about Manchester United's appreciation of Sir Matt Busby being a lot less than it should have been. I think if I were as badly used as Jock was at the end by Celtic, I would find it hard to be as philosophical or as generous as he was."

It is true that there seems little chance of Sir Alex Ferguson being asked to take over United's development pools, as happened to Stein at Celtic, and Sir Alex is financially more secure than either Shankly or Busby ever were, but his reference to Stein's plight is in many ways the crux of the United manager's new autobiography*. For the last third of the book is startling in its frankness, not simply in relation to the generally bland football books we are accustomed to, but because a serving manager is so open about his less than perfect relationship with the employer he describes as "the corporate monster it is now". The manifestation of the unease is a running dispute between the manager and the club over the terms of his contract – the size of the pay cheque and the length of the deal. But the essence of the dissatisfaction seems to be due to appreciation.

The first disagreement came about after United's ground-breaking title success in 1993, when Ferguson found himself earning less than a number of other top managers, and only one-third of the salary of Eric Cantona. But United's offer of a new contract was non-negotiable, and despite having described himself as "too timid" in negotiating earlier deals, leaving him with "very little in the way of financial security", Ferguson felt compelled to accept the terms on the table: "I was, I suppose, a captive of my own passion for the club and the job I was doing there." But you get the feeling that a perceived lack of appreciation, and not financial matters, hurt the most.

The subject was raised again in 1995, shortly after the departure from United of Hughes, Ince and Kanchelskis. Alex Ferguson was not enjoying his most serene period in management when he again sought equity with the terms George Graham had enjoyed at Arsenal. Ferguson writes: "Conversations with Martin Edwards are usually straightforward and pleasant until you ask him for more money. Then you have a problem." Referred to plc chairman Sir Roland Smith, Ferguson produced a copy of Graham's Arsenal contract, but the response to the manager who had won two titles and reached three FA Cup finals in the previous three seasons was "Do you think you have taken your eye off the ball? … some people at Old Trafford think you are not as focused as you have been." Ferguson believes the decision to sell Ince had been unpopular in the corridors of power, and his request for a six-year contract was refused on the basis that United managers are never offered more than four years. Furthermore, and here there are echoes of Stein, he was told that "having any role in the club after I retired as manager was totally out of the question". Unbeknown to the fans, Ferguson left Smith's home "flattened, confused and worried. My mind was working overtime, sifting through the debris of that shambles of a meeting, searching for fragments of hope that could motivate me to get on with my job."

This is desperate stuff, desperate language. You wonder how a club blessed with the best manager of his generation could be happy to see this situation develop. Surely everyone connected with Old Trafford – those who have grown rich from the success of the Ferguson years and the fans who thrive on glory alone – should be on their knees each night thanking God for Alex Ferguson, not bringing Ferguson himself to his knees.

But more was to follow. On the eve of the double-Double-clinching FA Cup final of 1996, Ferguson says a "furious row" erupted over the terms of another new contract offer. He recalls being "absolutely disgusted", and describes the affair as "pathetic". He continues: "The directors were armed with the knowledge that I didn't want to leave. I had put so much into the rebuilding of Manchester United and it was agony to think of walking away from that. But this time around it got to the point where I was not prepared to be ridiculed and felt that on a matter of principle I might have to resign. I was not going to accept a repeat of the previous nonsense over the contract." And in the end: "I was not given what I believed I was worth, but nonetheless I had made huge strides in relation to my existing agreement."

But other battles remained. Ferguson recounts his difficulty in persuading the club to support his bid for Dwight Yorke, and his account of the protracted affair does not reflect well on his assistant, Brian Kidd. He even reports that Eric Cantona had cited dissatisfaction with United's corporate face among the reasons behind his decision to retire: "He said he felt he had become a pawn of Manchester United's merchandising department, and that he was not going to accept such treatment any longer. His second complaint was that United were not ambitious enough in the purchase of players. I had a lot of sympathy with him on both counts." And so the investment that was finally made in Yorke and Stam, and which repaid the most glorious triple-dividend, was a triumph for the manager over the accountants: "In the summer of 1998 I decided that I had to assert myself on the need for Manchester United to spend money in the transfer market. For all too long I had allowed the plc to overwhelm me, accepting too readily all the Cityspeak about institutions and dividends and the harsh realities of the business world." The fans, he believes, are the biggest investors, and they expect no return other than glory.

It is natural that any autobiography will present a sympathetic version of the subject's life, if not simply a volume of justification for past actions. And so it is easy to acknowledge that there is always another side to the story when Sir Alex Ferguson portrays his slant on past events. Perhaps one day the tale will be told from the view of the boardroom. But for now it is up to the reader to weigh up the evidence presented by the manager, and the evidence of the last ten years on the field of play.

It seems natural to assume that every single United supporter will be a Fergie man or woman. Can there be anyone who does not hold a debt of gratitude to the manager who has delivered the unthinkable in the last decade? Of course we did not always understand. Back in the dark days of 1989 there was little evidence of hope for those of us who could not see the foundations Ferguson was building. A few called for his head, but my own recollection of those times is that most of us did not; that there was simply a weariness that once again a new manager had not made a significant difference to the performance of the United first team. For whatever the noises about a revolution taking place at the junior end of the club, it would not be the first time such claims had been made, only to prove unproductive.

But that is in the past. Now there is no argument – Sir Alex Ferguson has delivered, and has delivered beyond our wildest dreams. And so my own view is that the achievements of the 1990s have been due to the work of one man, and that whatever the contribution of the players and coaches at the club during this time, Ferguson is the one irreplaceable variable in the whole equation. Well, perhaps not the only one – I concede that a certain Eric Cantona also falls into that category. But would Cantona have delivered without the guiding hand of Ferguson? The evidence of his earlier career suggests not.

Before I read the new autobiography I wondered what I could possibly learn, there being numerous earlier volumes of his story, and the exhaustive diaries of recent years. But the tale that emerges is a fascinating account of a great man, perhaps the last of his kind, for the breeding ground that produced him is no more. A physically tough place, where hard work and hard play were the norm. Where those from a decent home learnt the values of integrity and honest graft, but where delinquency also laid its trap. In Alex Ferguson, Govan produced a fighter for social justice, an anti-bigot, a worker; a man with skill in his boots and iron in his heart, who chose to serve an industrial apprenticeship while carving a football career with distant clubs. Putting in the hours all round. Few take this route today, and Scotland seems no longer to produce great footballers.

As a manager he started at the bottom, at East Stirling, a club with no team and a mere two thousand pounds to spend on one. But he crafted a team (while also running a tough Govan pub), and he did the business at St Mirren before Aberdeen enabled him to proclaim his talent to Europe. Ferguson has done it all from scratch – in life as in every job he has ever held. Nothing was ever given to him easily, unless you include the ability to play football and to scrap your way to success.

And so it's sad to feel we may be approaching the latter days of Fergie. The end is in sight – he has said so – and very soon we will only be able to look back on it all. The man is monumental. It reminds me so much of how I felt in the late 1960s, when I was just a kid and when Sir Matt seemed like a really old man (he was about 60, as Sir Alex will be at the end of his current contract). I think Sir Matt was genuinely older than Sir Alex in terms of what life, war and Munich had taken out of him – but maybe time plays tricks on me. The autobiography and the testimonial may seem like the equivalent of a football manager's Greatest Hits album. But while Fergie remains in charge the fire will still burn. He's certainly had his moments, but not all of them yet we hope.

Managing My Life: My Autobiography by Alex Ferguson with Hugh McIlvanney, Hodder and Stoughton, 1999.

Wheel of Fortune

October 1999. Manchester United's seemingly relentless success in the 1990s didn't occur without the odd hiccup, and we had few neutral well-wishers along the way.

Before the recent Rugby World Cup match between England and New Zealand, the All Blacks' Jeff Wilson claimed that England had been "talking themselves up", and that this had served to motivate his team. "Forget 1995. Forget Australia … This is different, this is England – now. And, I promise you, we want this one." In fact he recalled that in the 1995 tournament feelings were running just as high. "In our dressing room before the game some guys were almost frothing at the mouth. They wanted to beat England that badly."

It seems there's something about England that the rest of the sporting world (and probably much of the non-sporting world) doesn't like very much. It's hardly a racial thing because the biggest England-baiters are our cousins from the antipodes, and our neighbours in the Celtic reaches of these islands. It's nothing to do with England being good at sport, either, as the Australians' ever-increasing delight in whipping the English cricket team proves. It's probably more akin to resentment towards a cocky elder brother, one whose achievements belie his self-importance. For despite the conclusions of *1066 And All That*, the English still consider themselves to be Top Nation, and it gets right up the noses of everyone else, from John O'Groats to Auckland. They love to give England a beating, but strangely the more they do the worst it gets for them, because the gap between English self-importance and English achievement widens still further.

Up until 1993 Manchester United could be described as the England of English football. United, despite having little to show for it since 1968, were football's Top Nation, and it got under everyone's skin. They all loved to beat United while the Reds were down, but the continued (and correct) belief among the Old Trafford faithful that United were the game's number one club (if at times a lousy team) seemed to add to the irritation. United just wouldn't climb down off that pedestal. And after a decade of unrivalled success, the reasons for hating 'Man U' (a more irritating abbreviation would be hard to imagine) become ever more inventive. The ultimate irony here is that the most visible manifestation of this national fad is the jeering of United players on England duty. For England, read Manchester United; for the rest of the world, read England.

And so Kenny Dalglish was able to proclaim his Blackburn team as the 'people's champions', meaning that the nation didn't care who won the league, not even a team as miserable to watch as the 1995 champions, as long as it wasn't Manchester United. As it happened, few beyond Old

Trafford (and Burnley) sought to disagree with him. The following season the 'crown' passed to Newcastle, who were styled 'Everyone's second-favourite team', largely because 'everyone' would have preferred them to win the title than United. I always believed that Alan Shearer, whom I freely admit to have been extremely competent at scoring goals (no faint praise intended), would not have achieved national icon status but for the fact that he prevented United from winning one title, and was the main hope of a repeat trick in later years. And although Arsenal have never been a popular outfit, their recent success has perhaps been made more palatable because they are not Manchester United.

All of which may sound a touch paranoid, but hey what's wrong with a little healthy paranoia when you're trying to develop a winning siege mentality? In any case, I'm no more imagining anti-United sentiments than the England rugby team is imagining that New Zealand are out to rip their heads off.

One fascinating by-product is that we gain some unlikely allies along the way. I have already mentioned Burnley, not a set of fans known for their love of United, whose dislike of Blackburn had them leaning towards the Reds in 1994 and 1995. Then in 1996, as the crowds gathered at Old Trafford to celebrate the title-clinching victory away at the Riverside, we were joined by a coach-load of Sunderland fans, so delighted that United had held off Newcastle that they diverted their journey from Tranmere back to Wearside to share in the fun. Perhaps the ultimate example was the Spurs support at Old Trafford for the final match of last season, happy to sacrifice the points to put a spike in Arsenal's wheel.

But just as English national teams rarely win at serious sport (by which I mean soccer, cricket and rugby league – though I'll throw in union while we're on the topic), even United supporters know that you cannot win every game, and every championship. (Indeed if you are a United supporter who suffered the 1970s and 1980s you will know this all too well.) Juventus don't win their league every year, neither do Barcelona; Milan and Real Madrid must take their turn. But as a United supporter it's becoming essential to win every game and every title because the feeding frenzy that accompanies the club's occasional failures is getting out of hand. And United have this habit of needing a kick up the shorts at least once a season, which normally results in us getting a thumping before normal service is resumed and we go on to lift the trophies.

It's odd how, in recent seasons, the various pretenders to the throne have raised their own hopes and the hopes of the non-Red nation, by giving United a bloody nose. Blackburn's 2-0 win at Easter in 1994; Newcastle's 5-0 in 1996; Arsenal's 3-0 in 1998; and, with Massimo Taibi making a start of Roche proportions to his Old Trafford career, a recent tonking at Chelsea. Comfort can be drawn from recalling the recent *Match of the Nineties* interview with Newcastle's John Beresford, who said that although some players ended their careers with championship and cup medals, he would remain proud of his 5-0 video. Nice for him.

There was a time, of course, when we had to take the hammerings without the consolation of silverware. In February 1972, having led the league at Christmas, United were in freefall, and suffered the ignominy of a 5-1 reverse at Leeds; fortunately Leeds were in their arrogant pomp at the time and managed to stick seven past Southampton, thus putting the United result a little in the shade. By December of that year our team had become a rabble, and was finally exposed in a dire 5-0 away defeat against a Don Rogers inspired Crystal Palace. The presence of the ITV cameras at that match (Frank O'Farrell's march to the scaffold, as it turned out) ensured that we would never be allowed to live it down. And if you believe that delight in United's infrequent present-day disappointments is simply down to a natural desire to favour the underdog, then listen to Brian Moore's screaming commentary on that Selhurst debacle.

The following season saw United relegated. We were so bad we deserved it, but in truth we'd only been bad for two seasons. It never ceases to amaze me how the likes of Coventry, Southampton and (more recently) Everton, can be hopeless year after year, yet keep getting away with it. United lost 20 out of 42 games in 1973/74, and were a very poor team, but 16 of those 20 defeats were by a single goal, which is an interesting statistic. We lost two games by two goals, and we suffered two 3-0 defeats, one on the opening day of the season, and the other on New Year's Day (as you probably predicted). It all puts the current trend towards a once-a-season nightmare in perspective: better to lose one game 5-0 than to lose five games 1-0. Though after a result like Chelsea this can be difficult to accept.

The passage of time is the cure. Few now recall a 5-1 lashing at Birmingham in 1978, not even the 6-0 humiliation at Ipswich the following season (where a couple of Gary Bailey penalty saves actually kept the score down!); and the 5-0 at Everton in 1984 was promptly avenged in that season's Cup final. Even the Maine Road nightmare of 1989 (now repaid thanks to a nice five-niller) is beginning to serve as a benchmark for the last time City beat United, and for how far United travelled since, rather than as a reminder of the embarrassment that we suffered at the time.

If ever we need a reminder of how setbacks can be an inspiration we need look no further than the 4-0 drubbing in the Nou Camp back in 1994. Little did we imagine that less than five years later this arena would become the scene of The Best Night Ever. I'd rather United be European champions than 'people's champions' any day.

Stand Up for the Champions' League

November 1999. The Champions' League ... well, what do you know?

An acquaintance remarked to me recently that a top-notch human brain is capable of storing up to 70,000 items of information. This sounded pretty impressive until he pointed out that around 30,000 of these slots are taken up by vocabulary. He said that average brains have a more limited capacity, but I reckon that this does not particularly disadvantage anyone, since the fewer the number of slots, the more limited the vocabulary is likely to be anyway. For some, the words 'effing', 'blinding', 'hate' and 'Man U' need only be supplemented by a vague recollection of the direction home and the price of a packet of Benson's.

All of which is highly unscientific given that my acquaintance was probably talking rubbish anyway. I mean, who counts these things? And why? And if you did, and if you found the answer, wouldn't it only use up one of your valuable information slots that could be more usefully employed in learning the name of the unit of currency in Burkina Faso (handy in a pub quiz, and a probable destination for a United pre-season friendly in 2002)?

But it did get me thinking. Suppose my own capacity amounts to 60,000 slots (I'm being optimistic here), and let's just pretend that I know 25,000 words. This leaves me with a mere 35,000 remaining slots (minus one for the fact that I seem to know 60,000 minus 25,000). The worry is that I seem to have filled up the rest with thirty years' worth of football results, goalscorers, and reserve-team player biographies. How the hell do I remember which is the hot tap? And why are my baths always so cold?

Here's a handy piece of information from one of my knowledge slots (and it's not as useless as it first appears, as I will shortly explain). In 1727 the early import from the Bundesliga, George Frideric Handel, composed an anthem for the coronation of King George II, entitled *Zadok the Priest*. It was such a hit that the work has been played at the coronation of every British monarch ever since, and rousing stuff it is too. But what's this all got to do with football? Well, I happened to hear *Zadok* recently and I thought it sounded strangely familiar. And then I realised why. Because crafty old Handel was clearly not simply your average Baroque composer but was apparently also the owner of a time-machine. It seems he zoomed forward to the 1990s, listened to the most rousing anthem of the era, then popped back to the 18th century to write *Zadok* based on what he'd heard. And what does *Zadok the Priest* sound remarkably like? Only the stirring UEFA Champions' League anthem that causes the hairs on the backs of our necks to rise with pride before each and every fixture (not to mention highlights programmes, preview shows, and what have you). I was so struck by the musical similarity that I took a tour of the UEFA web site, expecting to find some information on their theme tune. I drew a blank, unfortunately, but I did manage to while away a good hour playing multimedia files of Champions' League highlights – each prefaced by that damn tune.

It's hard for me to convey just how much I dislike the UEFA Champions' League anthem. I hate the fact that it's so pompous, and the fact that it is imposed on us at every opportunity; I hate the fact that it is accompanied on TV screens by the same sponsors' images – majesty being used to sell German tyres. But what I hate most of all is that when they play it at Old Trafford, the crowd all stand to attention, then applaud wildly as it reaches that nauseating (and incomprehensible) conclusion. Why do the fans react like that? It's not the Manchester United Calypso for God's sake! The players are all required to stand to respectful attention in a line, but why do the supporters do it too? And how long will it be before they are looking tearfully heavenwards, with right hand over left breast?

I don't wish to decry the Champions' League as a football competition, not least because when you win it they give you the European Cup, and there's no feeling in football better than that. But the peripheral nonsense, the marketing as opposed to the football, is all a bit irritating, and surely impresses no one. (Cue some UEFA financial statement to disprove that last bit.) Why, for example, are substitutions referred to on television captions as 'Player In / Player Out'? Have you ever seen a player go 'in' a football field, or 'out' of one? Surely it should be 'on' and 'off'? But that just wouldn't be American enough, would it? And thank goodness those woeful Champions' League match programmes seem to have disappeared this season. Did you ever spend more than about two minutes reading one? There's surely a more riveting read to be found on the back of a bus ticket. And could you imagine anything less worthy of a competition that should celebrate the diversity of footballing culture across so rich a continent? At least a heavy pre-match downpour can enliven the waving around of that big plastic logo-thing on the centre-circle while the UEFA anthem is being imposed on us.

I'm not a great one for anthems at the best of times. The first time I went along to watch Manchester's ice hockey team I thought I was present at a cup final or an international match – until I was told that the spectators were required to rise for the national anthem before each and every game. Could this ever happen at the football, I wondered, and if it did, where would you draw the line? Premier League? Nationwide League? Eccles and District Sunday League? It helps if you get a decent tune though, and I envy the French their stirring Marseilleise. A memorable highlight of Euro '96, was, for me, the playing of the French anthem before the semi-final at Old Trafford, with the United fans doing their best to sing the Ooh, Aah Cantona version against the grumbles of nearby Scousers and Geordies (bloody cheek, or what?).

World Cups are always good for checking up on the anthems, many of which are dire in the extreme. I take a curious interest in those central and south

American tunes that seem to be played on out-of-tune brass by a hung-over band. But you always know it's World Cup time when the Brazilian theme, so evocative of great football in the past, gets an airing. (I'm not so sure about the hand-holding by the players, however.) One of these days it would be fun to observe the anthems at a World Cup match between England and Liechtenstein since (and here's a bit of trivia from one of my more remote information slots) the national anthem of the tine alpine principality shares the tune to God Save the Queen. It could be amusing watching the players as the music starts up – well, who'd start singing first?

As well as being showcases for dodgy tunes, World Cups often serve as glorified catwalks for football-related fashion. Yellow away kits, previously rare, became the norm in the early-'70s as clubs went for the Brazilian blend, and United were one of the teams to fall victim to this vogue. I actually owned one of these most un-United of kits, and I thought I looked pretty neat at the time. But it was at Italia '90 that things went a little too far, as jazzy goalie shirts replaced the plain yellows, greys and greens (even blacks, recalling the Russian keeper, Yashin). So it was nice to see the Feyenoord goalkeeper in this season's Champions' League. He was wearing a plain(ish) grey jersey and (amazing this) the same style shorts and socks as his team-mates. Decked out like a proper goalie, he was, and in the Champions' League too. There's hope for football yet.

Worldly Matters

January 2000. United travelled to Brazil to compete in a world championship for clubs. It was the cue for more unbridled criticism of the trailblazing Reds. But we were already able to call ourselves World champions, 31 years after coming a little unstuck.

There's an uncomfortable little trend beginning to emerge around matters concerning Manchester United. Yes, another one. Rather as opposing sides in war claim to have God on their side, it seems that arguments about United are increasingly containing references to What Matt Busby Would Have Done. You will have heard it said that Busby would have shown Cantona the door after Selhurst Park, while others argued that if Matt was prepared (and able) to accommodate the fire of Stiles, Law, Crerand and Best then he'd have had no problem putting an arm around Eric's shoulder.

The latest claims to the spirit of Sir Matt have come in the wake of United's global adventures in Japan and Brazil. Some claim (leaving aside the disappointing decision not to defend the FA Cup) that embarking on the World tournament in Brazil bears comparison with Busby's European pioneering. Others have argued that the Club World Championship in Brazil is a contrived exercise designed to generate TV revenue only, and that Busby would have treated it with due disdain. You have to be suspicious of the motives, of course. Certain tabloids with a current grudge against United have a bit of a cheek in claiming the moral high ground, proclaiming that Matt would be turning in his grave if he were able to witness the 'disgraceful' antics of United and their manager in South America. Who knows what the great man would think of it all? Maybe he'd just be angry to hear his name taken in vain. I suspect that Busby, a man of his time but also ahead of his time, would have found a way to operate in the modern context, keeping the game at the forefront of his priorities. A bit like Alex Ferguson in fact.

The trouble is that the argument tends to get muddied because it's United. The hysterical coverage of the Brazil tournament has again highlighted the fact that United will be damned by their enemies whatever they do. Having made the trip at the behest of the FA and the government, United were vilified in sections of the gutter press. Once out there we get slaughtered again, this time for approaching the tournament with a determination to win it (ie treating the football tournament with some respect), rather than going round handing out the bouquets. What's becoming clear to some is that if (perhaps when) England is not selected to host the 2006 World Cup, then it will be the fault of United and their nasty manager for going out to Brazil, taking it seriously, and trying to win.

Leaving aside the World Cup bid baggage, competing in the Club World Championship will, I suspect, be to United's long-term advantage.

Realistically it was always likely that the winners would come from Brazil, just as I would expect United to have won the thing if the games had been played at Old Trafford in the freezing cold. No European nation has won a World Cup on that side of the Atlantic Ocean, so there's no real discredit in having gone out there and given it a go. The hard way is often the only way to learn, and I suspect we'll acquit ourselves better next time around.

In many ways the tournament was reminiscent of United's early experiences in the Champions' League, with particular parallels to 1994. For Necaxa read Gothenburg (chasing the game against so-so opponents, with an unnecessary red card not helping at all). The Vasco defeat had shades of Barcelona – a calamitous first half, with United failing to muster a shot, and Romario strangely providing the link. Then the slim consolation of a young United overcoming South Melbourne, a reminder (albeit without the flourish) of the 4-0 win over Galatasery in which a young boy called Beckham scored his first European goal.

So disappointment in Brazil but (it's getting a bit like the boxing), United do hold another version of the World Championship, and it is to be hoped that the great achievement of beating Palmeiras back in November isn't to be forgotten too easily. United jumped off the plane, won the game in Tokyo on a Tuesday, and were back scoring 5 in the Premiership on the Saturday. No mean feat against a Palmeiras team that was desperate to win. For those of us with long memories this was a very sweet experience. Before mini-tournaments in Brazil had been dreamed up, the contest between the European and South American champions was justifiably referred to as the World Club Championship. And few European sides were allowed to get through the two-legged encounters unscathed.

United's turn, of course, came as European champions in 1968, when our Argentinian opponents were the fearsome Estudiantes de la Plata. United were stitched up good and proper over there, though only lost 1-0. Nobby Stiles, apparently described in the match programme as "brutal, badly-intentioned, and a bad sportsman", was later dismissed for being given offside and waving an arm in protest. Perhaps there is a hint of Ferguson/Beckham in the comment of Sir Matt after the game: "They are crucifying Nobby Stiles because of a reputation he has been given which is quite unfair. He was sent off in this match because of a reputation and build up … which is quite disgraceful." Unlike modern times, the English press was highly supportive of United, so much so that the Argentinian FA complained to FIFA about their coverage.

At Old Trafford there was more of the same; the game ended 1-1, and Georgie (appropriately sporting a bandido moutstache) was sent off. It was a game that mattered to us at the time – United wanted to call themselves World champions – and for those who remember it remained a bit of an itch that the club had never attained that title. The Estudiantes experience, with our lads on the other side of the world, was truly exciting, and its one-off nature left the memories particularly clear in the mind. Much was made at the time of the armed police and (such things being unheard of in Salford at the time) the moat around the Estudiantes pitch. It all served to conjurer up the image of our team playing in a bear-pit, reinforced by Busby's comment that "Holding the ball out there put you in danger of your life". The programme notes for the home leg did not identify the referee, since his name was to be drawn out of a hat 30 minutes before kick-off (losers getting to be linesmen). Cloak and dagger stuff, indeed.

The programme for the home leg against Estudiantes refers to the match by its official title 'European/South American Cup', also the official name for the Toyota Cup match against Palmeiras. And it's a neat twist that Estudiantes qualified to play United by winning the Libertadores Cup against Palmeiras of Brazil. So for those of us with a 31-year itch, the Palmeiras game mattered. For two generations of United fans this contest was the World title decider – the cock of our street against the cock of theirs.

Palmeiras had prepared well for it, motivated by the desire from back home. Predictably United were decried in the English media for going out there to play the game (unlike Liverpool, who on two occasions were willed on to ice their cake, to win the World title that United had never won – failing each time). United, by contrast, had to motivate themselves. In England the game was dismissed as an 'exhibition' match (to quote ITN), a case of ABUs preparing the excuse for a United triumph, no doubt. But we won. It was a very good game against a very good team, and it was hard work. But we won, and as far as I am concerned that made us World champions. Memories of Estudiantes came flooding back, and another ambition was satisfied in 1999.

Straight after the game, feeling chuffed, I went down to Old Trafford. I don't know why, but there are times when it's the place to be for a bit of reflection. But it was cold and unwelcoming, blowing a gale, and resembling a building site rather than a football ground. I probably hoped that there'd be more people down there, some who remembered Estudiantes perhaps, but the place was pretty deserted. I wondered if it only really mattered to me after all. But then I went inside the North Stand, and passed Sir Matt's statue in its temporary home, and I thought: We did it Boss, we're the best, and I bet you are pretty happy today.

Not that I'd presume to know the great man's mind, of course.

Public Image plc

February 2000. United weren't getting a good press. Now there's a surprise. By the following year United did indeed have a Director of Communications.

I feel I'd better start with an apology. Much as I'd love to explore some fun or whimsical topic this month I feel the need once again to return to the weary old topic of United-hating. I know, I know I should just rise above all this, and I know, I know that it's all of reflection of just how much United matter, but the fact remains that United have been well and truly turned over in the press in recent weeks, and it is probably the duty of us all to put the Red case. I was going to mention something about the sword of truth and the shield of honour, but I think that's been done by someone else with less than convincing results. At least you know where I'm coming from: a standpoint which is based on United first and last, though that's not to say fair-mindedness is an impossibility. The trouble with the recent media pontifications (often by writers who style themselves 'The Nation's Greatest and Most Number One Football Reporter, So You'd Better Believe All This') is that their agenda is not always clear. Claiming to speak from some moral high-ground, it's hard not to conclude that the real agenda is to hammer Manchester United.

Of late the vilification of Manchester United has reached a new depth of intensity. Since Christmas United have been accused of devaluing the FA Cup, soiling the glorious reputation of English sport by their mean-spiritedness in Brazil, and corrupting the fresh-faced and innocent young lads from Leeds, who became a snarling and violent mob solely as a result of watching Roy Keane on *Match of the Day*. It seems United were responsible for four loveable Premier League sides being charged with misconduct, a fact underlined by the pictures of Keane that accompanied TV news stories of the FA's action. Forgive me if I seem to have read a little too much into this, but I'm sure that Alex Ferguson hi-jacked an aeroplane in Afghanistan recently to deflect attention from Dennis Irwin's attempts to scupper the Northern Ireland peace process. And the latest media campaign stems from that Middlesbrough penalty incident.

As it happens, I've yet to be convinced that the kick was correctly awarded, though many journalists and commentators have now decided that it was clear-cut. To me, one inconclusive camera angle does not out-weigh my view on the day that Stam played the ball first. But that is not the issue. After all (and here I go being all fair-minded), United had the benefit of a dubious penalty award against Boro last year – when the main camera angle suggested the decision had been correct. The fact is that the penalty was given to Middlesbrough and United over-reacted – it's as simple as that, and Fergie has acknowledged as much. As Monsieur Houllier (a good guy, according to Alex) has observed lately, there is a distinction between commitment and stupidity, and our lads effectively made a rod for their own backs. But Sir Alex's acknowledgement of the indiscretion has been treated with disdain; no doubt a similar statement from a Wenger or a Vialli would have been presented as proof of their sporting good nature. And Fergie's reaction to the incident was much at odds with David O'Leary's refusal to countenance any suggestion that his players had taken commitment several steps too far in their recent game against Spurs.

A similar contradiction appeared recently in the public demeanour of the respective captains of Manchester United and Newcastle. Roy Keane, not always beyond reproach, at least has the habit of holding his hands up and taking his punishment. His blood vessels may have been bursting after the Boro penalty award, but he accepted his unlucky (or totally and utterly justified, according to the proper writers) dismissal at St James's with good grace. It may seem a rum sort of compliment to pay, but Keane has seldom displayed any tendency to complain about his encounters with red cards. Arsenal players, on the other hand, are always hard done by if you listen to their post-match protestations. Keane, we must not forget, was wrongly imprisoned in Cup final week following a late-night incident that was lapped-up, if not actually set-up, by the newspapers. I have yet to hear him express the level of bitterness that would seem reasonable under the circumstances. Sometimes I think United could do worst than make the smooth Cork charms of the skipper available at every post match interview. The Newcastle captain, on the other hand, himself no stranger to the yellow card for dissent, gloated after United's recent defeat that the Reds do not like a kicking. A bit like Neil Lennon, then, although one should add straight away that the FA hearing assembled in private at the convenience of the Newcastle and England captain, declared that the Leicester player had not, after all, been the victim of a nasty boot to the face.

Let's go back to the subject of penalties, and the tedious myth that visitors to Old Trafford are consistently denied them. Peddlers of this nonsense have given Ruel Fox legendary status, for until the debatable Boro decision his spot kick for Norwich in December 1993 was the last given against United at Old Trafford in the league. I'll leave aside for now the fact Fox's goal was rough luck on United after Chris Sutton had gone to ground after the flimsiest of challenges from Gary Pallister. What I will say is that I have seen every game at Old Trafford since, and I can recall just one decent appeal for a penalty being turned down – a far cry from the mythical scenario of United constantly being given the benefit of the doubt by referees who fear for their careers. In this period United have conceded a number of penalties in European ties, suggesting that the lack of league penalties is simply due to United's domestic superiority – a step up to continental class (and we're talking about Juventus and Barcelona here) means more defending against better teams, with more penalties as a result. Perversely, even one penalty awarded against United in this period – against York City in the League Cup – is used to substantiate the argument that the establishment is in United's pocket. For despite TV proving Pat McGibbon's challenge on the York forward to have been well outside the box, and despite the fact that United simply got on with the game, the linesman who awarded it is often wheeled out by the newspapers to tell how that decision cost him his place on a non-league referees' list. As if.

I've often reflected that every time United are four-nil up at Old Trafford we should give away a gratuitous penalty, just to satisfy the statistically-inclined United-haters (and these people do love to pour over the record books, carefully ignoring attendance figures at Old Trafford in the last forty years). If they were truly interested in objective facts they would find United well down any list of penalty recipients (I think we had five in over 60 matches on the way to last season's Treble – and we missed two of those!). But as I said, I'm nothing if not fair-minded, so I'm happy to acknowledge that Barnsley were denied an FA Cup victory at Old Trafford after being refused a clear penalty. By my reckoning that makes one bad decision in six years (and they won the replay anyway), but staggeringly it led to questions being raised in Parliament. The honourable and right honourable members have been less agitated on other occasions, of course, such as last season when United were crazily denied what would have been the only goal of the FA Cup semi-final.

The ongoing media battering, plus the communication problems that exist between Manchester United and its own supporters, have led to serious suggestions that the club needs its own media master to lead a counter attack, or at least to defend our name. It has probably got to happen, so who is it going to be? The modern Manchester United needs a professional channel of public communication – the waters are simply too shark-infested to allow the club's various officers (directors, secretary etc) to go wading out there. But it is paramount that the appointed person should have impeccable credentials, with honesty and trustworthiness at the top of the list. Given the importance of repairing broken bridges with the fans, any new 'communications officer' should be able to relate to supporters as football people – it will not do simply to have a sharp suit and a crafty turn of phrase. By the same rule, United need to appeal to a broader constituency, and we need a public figure that can inspire general good-will. We need a diplomat, a consolidator, someone with no axes to grind, and someone with no enemies; he must have a thick skin and a cool and polite demeanour. A footballing gentleman, if that is not too cute an expression. But who? You'll no doubt have your own preference, but if I were Sir Roland Smith I'd be drawing up an employment package right now that would be attractive to one Mr Raymond Wilkins.

A surprise call? Well, remember that Wilkins was a very good player for Manchester United. He knows how special this club is, and I believe he retains an affection for Old Trafford despite his many other ports of call, and in spite of the fact that he suffered a hurtful, and undeserved, level of media and crowd disdain during his time in the Red shirt. Apart from anything else,

I can't think of anyone other than the Queen Mother who gives less offence than Ray Wilkins, and I doubt that she's a closet Cockney Red.

Painting the World Red

March 2000. How best to take your mind off the football? Not by decorating your house.

I finally got round to painting my kitchen walls recently – well, there was no football on the telly – and like one does when mindlessly applying the emulsion I started to daydream a little. I began to think how inevitable it was that I would run out of paint before I'd quite finished, yet had I saved myself the extra trip to the DIY store by buying two tins in the first place I would almost certainly not have needed the extra one. So I would have to go out for another pot of paint, knowing that I'd be left with three-quarters of a tin of relatively expensive vinyl silk, and that I'd probably shove it in the garage just in case … just in case what I am not quite sure. I can hardly get my car in the garage these days, for all the three-quarter-full pots of surplus paint that are stacked up in there.

Maybe it was the effect of the emulsion fumes, but it struck me that Alex Ferguson has faced a similar sort of problem. A few years ago, planning United's conquest of Europe, he probably wondered just how many tins of paint would be needed to complete his canvas. I apologise here for shifting the analogy from my kitchen wall to a burgeoning artwork, but daydreams seldom follow a logical thread. Anyway, in the event Alex decides he'll get two extra tins because, well you just never know. It seemed like a good idea at the time, as the shades he selected seemed to fit in with the grand design, and a little continental style was therefore added to the palette.

Signing footballers is a chancy affair, and things often don't turn out quite as you'd expect. A bit like choosing your paint from one of those bewildering colour charts. Once in a generation you'll find a Cantona Crimson, it not only blends in with the surroundings, but enhances and beautifies them to such an extent that time and weathering only serve to sharpen the memory of how wonderful it all was. Then again, a coat of Hazy Milne can soon leave you with the urge to redecorate. Alex's colour chart included the seductively named Hint of Cruyff, with an appealing sheen of a finish. He was tempted enough to try a tin, and although he has dabbed it around here and there, he seems unsure of where it would be best placed. It appears bright in dimmer surroundings, but quickly seems to fade under the gaze of the very brightest lights. Perhaps it wasn't the full all-weather version, or perhaps a Hint of the real Cruyff is all we could have expected anyway. And so it keeps getting put back into the garage, taken out for the occasional musing, and then returned. It could be something to do with application.

Alex's other extra tin reminded me of the old trick traditionally played on first-day apprentice tradesmen – you know the one, where they are sent to the stores to fetch a tin of chequered paint. In this case United went for the

---

Czech paint, only to find that Bohemian Red was prone to run in all directions whilst lacking any true consistency. Not even fit to be banished to the back of the garage, it wasn't long before Alex went and got his money back.

In Karel Poborsky United were probably hoping for a new Andrei Kanchelskis, a pale, white spirit from a cold faraway land, where two coats are often recommended. But memory plays its tricks, and the abiding recollections of the darting Ukrainian cutting a dash on the way to the 1994 Double tend to outweigh some of the paler shades of play witnessed either side of that season's great finale. In other words, not even Andrei Kanchelskis was Andrei Kanchelskis half of the time.

Thoughts of the hirsute Poborsky caused me to reflect that the shaggy one held more than a passing resemblance to the sheepdog on the Dulux tins, and I began to feel that this whole paint analogy was becoming a little spooky – or, more likely, I've probably just spread it a little too thinly. But what the hell – this is a bloody fanzine, not your actual Literary Review, you know. At least United players don't tend to rely on a Roller to move themselves around, not when there's a Ferrari waiting on the driveway. And speaking of Ferrari drivers, I can't not add a few words to the several million that accompanied the most breathtaking news item of recent weeks – the unveiling of David Beckham's latest hairstyle. Despite his short stay, Karel Poborsky will at least be remembered for one of the notable (non-) haircuts to have graced Old Trafford, but perhaps his greatest achievement was to offer us a style that even David Beckham would find it hard to carry off. So stylogenic (I think I've just invented a new word there) is the lad Becks, that in his various incarnations (from potential Baywatch extra to Ivan Denisovitch stand-in) he has yet to appear anything less than totally cool.

You wonder what Dennis Irwin makes of it all, Dennis being a man who probably regards Martin Buchan's barber as ever so slightly over-adventurous. But a man with more medals than even David May, and who remains first choice left-back when the chips are down, can probably afford a benevolent smile. While Becks hit the headlines for getting his hair cut, Irwin's retirement from international football caused barely a murmur, and that sort of sums up the way things are these days. All references to painting and decorating go out of the window when you are talking about Dennis Irwin, the uPVC of the United team. Back in 1992 Fergie thought he looked neat, had him installed, and was able to leave him to it, knowing that the full-back slot was maintenance-free and long-lasting. He's served us well and is reliable still.

Pots of paint and Manchester United. An odd train of thought, I agree, but it proves two things. First that spending too much time alone painting your kitchen walls can cause the mind to meander a bit, and secondly that my mind never wanders too far from Manchester United. The good news is that the walls are finished and I'm through with the emulsion. The bad news is that I'm starting on the woodwork next. I think I'll go for the Roy Keane, a tough, hard-wearing gloss – non-drip guaranteed.

Just Champions: A Review of 1999/2000

April 2000. United had won the Premiership again. No Treble this year, but miracles don't happen all that often.

We gathered at Goodison Park on a pleasant Sunday afternoon last August, wondering what we had the right to expect. Most of us had glided out of the Nou Camp only nine weeks earlier accepting that things would probably never be as good again, and the early start to the new league season seemed a cruel curtailing of a summer devoted to basking in the glow of Treble glory – did we really have to get back to business so soon?

Looking back over the Treble campaign, it was impossible not to be struck by the awesome extent of the challenge we met. But it went on and on, from seemingly insurmountable peak to beautiful new vista. Having reached the promised land and captured the Holy Grail, the team that launched a thousand cliches (giving Clive Tyldesley and Big Ron a place in Old Trafford folklore) were asked to go and do it again. But, as Alex reminds the players, you have to keep on striving, because the alternative is to throw it all away – as we'd done 31 years before.

Emerging from Everton's ground into the mild evening, having seen United totally out-play the home side, but fail to secure the match before conceding a messy equaliser, there were no voices of discontent. In the context of the football match United may have tossed away two points, but these lads were all legends now, and the least we could do was to be a little patient.

The reward followed immediately, with United winning the next six games, including enormous wins at Highbury and Anfield, and three points against Leeds that would come in useful later on. United were banging in the goals, but against lesser opposition (Sheffield Wednesday, Coventry and Gullit's Newcastle) it seemed to be achieved without really reaching top gear – a recurring observation as the season sped by.

Few, then, were surprised when the league campaign stalled as soon as the Champions' League resumed. The hiccup period may ultimately amount to Massimo Taibi's entire United career. Whether the Italian is a bad goalkeeper or simply unlucky, we may never get to find out, but he certainly enjoyed a rougher stroke of luck than Mickael Silvestre, signed around the same time, whose defensive indiscipline contributed to disappointing home draws against Wimbledon and Southampton. As for the 5-0 defeat at Chelsea, an annual hammering seems to be written into the script to give championship pretenders a little false hope (remember Newcastle?); but it was nice for them that they enjoyed their big day.

A routine demolition of Watford (with the Old Trafford atmosphere reaching an all-time low) was followed by another day of October gloom at Spurs. The fact that Giggs had opened the scoring also ruined the famous quiz question: When did United last lose a league game having scored first? (It had been at Chelsea in March 1991).

As quickly as results had stuttered, they began to pick up. From late October United won another six on the bounce before ending the wondrous year of 1999 with a comeback draw at Sunderland. Highly appropriate too, because as well as so many other things, 1999 will be remembered as a year of glorious fightbacks. The latest run of results was all the more creditable in the context of a Champions' League campaign that had reached the second group phase, and a detour to Tokyo to claim a World title. We'd played reasonable well without starting any fires, but the lack of credible opposition led us to wonder if another title was beckoning, and the feeling grew that the league was there to be claimed. This despite all pre-European Cup final promises to anyone listening that if we won the Treble we'd never ask God or Father Christmas for anything else ever again.

And so with United riding high the team set off for the unchartered waters of Brazil and the FIFA World Championships. Although the wise and considered Monsieur Wenger has since declared that the arrangements surrounding the whole jaunt were contrived to ease United's title chances, the pre-tournament tales were mostly filled with doom. For a start, United's rivals would have the opportunity to pull ahead in the title race, leaving the returning Reds to play catch-up. And the reports of previous visitors to Brazil going home with all manner of mystery viruses added to the fears. With a significant Champions' League schedule to accommodate as well, I recall no one suggesting beforehand that United were about to receive the boost of a sunshine break that would see them return refreshed and raring for action. For sure, United made the most of the climate and the disappointment of an early exit from the competition, but it was hardly Alex Ferguson's fault that the alleged challengers did not take advantage of United's absence to build up a points lead. Presumably, had Arsenal been in our shoes, the honourable Monsieur Wenger would have made his squad return on foot via the South Pole without benefit of sleds and huskies, just to make sure they were unfit to compete on their return

Despite the suntans, United did take a couple of games to re-acclimatise. A gruelling home draw with Arsenal and a scrappy win over Middlesbrough, were followed by victory over Sheffield Wednesday in our game in hand. United went top, and that was how it would remain.

But not before a tricky February and early-March had been negotiated. A sloppy home win over Coventry, then a kick-up-the-backside defeat at Newcastle represented our preparation for the important trip to Leeds. With Becks in the cooler we'd have taken a point gladly, but Cole's winner told us our team was determined to go all the way. Bizarrely, though, we again failed to beat Wimbledon the following week. I mean, everyone just goes out and beats Wimbledon, don't they? And does Neil Sullivan just save up the heroic goalkeeping antics for our visits?

There remained the need to keep Liverpool at arms' length, and a 1-1 draw was all it took. We had to have a final silly-session, at home to Derby, when we invited an equaliser for ages, then ran up the other end and scored two more as soon as we'd surrendered the advantage. But finally all the lights came on at once and United ran away with it. Twenty-four goals came in the next six matches, including the title clincher at the Dell. With four games still to play, United were out of sight, and (as I write) we need just ten more goals from three games to make it 100 for the season in the league alone.

That final statistic is perhaps the most remarkable. The swashbuckling Double-winning team of 1994 is remembered for its attacking flair and goals, but they scored 'just' 80 in 42 league games that season. To be on for a ton in a 38-game campaign, is made more remarkable since the team has played in spurts for much of the season, with Watford and Everton among those let off the hook in the latter stages of big defeats at Old Trafford.

On the day the league was won, the gloom merchants spoke of their dread that United would embark on a Scottish-style domination of the Premiership. Well, we all hope that will come to pass, but we also need to keep our feet on the ground. United have now won two consecutive titles, not 9 as Glasgow Rangers did in their league, and although we've won it in six of the last eight seasons, we've always passed up on the opportunity of a hat-trick. So let's hope that particular milestone is achieved next term – another sort of Treble – and that we can break a new record by going on to win a fourth.

Although exit from the European Cup was a disappointment, it shouldn't overshadow the achievement of topping the league. Winning the English league is always special, and each triumph should be savoured for all it is worth. One of these days the wheel will turn, and it will hurt like hell, so I'm celebrating while I can. As Ryan Giggs remarked, the sheer awfulness of not winning it makes victory essential for Manchester United. If, on the afternoon of the 1999 European Cup final, a genie had appeared and offered us the Treble with 'only' the English title to follow one year later, I think we'd have gladly settled for 'just' the championship this time around. In more ways than one we can proudly say we are Just Champions.

Resting Assured

July 2000. Summer holidays, and a time to forget about football. Or look forward to the season to come.

Much as I love football, and much as I love Manchester United, I relish the summertime. Apart from the fact that it's ever-so-slightly warmer than the rest of the year (I enjoy the cold months as much as I enjoyed City's promotion) I actually need a break from all the stress. Some stress, with six titles in eight years, I hear you cry from the direction of Anfield, but I mean it. The fan's weekend may have become a modern cliché, but only because it is true. You look ahead nervously to the match, go to the game and worry until it's in the bag, then go home and check the next five fixtures, working out how many points we need to gain and where the pitfalls lie. Following United may have the advantage that few post-match evenings are spent mulling over a devastating defeat (though I've sulked through many a weekend in the last thirty years), but the national outpouring of joy that tends to accompany our occasional reverses these days more than makes up for that. The summer is particularly delightful after a successful season, when you can sit back in your deckchair knowing that United are champions, and there's not a damned thing anyone can do or say to alter the fact.

It's nice when it's a World Cup summer or, as this year, a European Championship. That way you get to watch some decent football without the anxiety. I mean, Spain versus Yugoslavia was great fun, but I can't say I was suffering the apoplexy being experienced across Belgrade and Madrid. I had to laugh, though, when the commentators said they'd never seen anything like it as Spain scored twice in injury time to win the match. Didn't Ole put the ball in the Scousers' net in similar circumstances? And in the Germans' net when there was a serious trophy at stake?

Euro 2000 – what a bloody awful name for a tournament. Everything is Euro-this and Euro-that these days. Even the new-fangled money is being called the 'euro'. If ever we have a global currency, will it be called the 'worldo'? All right, I'm a miserable old traditionalist, and I can't stand seeing numbers on the front of players' shirts, but wasn't the original name of the competition, the *European Nations Cup*, so much more splendid?

Talking of shirts, the players themselves are beginning to resemble grand prix drivers, so festooned are the kits these days. The jerseys are adorned with numbers, front and back; team badges and manufacturers' badges; the tournament logo on one sleeve and, best of all, the Fair Play badge on the other. It's sort of ironic to see the Fair Play badge above an elbow which is about to strike an opponent's face, or to see it waving around in the air as its wearer brandishes an imaginary yellow card in the hope of getting an opponent booked. Sometimes the Fair Play badge will be sprawled across the deck in the penalty area alongside a pair of pleading eyes, imploring the referee to give an undeserved spot kick. We could soon clamp down on this, you know, by stripping persistent offenders of their Fair Play badge, and making them wear another that says Cheating, Diving Bastard. Let's go the whole way in fact. Instead of showing players yellow cards, why not pin them on their foreheads for the rest of the match? It may not shame them into repentance, but at least the crowd will have a better idea what's going on.

It would seldom happen at Old Trafford of course, as United are the current Fair Play Champions of the Premiership. You may have missed this announcement, as it was hardly broadcast from the rooftops, except by those who claimed it as proof that referees are simply intimidated by the bad boys of Old Trafford. This is yet another example of a rapid riposte from the stack of anti-United myths that seems to offer some comfort to the bitter and the twisted. For example, after England's elimination from Euro 2000, the Guardian printed a highly unamusing and totally unoriginal letter, blaming the referee for forgetting that penalties must not be awarded against United players. It would help if half our domestic opponents could get into our box – the likes of Barcelona, Vasco de Gama and even Sturm Graz seem to manage all right, and find penalties coming their way.

It was always on the cards that England would go out of Euro 2000 early, not having a good enough set of players (at the right stage of their careers) and failing to get the best from those selected. But it was almost inevitable that the fall guy would have to be a United man, and I bet poor Phil Neville doesn't get the pizza contract that went Southgate's way. Perhaps Phil should have lived up to another weary myth, and harangued the referee in the company of Gary, Becks and Scholesey. As it was, the honour of most-pointless-protest-against-blindingly-obvious-penalty went to the otherwise excellent Portuguese. Their ballistic reaction to a correct penalty award in the semi-final made the average Roy Keane protest look like a polite request for more tea. I awaited the condemnation that would surely follow, but the general conclusion seemed to be that it was a very disappointing way to lose a semi-final and 'you have to feel sorry for them'. Er, right. I imagined them in the dressing rooms later, contemplating pointless suspensions, and having seen the replays on TV. Did they all turn to Abel Xavier and say "You peroxide bastard, you said you never touched it!"?

At least the Dutch are likely to be kinder to Jaap Stam after his spectacular shoot-out failure, perhaps the worst consequence of which was the predictably high number of witty people who claimed to have seen the ball flying past their fourth-floor office windows during the following week. It was an unfortunate conclusion to what had been a flawless performance by Jip Jaap against Italy; I even heard myself use the word 'immaculate', a phrase which recalled my common adjective for the great Martin Buchan.

If Euro 2000 had one positive for United fans it was the chance to cast an eye over Fabien Barthez. The first opportunity came as the French team lined up for that excellent national anthem, with me and the kids singing out loud the Eric Cantona version (and I'll bet we weren't alone). First impressions were to wonder if he has the height, but once the games were underway he looked agile, safe and in control. Just nutty enough, in fact. It should be fun. But nice too to see the rejuvenated Schmeichel, virtually representing Denmark on his own. He's still a great goalkeeper, and is looking in fine fettle after his year in the sun, lucky man.

Which is sort of where I came in, relishing the summertime. I'd just got my deckchair out, closed my eyes and started to daydream about 18 point gaps at the top of the Premiership, when our esteemed editor got in touch to mention deadlines for the first Red News of the season – thanks, Barney. But that's enough of my musing; I'm off on my holidays now, and when I get back the new season, the months of stress, the cold and the damp all await me. Along with Fabien Barthez of course – I hope he remembers to bring his overcoat. To all fellow Reds, let's hope the months ahead bring us plenty to savour in the summer of 2001.

Style and the Council Pitches

September 2000. Recalling football as I learned it.

Matters of style have been in my mind of late. This was prompted because I happened to revisit recently the playing fields where I'd kicked many a football as a primary school kid back in the late 1960s. It was the first time I'd walked on the pitches for over 30 years, but other than the fact that the place did not seem so vast, it was surprisingly familiar. It was an inevitable cue for a nostalgia trip, needless to say, and so I retreated into my own memory to spend a little time back in that fondly-remembered world. I can never escape a tingle of poignancy when I find myself playing the role of a middle-aged adult on a stage where I was once the child. It's difficult not to recall the cast of characters back in former days, and to reflect with sadness that time has left many of them behind, though the joy of beholding the new blood is undiminished. And so the scene brought back the routine and the incidents that had happened such a long time ago.

For some peculiar reason one defining image was of the plastic bus tokens which were issued to our school football team on a Friday afternoon – these were like toy money, coloured green, and valid for fares on Salford Corporation buses. There were different tokens for pre-decimal pennies and ha'pennies, and they were useless for anything other than bus travel. Among my mates, few (if any) families owned a car, so the tokens were a smart idea; unfortunately the old green corporation buses were no more reliable than the deregulated fleets of today, and we often ended up walking a couple of miles home in our muddy kit.

But what a kit, or so we thought at the time. The shirts were white, with a black round collar and black cuffs; classic late '60s in fact, and not unlike those worn by the West Germans of the time. The socks were white too, but the really stylish touch came with the ultra-modern black shorts, which were made from a silky sort of material. We were in no doubt that the shiny shorts marked us out as a thoroughly modern outfit, a view reinforced by the disbelief expressed by our old parish priest that such modish decadence had manifested itself in our attire. It's what you're accustomed to, I suppose, and for many years previously the school team had worn an altogether different sort of outfit. The old kit was still being worn by the younger school team, and so we'd played in it the previous year. Regarded as uncool and antique at the time, I actually have a fond regard for it now, its early 1950s styling being reminiscent of some old Boys' Own comic strip. The baggy blue cotton shirt had a button-up collar, there were baggy white shorts, and socks that had been worn and half-washed so many times I no longer recall their true appearance.

I really don't know if football boots were so much more expensive than today in relative terms, though that was how it seemed to me. It was a really big deal for our parents to buy our boots, but we got the neatest-looking style we could find (I think the old priest said they were no better than carpet slippers). The truly cool would turn out in Georgie Best's Stylo Matchmakers, with the laces up one side, but this was a little ostentatious even for most of our tastes, and certainly for our mothers' purses.

I'd never decry the teachers who took us for football, for they were keen and hard-working, but we were never taught to play football, as such. What I mean is, we were never taught to play with a football, to be comfortable in its company. The 'coaching' was very much of its time, and my main recollection of playing in these games was being urged to lump it forward. It seemed that skill was regarded as something you were either born with or you did without; I now know that although some people are inevitably naturally skilful, almost anyone can be taught to learn and develop some degree of technique and skill. It's a lesson that the whole of English football has only seemed to grasp in recent times, and so for many of us the shiny shorts remained the most stylish part of our game.

England's World Cup winning tactics, to say nothing of the Italian catenaccio of the era, had failed to make much impact on our part of the world. We may have been kitted out like thoroughly modern 1960s players, but we still played 'proper' football: 5-3-2. Not that this mattered half the time, when the key thing was to imitate Denis Law as closely as possible. And so the cuffs were tucked into the fists and the single finger pointed to the sky in salute of any goal. Looking stylish was the key, and if you could look the part and play as well, then you'd just about cracked it.

So here I was over thirty years on. Not much had changed in my head. I was still mad about the football, I still loved Manchester United to bits, and the week earlier at United's opening game of the season I'd watched Denis Law scamper around the pitch at half-time, still my hero. I wonder whether, thirty years from now, today's young lads will reflect on their worship of David Beckham, and recall fondly their trendy Adidas boots, laced carefully to hold the tongue of the boot down flat? I asked my modern-day 'style consultant' – one of the local kids – about this recently, and he told me he prefers to lace the boots in normal fashion, but wear an elastic band around the boot to hold the tongue in place. I found this amusing and touching at the same time. It's great to know that hero-worship is still going strong, and I hope that Becks remains a hero for him, as Denis has for me. In fact it's not difficult to imagine, thirty years from now, David Beckham, Gary Neville and Ryan Giggs on the pitch at half time drawing the raffle (or whatever else they dream up in the meantime), with today's youngsters, greying and balding, doing their own nostalgia trip. Sounds bizarre, but as sure as anything it will happen.

Their memories are likely to differ considerably from my own. Things vary from place to place, but it's probably safe to say that opportunities for young kids to play organised football have never been greater than today. Junior football has undergone a remarkable expansion in recent years, with many local clubs offering a game and some coaching to kids from as young as five years old. The enormous number of junior football tournaments taking place every weekend of the summer, and the highly organised leagues in the winter, are a far cry from the way things once were. It's possible to be delighted for the kids and envious at the same time. Today many a half-decent lad of eight years old is likely to have a couple of years' experience with a junior club, and kids have often played for a full four or five years before they are old enough for the school team. If there's a down side it may be in the demise of street football – because of the traffic if nothing else – and the feeling that the parks may be less safe places than they once were.

Perhaps the biggest difference today concerns the opportunity kids have to get into Old Trafford to see United play. Or at least to do so every fortnight as I did, developing a habit (an obsession then, I confess) that has remained to this day. It's to be hoped with increasing capacities (though sadly increasing ticket prices too), that this can be addressed. For you've got to fuel the dream. Football must be magical or it is nothing. Old Trafford will remain an inspiration for all and an aspiration for some, but the scruffy council pitch will remain the real theatre upon which all our dreams are played out.

Recalling Scarlet Ribbons in the Merry Month of May

October 2000. Wembley Stadium was closing down. We'd had some good times there.

Although Old Trafford and its surroundings have changed dramatically in recent years, so much so that anyone who has been away during the Fergie era would scarcely recognise the place today, it remains a place where I can feel at home. Come to think of it, Old Trafford is the single place in the world with which I have had the longest-lasting bond of attachment, and as long as there is grass on that pitch I suppose that is the way it will remain.

Are things changing faster than ever these days, or am I just getting old? On my way into London recently, my train passed Wembley Stadium. I'll probably see the towers a few more times before they finally bite the dust (and there is now talk of rebuilding them in Widnes in honour of rugby league), but this would be my last sighting before the England v. Germany game, officially Wembley's final curtain. The thought struck me that apart from Old Trafford, Wembley is the ground at which I've most often seen United play. Now that's a fairly amazing statistic given my routine visits to places like Maine Road, Villa Park and Goodison Park over the years. If my arithmetic is right, I've made 21 trips to Wembley to watch United, starting with the FA Cup final of 1976. There have been 10 FA Cup finals and two replays; four League Cup finals; the FA Cup semi-final of 1994; and four Charity Shield matches. Remarkably it could have been many more had I not abandoned several Charity Shield games on account of the cost and time given up to watch a fairly meaningless match. All right, it's United, but you have to draw the line somewhere when the money is tight.

Part of the allure of Wembley has always been its crock of gold appeal, lying as it does at the end of the FA Cup's rainbow. You don't yearn entirely for Wembley itself, but for what it represents as an achievement for your team. When your team is playing at Wembley, everyone sits up and takes notice. These days it can be hard for young United fans to appreciate the thrill of a first-time Wembley visit after years of unfulfilled expectation, though many other clubs are still waiting their turn. To some extent this thrill-factor has lessened in recent years, with all manner of dubious cup finals and play-off matches increasing the opportunity to experience a Wembley trip. But not so long ago the very idea of Wembley set all hearts racing, and it seemed something of an impossible dream even for supporters of Manchester United.

From watching the 1968 European Cup final on TV at the age of 9, it took me almost another lifetime, until I was nearly 18, before I actually got to visit Wembley for myself. During that footballing dark age Wembley was a place for other teams, for other fans. If, by 1993, it seemed that championships were the domain of others, and if upon losing to Monaco in 1998 it seemed that the European Cup was never to be recaptured, then a similar feeling existed towards Wembley in the mid-1970s. With league championships in the realm of pure fantasy, the big hope back then was for a cup run to Wembley, and unlike today we'd have jumped through hoops at the idea of reaching the League Cup final. Several times Wembley loomed, but League Cup semi-final defeats against Manchester City in 1970 and third division (yes, third division, God help us!) Aston Villa in 1971 saw us miss out. 1970 also brought the heartbreak of FA Cup semi-final defeat to Leeds, and the closing minutes of the second replay remain in my list of most-painful United moments. There was more disappointment in 1975, when United met Norwich in the League Cup semi-final over two legs. Norwich were one of United's closest rivals in the second division that season, and eventually were promoted with us. Their team included Ted MacDougall, released by Tommy Docherty after briefly offering us hope that we had found ourselves a decent goalscorer. MacDougall was undeservedly taunted in the first leg at Old Trafford with cries of 'United reject', but in truth I recall most of us had been sorry to see him off-loaded. Needless to say he had a long and successful career, and managed to break our hearts with a late equaliser to give Norwich a 2-2 draw, and a platform for a close victory at Carrow Road. Once again Wembley would have to wait, and once again we were left to discard our token sheets, lovingly completed on cold winter nights at youth team matches, all to no avail.

Once we finally made it, however, the Wembley trips came thick and fast, and within a few years the sense of occasion was quickly replaced by the straightforward need to see United win an important football match. Nevertheless the years of hankering ensured that my first visit to Wembley remained the most memorable in terms of events off the pitch. I can recall so much about the day. The expectation of victory; the winding route of the coach from the M1 and North Circular Road; the masses and masses of Reds lining every pavement. And the awful crush at the turnstiles – I suppose it was the first Wembley trip for a whole generation of us, and we hadn't yet developed the laid back style of strolling to the ground in our own good time. Once inside, the gloomy ugliness of the area below the stands was fairly shocking to anyone whose only previous experience of Wembley was the glorified TV version. But this was offset by the scale of the arena itself. Unlike any normal football ground this place was expansive, and I do recall a sharp intake of breath. I'd waited so long to be here, ever since watching the World Cup final of 1966 as a youngster, and the glorious 29 May two years later as a still-young, but by now confirmed, Manchester United supporter without a ticket. I was finally here. But United came out and forgot to play against Southampton, and the following day I lay at home on my bed wondering if I'd have to wait another ten years, or longer, to get another chance. Would I ever see United lift a trophy before my own eyes?

How sweet it was, then, to be back the following year. I trained my eyes on Martin Buchan as he lifted the Cup – a faint glimmer of silver so far away, but confirmation that United had finally won something again. At Wembley that afternoon I could not have been happier. At Wembley I finally saw United victorious. And it now seems like a strangely distant time, as the defeated Liverpool team did a lap of honour to be greeted by the magnanimous United crowd chanting 'Liverpool, Liverpool ...', as if to honour our rivals' efforts that day. It really did happen like that, and the Liverpool players, though clearly gutted, applauded the United fans in turn. Perhaps they appreciated less our last ever rendition of 'Oh, Man United, the only English team to win the European Cup', because four days later that particular ditty had passed its sing-by date.

For the next dozen years Wembley represented the peak of our achievements, if not our ambitions. For as every championship challenge fizzled away, there were at least regular trips to Wembley to lift the spirits, even if the final experience often proved unsatisfying. The agonising last five minutes of the 1979 final, when a two-goal deficit was rescued then thrown away; the empty feeling of unfinished business after the 2-2 draw with Brighton in 1983. But we enjoyed the fun of the replay when Robbo led the charge, and the brilliant Norman conquest of Everton in 1985. Then Wembley came to Fergie's rescue after a horrible couple of seasons, as the 1990 FA Cup bought the manager time, and opened the door to the European glory of Rotterdam one year later.

I shouldn't forget to mention the League Cup, though our four finals, including three defeats, are hardly etched on the memory. Perhaps the most notable game came against Liverpool in 1983, the first of four Wembley appearances in just a few months for United that year. Taking place in the era when Ron Atkinson's Reds were vying unsuccessfully with the enemy for league honours, the match kind of summed-up the entire period. Norman put us ahead with a beauty, but United ran out of luck, as injuries and some unpunished antics by Grobbelaar contributed to our extra-time defeat. Forgive me for indulging in a particularly personal recollection of that game – this was the only Wembley match I watched with my late father (a devoted Red who missed out on the glorious Ferguson era). Except for this game, my dad and I always found ourselves in different parts of Wembley, so result apart the 1983 League Cup final does hold a warm memory for me. When United did finally win the trophy for the only time it was an unreal sort of affair, with the team wearing the psychedelic blue kit, and with victory celebrations muted by the over-riding anxiety of a title challenge that would eventually break our hearts. Odd, too, to think that Sheringham and Keane both played for Nottingham Forest that day. Their time would come.

I don't need to describe all the games – you were probably there yourself. Wembley had by now become something of a home from home, but we were no longer grateful just to be there; higher and higher prices were being paid with every visit, and we began, justifiably, to grumble about the facilities. Dragging my then eight year old daughter through urine-flooded stairwells at the 1995 FA Cup final was perhaps my lowest point. Inadequate sightlines from newly-installed seats behind a visually-intrusive fence ruined many an expensive Wembley outing, but complaints were often brushed aside by the stadium authorities, who simply recounted their expenditure on a venue no longer worthy of its reputation. Far from relishing the experience, United fans (whilst grateful for the footballing glory) began to dread the expense and inconvenience of each trip, and I spent as much time hoping not to be seated behind an iron post as I did worrying about the actual game (and those who know me know that I do like to worry about the game).

But even if it's fair to welcome the demise of the old Wembley, and to hope that we eventually get a new stadium worthy of the prices we pay, it would be wrong to let negative thoughts overshadow the great days we have spent there, and the memories we'll carry forever. The Double of 1994 was won as much by Mark Hughes's injury-time equaliser in the Wembley semi-final against Oldham as in the final itself. And but for a damp squib of a League Cup final against Villa, we'd have grabbed a Treble that year. If that was dreamland, Eric's beautiful goal to capture a second Double two years later was the stuff of fantasy; and this time there was no magnanimity towards Liverpool, who didn't really bother with a lap of honour.

As United completed the second leg of the incredible Treble of 1999, easily beating Newcastle on the only occasion I went to Wembley just knowing that we were going to win, the distance we'd travelled from the pipedream days of the early 1970s was incalculable. But you never know what's around the corner, and my eyes were as fixed on the distant silver glimmer as they had been twenty-two years earlier. Being there when United win is what the agonies of any season are all about.

I've made only a handful of journeys to Wembley when United haven't been playing, but there have been strange little United connections each time. In 1992 I was there to see Barcelona win their first ever European Cup, reaching their own Holy Grail to scenes of celebration and relief that would be matched in their own stadium seven years later. One year later I saw Parma win the Cup Winners' Cup against Antwerp, a club soon to be linked to our own. I have only attended one England match at Wembley (indeed anywhere). France were the visitors in 1992 when their team included a bad-guy from Leeds called Cantona – little did any of us know. And I was at the Euro '96 final when a little Czech called Poborsky continually caught the eye.

So that's my Wembley. Its time has passed and it is right that it should leave us now. We deserve, after all, to see the pitch on Cup final day. Perhaps Wembley's greatest days, and United's greatest Wembley days, were before my own time: winning the acclaimed final of 1948, just being there ten years later, and then achieving a sort of immortality in 1968. It is for someone else to record those occasions. What I do know is that in 1977, and again in 1994 and 1996, I went away from Wembley thinking that my wildest dreams had come true, and that things couldn't get any better than this. But each time I was wrong. Still greater things kept coming our way, and I only hope that the new Wembley brings as much glory to United as the old one did. What is certain is that I'll savour each and every future success as though it were our last, because you just never know.

The Luck of the Draw

November 2000. Does fate really determine the outcome in football? Are we getting all worked up about events that are pre-ordained? Sometimes you have to wonder.

At Old Trafford we have become accustomed to intellectual Frenchmen imparting the occasional cool one-liner, but it's not a recent phenomenon. A couple of hundred years ago, even before Guy Roux set up his footballing shop in Auxerre, there lived a man of letters called Jacques Delille. He may not be up there with Voltaire, Hugo or Cantona, but he must have been doing something right to get a mention in Red News nearly two centuries after he popped his *sabots*. Delille wrote this: "Fate chooses your relations, you choose your friends". Now I'm sure he wrote a whole lot else, but it was this that got me thinking. For if Jacques had been around today, I wonder if he'd have refined his observation to reflect modern times? Perhaps he'd have written "Fate chooses your football team, you choose your friends".

If so, I think he'd be correct. I know that I did not choose to support Manchester United, and I don't remember an occasion when the realisation actually dawned. Supporting United was just what I did; what everyone (surely?) did. It was a sort of understanding I grew up with. And I think this is good, because it leaves no room for doubt. Like Gary Neville, I'm a Red. You can't deny what you are. Now you may argue that this is not down to fate at all, but is simply a product of upbringing (or parental brainwashing, as I've heard it referred). But Jacques' point was that fate is the hand you're dealt, and I'd say that football allegiances fall firmly into this category.

I agree that this is only true for some of us. And it is perhaps here that we come to the crucial point of difference between the 'hard core' and the '1990s new fan'. The phrase 'hard core' has a bit of an unpleasant edge, a hint of 1970s nastiness, but I think that is misleading. 'Hard core' to me means simply that the team is a part of you, that it was chosen by fate, and that there ain't nothing you can ever do about it. You can be a sixty-five year old Esperanto-speaking Quaker, and still be a hard core Red. You've been there for as long as you can remember, and you can't imagine life without it. For the 'new fan', however, football is indeed about choice rather than fate. Football is as fashionable now as it was contemptible in the 1980s, when it was left to the hard core only to keep the turnstiles ticking. The new fans have come along to ride the bandwagon, and have picked their teams.

Here's an example of the outcome. On 26 October 1986 the Manchester derby was televised live for the first time. I remember it well, not for the game (an unremarkable 1-1 draw between two struggling sides), but for the fact that there were about 10,000 unsold tickets for the match. The attendance was just 32,440. Live TV tended to have this effect on crowds in the days before football became fashion, but I was staggered and sad that so many people were prepared to miss this particular game. I think it's safe to say that the hard core were there that day. Not that we had any choice, you understand. United were playing in Manchester and fate had decreed that we would simply be there. Choice didn't enter into it. There was no 'shall we or shan't we?' about it. But that was then. For the recent Manchester derby (also televised live) tickets were like the proverbial gold dust, and I imagine that Maine Road could have sold out three times over. It would be very interesting to ask everyone aged over 30 in the recent crowd where they were in '86.

There's something altogether unappealing about bandwagon-jumping. Whether it's 'new lifelong' United fans or those proclaiming 'hatred' of a football team they seldom noticed until six years ago. It's based on the choice of (or alignment with) whatever is fashionable, rather than something truly heartfelt. And when you hear of people switching allegiances (from Fulham to Chelsea, being oft-quoted), then you could almost cry.

If fate hands us our teams for life, it also plays a part in the successes we enjoy and the failures we don't. Perhaps the most common (if oblique) reference to the part of fate in football is the idea of your name being on the cup. Or "Name on the Trophy", as Clive Tyldesley cried so memorably, so evocatively and so accurately as Teddy hit the equaliser in the Nou Camp Miracle of 1999. In the cold light of day (all right, it was more of a warm glow) in the weeks and months that followed that match, many United supporters found themselves unable to dismiss the thought that the victory had been pre-ordained. In fact the more they thought about it, the more likely, the less ridiculous, this seemed. It wasn't just the events of the final, as a couple of strokes of good fortune against Inter in the quarters (notably a disallowed away goal at Old Trafford) had played their part. Fate had declared it Manchester United's year, it seemed, and not just in Europe. It's impossible now to watch the FA Cup semi-final replay against Arsenal, so nerve-wracking at the time, and not be overcome by the sheer inevitability of the outcome. The same can be said of the 4th Round match against Liverpool, when United rehearsed the Nou Camp script to an uncanny degree. On the face of it United didn't enjoy the luck of the draw in Europe and the FA Cup that season, having tough games in every round. But maybe we were favoured in the unseen draw that matters – name on the trophies. If fate deals the hand, United got a Royal Flush that year.

The hand of fate can of course be cruel, and no club is more aware of this than Manchester United. But fate (chance, call it what you will) is at the essence of our club, having played its part in the rebirth of Manchester United out of Newton Heath. Harry Stafford, the team captain, persuaded a group of businessmen led by J.H. Davies to underwrite the relaunch of the club, but, according to legend, only after the hand of fate had led to their initial meeting. The story goes that Stafford's St Bernard dog, with a collecting tin around its neck, had strayed from a fundraising event, and was found by a tenant of one of Davies's pubs. Perhaps no one knows how far this particular yarn has been spun, but it seems clear that fate intended that the club would survive. But under what name? Geoffrey Green's centenary history of United suggests that the renaming of Newton Heath was the cause for some disagreement, with Manchester Celtic and Manchester Central being favoured. If we'd gone for the latter (and here comes an in-joke for all Mancunians with long memories) we'd probably be known as Manchester G-Mex by now. Green says that it was Louis Rocca, United stalwart and Chief Scout from 1907 until 1950, who claimed the credit for the new name: "I got up and suggested Manchester United. The name was taken." So there you have it, without a wandering dog and a bit of inspiration from Louis Rocca there would be no Manchester United at all. Fate, surely.

Perhaps things just turn out the way they are meant to. Here's another example. In 1945 Liverpool offered Matt Busby, one of their senior players, a five year contract as coach, an offer that Matt verbally accepted. But before he was able to put pen to paper, he was given the opportunity to become a manager in his own right at Manchester United. Of Liverpool, Matt wrote: "Had I signed that contract, who knows what would have happened?" Who, indeed.

The 'what ifs' are endless. What if Matt and Jimmy Murphy had responded to lavish overtures from Spain and Italy in the 1950s? What if Jock Stein had been persuaded to follow Sir Matt at Old Trafford? What if United had signed Dalglish in 1977 or Shearer in 1993? If Kidd had not left to be replaced by McClaren, would we have won the Treble? If you are looking for one moment in one game, what if Denis Law's 'equalising goal' in the European Cup semi-final 2nd leg of 1969 had been allowed to stand (because it really did cross the line!)? Would we have gone on to win the tie? Would we have beaten the inexperienced Ajax in the final? And would we have been reduced to relegation five years later?

If, as it sometimes seems, things are written in the stars, it makes me wonder whether I should give up worrying before every big game (all right, every single game). But if I can't choose to change because I am fated to be the way I am, perhaps there is a little solace to be found. Maybe, as the song goes, whatever will be will be.

Jingle Bells

January 2001. The Christmas period is over, and another Premiership is already on the horizon for United.

One of these days English football may take up Sir Alex Ferguson's suggestion, and introduce a mid-season break. But even if it leads to fewer matches in the festive period, Manchester United will no doubt remain at the forefront of our minds each Christmas. Here's a true story. A United supporter and a Liverpool supporter are comparing Christmas presents, when the United fan complains that he's getting a bit fed up of receiving the same gift year in and year out. The Liverpool fan sympathises: "I know what you mean – more socks and after-shave, eh?" "No," grins the United supporter, "yet another 'Champions' video."

In reality, none of us will ever grow weary of the 'Champions' videos, and as United moved 11 points clear of the pack on New Year's Day, I've no doubt that the video manufacturers began sketching out the cover for this season's version. But never one to count my chickens (and with 1998 being far too vivid in my memory), I was certainly not joining in with the chant of 'We won the Football League again, this time on New Year's Day' – excellent song, though it is.

In years gone by my Christmas stocking always contained the latest edition of David Meek's Manchester United Football Book. I've got the full set, from the first issue in 1966 until the title faded away in the early 1980s, though I was missing a couple of volumes until fairly recently – it says a lot about those days that Number 12 from 1977 was sold out before Christmas because United had actually won something that year. The Manchester United Football Book was special because it represented a neat resume of the previous season, and focused on the hopes of our heroes for the campaign ahead. In its day it was the equivalent of the season review video – it was a book of record – and I still refer to my volumes when I want to settle an argument or look up a classic photograph. As it happens, my favourite book isn't Number 3 (the European Cup winning season), but Number 8. Although it recorded the miserable decline of 1972/73, I managed to get this one autographed by almost everyone at the club, including Sir Matt.

Perhaps the most poignant image in the book is the autographed full-page picture of Jim Holton, with a face full of mud, looking up for the battle that United faced in those days. A young fans' idol, was Jim Holton, and (I'd practically forgotten this) I even had a silk scarf with his name and face printed on. Probably my clearest recollection of Jim is not one of his titanic battles in the mud, or even the time he was sent off for nutting Malcolm MacDonald, but the day he signed my book. It was at the Cliff, in a time when the players were truly accessible, and he was getting out of his car – it was a Vauxhall, received as a member of the Scotland squad that had reached the World Cup finals that year (1974). There were a number of identical cars in the Cliff car park in those days, as Doc's Tartan Army was well represented in the Scotland team of the time. His was a meteoric rise following a United debut (along with Lou Macari) against West Ham in January 1973, but a broken leg at Hillsborough in December 1974 led to wretched misfortune with injury. He never played for United again, and was of course lost to us at a tragically young age. The legendary Jim Holton is recalled with each season's visit to Coventry, when United fans pop into his former pub. He was a good player (or a "rugged, fearless 6ft 2ins tank of a player" to quote from the book), and I remember him fondly.

It's the recollection of years like 1973 (and the even worse season that followed) that make all talk of anti-climax when United 'only' managed to win the league in 2000 so absurd. That thought was also brought to mind recently when I watched the late-1980s version of the History of Manchester United on a BBC video. The film ends with Alex Ferguson describing his hope that one day United can reclaim the championship, and with the narrator wondering if this will ever happen, or whether the burden is too great. These things can leave me suffering from an awful sense of perspective – all those clips of games from the seventies, and knowing I was in all of those crowds. The energy I've invested in all these years. It's better not to think about it too much.

One thing that did come out of the video was the answer to a question I posed in the last Red News: was the story true that JH Davies saved United in 1902 having met the club captain, Harry Stafford, through finding Stafford's wandering St Bernard dog? Well I'd obviously forgotten all about the clip, but the video includes an old interview with the daughter of Mr Davies. She confirmed that the dog did indeed find its way to her family home, and added that Harry Stafford was persuaded to let her keep it in return for her father's efforts in support of the football club. So now I know.

I may be in my forties now, and the Manchester United Football Book may seem like a bit of a period piece, but my typical Christmas presents haven't changed too much. I'm a bit too old to start growing up now, so (when I wasn't watching old United videos) I spent all of this Christmas reading the new books about Roger Byrne, Roy Keane and David Beckham. For serious Reds, Ian McCartney's biography of Roger Byrne is essential reading. It's not often that I read a book on a United topic and feel that I'm really learning something new, but this short biography presented the human side of Roger Byrne and his team-mates. I'm not sure if being born in 1958 has given me a particular bond with the team we lost, but I am aware that these are the lads I'd have started watching in the 1960s if things had turned out differently. Although I arrived soon after they'd gone, they were my loss too.

Which brings me on to the obnoxious references to Munich in a recent Manchester City programme. I didn't really want to mention it, but here I go anyway. I just find it sad, that's all. Manchester City's hierarchy have moved to distance themselves from the offensive remark, but is there a real determination to wipe out this sick mentality? It's no good United fans asking if these people understand that Frank Swift, probably Manchester City's finest goalkeeper, was also a victim of Munich. The perpetrators probably do not know who Swift was, or do not care. And I'm not sure that we're talking just about an underclass here, as references to Munich are bandied around all too incautiously. A high-profile example occurs in another book I read over Christmas, Mihir Bose's 'Manchester Unlimited'. On the proposed (and thankfully defeated) Sky take-over of United, Bose quotes Howard Davies, head of the Securities and Financial Authority, as follows: "I am so glad it is happening. I have hated Manchester United all my life. Manchester United was born in Munich and will die with Murdoch". Can he really have said that? Can any educated person really use the words 'born' and 'die' in the same sentence as 'Munich'? Would anyone in such a position risk a similarly bitter and twisted reference to one of British football's other tragedies (Ibrox, Burnden Park, Bradford or Hillsborough)? Human nature certainly has an infinite ability to depress.

There may be times, though, when United supporters also need to think things through a little more carefully. I confess I have a real problem with the 'Russian submarine' song, so popular at the moment. It may not have reached and offended the populations of St Petersburg or Murmansk, but you have to wonder if it would be sung (thoughtlessly if not with malice) if we happen to visit Spartak Moscow (or some such place) in the near future. Is the song so funny that we just can't discard it? I'm only asking. I think someone has to.

Oh dear, this article has now taken a serious turn, when I only really wanted to reminisce about Christmas Past and Jim Holton. Never mind, United are top of the league, and with a bit of luck we'll be able to sing Jingle Bells at away games all year long, while dropping hints that the latest 'Champions' video will do nicely for next Christmas. Happy New Year.

Yankee Doodles

February 2001. Manchester United announce a commercial partnership with the New York Yankees baseball team. Now what's this all about?

It takes me quite a while to get worked up about a lot of the stuff in the newspapers these days. In fact I seldom give a second glance each time I see splash banner headlines about United's latest crime of treachery. It usually is tantamount to treachery, of course, whether it's competing in Brazil at the behest of the FA and Government or simply winning too many football matches, thereby being 'too dominant' and being 'bad for the game of football in England'. How dare we. And wasn't football so much healthier twenty years ago when lovable Liverpool were strutting their stuff? So it's only once in a while that I stop and think that a story may truly be significant. The Sky deal was once such case, when (for about thirty seconds) I dismissed it out of hand as paper talk, only to get this sinking feeling before reaching for the worry-beads. Then recently came the news of the commercial link-up with the New York Yankees.

Do any of us really know what we feel about the Yankees deal? Its announcement was accompanied by several days of media frothing, most of it speculative, if not simply ill-informed. Hearing the professional 'business analysts' on the radio simply making it up as they went along, doing their couple of minutes in front of the microphone and hoping they'd bluffed their way through, at least offered amusement along with the consolation that as a mere United supporter I wasn't alone in wondering what it all meant. At least I knew more about United than the paid commentators. I think it's fair to say that the first feelings of many fans were simply those of unease. What were United playing at? Was there a wider agenda? And have we all simply become too attuned to suspicion?

I decided to ignore all the analysis, all the guesswork, and take a close look at the press release issued by United and our new chums from across the ocean. The first thing that struck me was that we weren't just talking about the New York Yankees here. The Yankees are a well-known team even in these baseball-free islands, but less is known about their corporate body. So we learn that the Yankees are part of a set-up that calls itself YankeeNets LLC, and that the 'Nets' bit refers to *"a premier integrated sports-based media company that was formed in 1999-2000 to combine the ownership of the World Series Champion New York Yankees Major League Baseball (MLB) team, the New Jersey Nets National Basketball Association (NBA) team, and through an affiliate Puck Holdings, the 2000 Stanley Cup Champion New Jersey Devils National Hockey League (NHL) team"*. Blimey. So the Yankees and the New Jersey Nets basketball team are somehow affiliated to an ice-hockey team called the New Jersey Devils, and there are blokes in suits who somehow represent the whole caboodle.

Needless to say, it's all about selling TV rights. Well, OK, that's up to them I suppose, as long as no one is thinking of expanding their 'premier integrated sports-based media company' into something called YankeeNetsUnited.

All of which is pretty exhausting stuff, and I've not even started on the nitty-gritty of the press release yet. But there's more. We learn that YankeeNets have recently established a "*marketing alliance partnership*" with the New York Giants (they play American football), and that the aim has been to develop marketing, sponsorship and retailing. These are also given as the precise aims of the 'alliance' between Manchester United and the corporate body representing all those New York/New Jersey Thingies. This makes, I'm sure you'll agree, very dull reading (the press release was probably designed to be read from beginning to end by no one), but I found its very dullness rather reassuring.   For if all they were going to do was sit around boardrooms watching each others slide shows, while maybe trying to offload souvenirs in each other's shops, then we probably wouldn't have too much to worry about.

But that's not quite all they will be doing. We are told that YankeeNets, and their affiliated company called ChampionsWorld (no, I've no idea who they are either, nor do I know why American companies' names never seem to have spaces between words) will "*also provide assistance to Manchester United in the planning of their youth and community relations initiatives in North America, and the two clubs will share sporting knowledge in areas such as player training, fitness and health. They also plan to work together to develop a Manchester United pre-season tour of North America in 2003*". On the face of it there is nothing too scary here. If United want to crack America by getting involved in youth football (I assume 'initiatives' has something to do with football!) then that's fine, but 'North America' is a big place – even bigger than the Maine Road pitch – so I suspect they will need to focus their attention on targeted localities. The idea of pooling expertise on sports science is something that goes on anyway – Brian Kidd was a regular visitor to European football clubs, and Steve McClaren is a well-known student of coaching, whatever the sport. So still no reason to take to the streets – maybe this is all fairly sensible stuff, and we were just too wary of business-speak?

If United are looking for a shoe-horn into American markets, the press release is less specific about the benefits the Yankee people are looking to gain from the relationship. The Yankees side refers to the strong brand name of United in the international sports world and point to United's success in "*internationalizing their business with the sale of sponsorships and merchandise*". An educated guess would therefore be that while it would be nice for them to sell a few more New York Yankees baseball caps in the shop at Old Trafford, they have more of an eye on the potential for taking some advantage of United's merchandising networks in Asia, and maybe flogging televised games to places like Thailand and Singapore. Again, no major problems there, but I can't help thinking that the Yankees will have more success in Asia than United will in America, where (despite the popularity of proper football as a participation sport for youngsters) the big bucks of baseball, American football, basketball and ice hockey seem none too keen to allow our game a professional foothold.

So why the furore? Reaction to the news came in two flavours, depending on whether you love United or claim to hate them. The more pessimistic of the anti-United faction gave rise to the usual nonsense about the inevitable global domination that would ensue. We would immediately sign Figo and Zidane, we would become unbeatable in England and would therefore break out into a European super-league (yawn!). It's nice to know that all those who profess to dislike us would miss us so much (they proved it when we missed the FA Cup), but they perhaps ought to get back to the real world. We've quite a way to go yet before we become unbeatable, before achievements such as the 1999 Treble are anything other than miraculous, and we face in twelve months' time the loss of the single main reason for all our success – Sir Alex himself. All Reds with a grasp on reality are praying for a successful transition, and are leaving the scare stories to those whose speculations are marked 'Kiss of Death'.

As I said, the reaction of United fans has not been to join the clamour, but to experience a little disquiet, a sense of unease. True, the bare bones of the press release don't give major cause for concern on the face of it, but it would be very dangerous to be complacent. And that probably explains why various fans' groups have not offered the move a guarded welcome, but have instead pointed out their insistence that the deal safeguards the tradition of the club and the interests of the fans.

We all recognise the direction that the club's wage bill is taking, and we are realistic enough to acknowledge that the boys' Ferraris have got to be financed somehow. That's why United fans don't join in the carping about new shirts every season – if people want to buy them, and if it helps to keep the team competitive then that's fine by us. After all, the replica shirts remain an optional expense. Ticket prices are another matter. Tickets are not an option for the longstanding loyal fans. So while we don't mind the players benefiting from any returns that a 'marketing alliance' will bring (and discounting all talk of 'billions' as idle hyperbole), it would be nice to think that someone would spare a thought for the riff-raff in the stands from time to time. If someone had predicted, twenty years ago, the money that would come into the Premier League from television rights, we'd have thought a ticket-price freeze for a generation would have been a possibility. Instead the admission prices soared as well, and much of the cash flowed straight through the club into the sports car dealerships and into the share dividends. If the club is looking for the fans to support trans-Atlantic commercial partnerships, a promise that this time the fans won't be forgotten would be a decent place to start.

When all is said and done there are two things that matter to Manchester United supporters, and it is around these that any unease is based. First we want United to win, but we want to do this the right way. That means we want to win gloriously, playing football taught by Matt Busby, and it means that we win as United and for United. We don't want to be part of a premier integrated sports-based media company, any more than we wanted to be part of Sky TV – we want to be a great Football Club. Simply that. Secondly we want the true fans, especially kids from Manchester, to have access to their team and to be at the forefront of the club policy. A business should not neglect its customers while chasing new ones who'll never enter its doors. Anyway, we're not customers – we are the club.

Hence the unease with all this 'internationalisation'. When a top European club coach (as happened recently) refers to the strength of the United 'brand', but adds that it's a shame about the Manchester connection, you have to hope this doesn't give anyone silly ideas. It may sound a crazy notion, but look what happened to the Manchester Guardian newspaper. And it was in the Guardian recently that our own Jim White reported the club's refusal to allow a plaque at Old Trafford in memory of the construction workers who tragically died building the new stand. Apparently the bizarre reason given was that this would be inappropriate as United may move away from Old Trafford one day. Is there something we need to be told?

A final thought. I was looking through an old football book recently, and came across a contemporary report of United's 1952 tour to the United States. In one match United (newly-crowned champions) were beaten 7-1 by Spurs ... at Yankee Stadium. If nothing else, let's hope that United's next trip west, announced along with the commercial link-up, shows America what Manchester United are best at – playing our football and winning with style.

Teams that Matter, Games that Don't

March 2001. What is sport? Well, sport is football, mainly.

I've often wondered why people get excited about some of those 'other' sports – your golf, your tennis, and all that. Yes, I'll watch these things from time to time, but only as I may observe a pub football match from the top deck of a bus – fleetingly, and totally uninterested in who wins. All I'm saying is that I don't know how people can get worked up about a tennis player, or a golfer, winning a nice pile of cash for himself. Events like the Ryder Cup are a bit of an exception, when the wealthy individuals (who earn a sight more than Keano or Becks without anyone batting an eyelid) work as a team, but I can never see myself getting too agitated about the outcome. 'Come on, Europe' hardly trips freely from the tongue. As for camping out in the street to buy a ticket for Court Number 614 on the first Tuesday at Wimbledon, well I think I must have been missing when they handed that gene out. Maybe it's just me.

I know I'm a fairly simple soul from humble origins, but a staple diet of Manchester United, Salford rugby league and Lancashire cricket has provided all the nourishment I ever needed. Perhaps it has something to do with these teams representing my own place and my own sort of people? It's a bit more specific than 'Europe', you have to agree. Or perhaps I'm merely unimaginative. Manchester United has always been my main passion, of course, and every single defeat (or home draw come to that – I always have an empty feeling when United draw at Old Trafford) has been a source of pain for decades. I admit that I have lost much less sleep over the rugby league, where my presence has been fitful over the years, but I'm always happier when I hear that Salford have won. Unfortunately this isn't as often as I'd like nowadays, but I can't shake off all those occasions when I sneaked into the Willows for the last five minutes of a match after the exit gates had opened. Nor the memories of the post-match fun, messing around on the pitch, charging into and bouncing off the padding around the goalposts. Salford provided one of my earliest experiences of sporting pain, in fact, when the team lost the 1969 Challenge Cup final to Castleford – the hurt was genuine, and one day I'd love to see the original Red Devils make up for that disappointment. That defeat by Salford was the first of a rotten treble – three cup final miseries experienced with my three teams.

In the late 1960s and early 1970s Lancashire's cricketers were a breath of fresh air, not quite making up for the dive in United's fortunes at the time, but at least giving me a team of winners to watch. Like United, Lancashire were a glamour outfit, featuring the incomparable Clive Lloyd and the charismatic Farokh Engineer, but the team was led by a man called Jack Bond who bore more than a passing resemblance to my granddad. I was a junior member of Lancashire in those days. It cost one pound – a measly quid – for the season, and for that I was able to gain entry into the Old Trafford cricket ground for every match, including Test matches. If that doesn't sum up the difference between then and now, I'm not sure what does. Lancashire had made winning the old Gillette Cup an annual event, but it wasn't until 1974 that I finally followed the team to the final at Lord's, when my second cup final misery unfolded.

The Gillette Cup final was always played on a Saturday in early September, and the weather was always glorious. It just was, I don't know how they managed to arrange it. But the year I went, no one had asked the sun to shine. The coaches left Old Trafford at about 5am on a filthy wet morning. It was raining all over the country, and it was clear that it was not going to stop. I've often wondered why we made the journey, but we duly entered the Lord's ground to brace ourselves against the wind and drizzle, while admiring the covers on the pitch. Within an hour it was clear we'd wasted our time, and thoughts turned to getting back to Manchester for 3pm – as United were playing Nottingham Forest in a Division Two fixture. But after abandoning the coach and dashing off to Euston, misery was to be piled on misery, as our train broke down and limped into Piccadilly Station around 5pm. We'd missed the cricket, spent a fortune on the train fare, missed the football ... and Lancashire lost the match against Kent on the Monday. But if the price of watching cricket has risen in the intervening years, and if United's second division days are now just a quirky memory, it is somehow reassuring to know that the trains are still as hopeless as ever.

The final leg of my treble cup final disappointment came, of course, two years later when the resurgent Manchester United came a cropper against Southampton in the 1976 FA Cup final. Two memories of this occasion, which don't involve the events at Wembley, have always stayed with me. At the crack of dawn before setting off for the match I was walking my dog in the park, and thinking the unthinkable – what if Southampton won? I tried to tell myself that it simply couldn't happen, that United were just too good, and that we were lucky to be facing such an ordinary team in the final. But a day that began with the dog soon went to the dogs, or at least to the underdogs, and the following day, with the heartbreak total, I vowed that I'd never, ever again support the little club, the giantkiller. My reasoning was simple – as a supporter of the 'giant' club my feelings mattered too. And although I could be tempted to set aside my principles on occasions such as Wycombe Wanderers versus Liverpool, I can honestly say that I've never supported an underdog for the plain fact that they were an underdog, in all the years since.

All the world loves to see a giant slain. If you excel in your field, a lifetime of hard work will not win you an ounce of sympathy, nor compassion. Excellence in a football team requires a mixture of qualities. A truly excellent side will include its sprinkling of natural flair and genius (Giggs, Beckham, Brown), but is founded on the more prosaic qualities of hard work, good habits, dedication, and basically making the most of what you have got. That goes for the natural-born geniuses too, of course, as many a player with magic feet has ended up in obscurity for want of a Giggs-like work ethic. In players such as Gary Neville and Nicky Butt the result of their efforts is a different type of excellence, but it is excellence, nonetheless. The trouble is that if you achieve excellence as a footballer (or as a football team) through years of graft and dedication then everyone will want to see you fall flat on your face. Especially if you play for Manchester United. It's true in the individual sports as well, where a flawed genius, such as a Nastase, will always be more popular than the charisma-free perfection of a Sampras.

The great thing about team sports (such as my three 'proper sports') is that natural flair must be backed up by solid graft and steady reliability to produce a superb end-product. It should be a perfect mixture. An excellent football team does not have to be a bunch of robots (although successive German national sides have tried hard to disprove this). Just as Lancashire's fine cricket team owed as much to Jack Bond as to Clive Lloyd, the solid talent of great players like Denis Irwin – an archetypal unsung hero – enabled the 1990s Manchester United, and its stars such as Ryan Giggs, to shine so brightly. I like this idea, the juxtaposition of genius and solid dependability. I like it in a democratic sort of way. It seems to show how the world ought to be run, with the artists and the artisans shoulder to shoulder, working to a common goal. I like it when I see the geniuses show that they are putting the graft in too. It seems a decent way to go about things, and it seems wrong to me when excellence is achieved in such a way, only for people to oppose it out of principle, always supporting the underdog no matter how flea-bitten a mongrel it may be.

And that's perhaps why I'm not too fond of those 'other' sports I mentioned at the outset. Where personal excellence is all, yet where fans prefer the flawed performer. Where the concept of a team is lacking, and where the fruits of success are enjoyed by an individual and his bank manager. It's so much more satisfying when success is shared by, and gives pride to, a whole community – in Manchester, or Salford or Lancashire. United may be a global phenomenon in many respects, but the homecoming following the European Cup win in 1999 showed that its roots are still strong. And when United are successful we can all skip along to work lighter of foot on a Monday morning – no Henman or Faldo will ever have that effect.

Three in a Row – Enjoy: A Review of 2000/2001

April 2001. Manchester United win an incredible third consecutive championship. But it's not enough for some people.

It's that time of year again. The daffodils are giving way to the tulips, the evenings are becoming lighter and brighter, and Manchester City are staring relegation in the face. It's also the final Red News of the season, and time for a few reflections on how it was for us.

The months have flown by. It seems incredible to think that a whole season has passed since I looked forward to marvelling at the tricks of Fabien Barthez (a prediction wonderfully fulfilled by the man who became a true Manchester United player so quickly), whilst expressing my usual fears that maybe this time glory would pass us by. A daft notion with hindsight, but previous back-to-back championships have been followed by severe disappointment. The Eric-less Double-devastation of 1995, and the spectacular collapse in 1998 with the title seemingly in the bag, were genuine seasons of anti-climax when we had all longed for the serious achievement of three titles in a row.

Anti-climax – I had to get that word in early. I'm sick to death of hearing about it, to be honest. Manchester United win a hat-trick of championships and there are actually United fans out there who wish we'd made harder work of it. Which is ironic, because the other reason for the supposed anti-climax is that we did make hard work of it in Europe. I'd quite like to take a look back at some contemporary reports of Huddersfield's third consecutive championship in 1926, or Arsenal's in 1935 – were fans of those clubs talking down the achievement? I have this bizarre image of a bunch of nonagenarian Huddersfield fans cheering up the younger generation, tired of Huddersfield's first division relegation fight, by saying "Aye, but it were bloody awful back in '26, a right sodding anti-climax when we won that third title in a row. At least we had the General Strike to keep us amused". As if.

I don't know about you, but I was desperate to see United win that third successive title. As it happens, I'm equally desperate to make it four next year, as I seriously doubt that the achievement will be matched in the next fifty years – not by anyone else, anyway! In the dark days of the not-too-distant past we would have sold our souls to Malcolm Allison (well, perhaps not) to witness just one championship in our lifetimes, and now here we are in the midst of an era that will be talked about for as long as football is played. I'll grant you that the football that delivered this season's title was not vintage by the standards of recent years, but the championship has been delivered in an almost routine fashion. We didn't really suffer any sort of bad run – in terms of results – and the title was all but assured from the turn of the year, assuming the home game with Arsenal was negotiated without defeat.

February's home game against Arsenal sort of mirrored the campaign. The result, like the final league table, was gloriously emphatic. The victory was practically achieved, like the title itself, with the battle only half-way through. And although the six goals were devastating in their execution and impact, we coasted through the rest of the contest, absorbing what pressure our rivals tried to apply. And I didn't leave Old Trafford that day talking of anti-climaxes, either.

But there is a serious point about all this anti-climax stuff, and where it is coming from. The point was proved to me on the evening when the third championship was confirmed, following Arsenal's home defeat by Middlesbrough. It wasn't great timing, as United had won a home game at lunch-time, but as the final score from Highbury came through I felt the urge to get myself back to Old Trafford. Why? Well, it was something about the memories of the gatherings on the forecourt in 1993, 1994 and 1996 – the spontaneous outpourings of relief and joy and all sorts of other irrational emotions. I felt, as I'd done last year, that if I didn't pop back down to the ground to mark the occasion, then I was guilty of taking it for granted – effectively betraying the hopes I'd expressed in the long, long barren spell that ended just eight years ago. But I should have been prepared for the worst. Last season, when United won the league at Southampton, there was a smattering of people at Old Trafford; the festivities of previous seasons were absent, but a few car horns were being sounded. This time it was awful, deserted. A steady rain fell, the sky was dark and heavy, and it was impossible to believe that almost 70,000 people had left the ground just three hours earlier. I didn't even park my car – there was no point – and I was back home shortly afterwards wondering why I'd bothered, but somehow pleased that I had.

I supposed I have to accept that unassailable leads by early January are not everyone's cup of tea. Even if I can't understand that point of view. Where I do understand the acute sense of disappointment this season is around the team's showing in the European Cup. Taking the positive side first of all, it's important to remember that United have done brilliantly in reaching five consecutive quarter-finals. Never mind the fact that four have not led to ultimate glory, this is a record that no other club in Europe can match. In effect, you can argue that United have been among Europe's top six clubs for the whole of that period – and that no other club in Europe can claim that. In fact only Real Madrid, with two Cups won, and going well this year, have a more enviable record. But it would be wrong to settle for that, because the four eliminations in the final stages have seen United fade out of the competition pretty tamely – you remember Dortmund, and Monaco, and Real, and of course Bayern.

This year the noises from the players sounded positive – the lessons of the Real defeat had been learned, they said, and this time we'd give it a better go. But the first group stage was poor, and we suffered a couple of embarrassing defeats in the Low Countries amid talk of how difficult it was for the lads to be fully motivated by the phoney war of the initial group phase. We were reassured when the second stage began brightly enough, and qualification seemed assured before the mid-winter break, but we staggered over the line in the end, and perhaps should have been prepared for a tricky time in the quarter-final. Again the players sounded up for it, ready for the true contest of the knock-out stage, with determination to overcome the failure of last year. But it would have been remarkable if a season's sporadic form in Europe could suddenly have been converted into the sparkle of 1999, and we bit the dust as we probably deserved. Fair enough, I'd take winning the European Cup under any circumstances, but our performances in Eindhoven, against Anderlecht, and away to Panathanaikos (none of them special teams, in any respect) would have cast a shadow over any ultimate triumph. It's always better, I think, to walk away, sort it out and come out fighting stronger next time around.

I see comparisons this year with 1998. Although we fell away badly in the league that season, the problem as I always saw it (and I'm not Sir Alex, so what do I know?) was that the team stood still after winning the championship fairly easily in 1997. The squad was not strengthened for the new season, and we lost Roy to injury, but the damp squib of a European Cup quarter-final exit at the (unexceptional) hands of Monaco stirred United into off-field action. It didn't take major surgery – a clear out of the squad – to turn an empty-handed United into Treble winners. The astute signings of Jaap Stam and Dwight Yorke, along with Jesper Blomqvist, augmented a solid squad, and we know the rest.

This season United have welcomed the magical Barthez to the fold, but otherwise (as in 1998) the team has stood still. Some predicted major changes after the European defeat in Munich, but Roy Keane's talk of the end of the road for the present team was indicative more of his disappointment, and determination to overcome it, than the signal for a major revolution. And sure enough, Sir Alex has moved quickly to recruit Van Nistelrooy, indicating that one or two more well-targeted signings will re-ignite the fires, just as Stam and Yorke did three years ago.

It's about predictability. The coaching manuals tell you how to win matches by making the play of the opposition predictable – making them play the way it suits you. Perhaps United were a little too predictable on the European stage this season – certainly Bayern were directing all the traffic for much of the game at Old Trafford. In contrast, the only thing predictable about the 1999 Treble winning side was that United would score in a minute. We all seemed to agree, as we left the Nou Camp on that hot evening in May 1999 that things could never be as good again. We were probably right, but we shouldn't allow lesser, though still triumphant, seasons to be dismissed as anti-climactic. The phenomenal events of 1999 should not be a benchmark against which anything else will inevitably fall short. Instead, the way United freshened up the team that year to staggering effect shows the way forward to 2002, and as we look forward to the final year of Fergie we should savour every minute. It will suit me fine if we have a twenty point lead in the Premier League by Christmas, because it won't always be this way. Anti-climax is winning nowt.

The Gaffer, the Wizard

August 2001. Sir Alex Ferguson was embarking on his last season before his announced retirement. Red News produced a tribute issue to our legendary manager. Little did we know we'd be smiling again when Fergie changed his mind after Christmas. Long may he continue.

Being an Alex Ferguson devotee I readily agreed to write a retrospective piece – a sort of overview of the overlord. It's impossible to contemplate a comprehensive resume of the Fergie regime, however, without knowing precisely how, or even when, it will draw to a close. Many of us still cling to the hope that the great man's reign won't end quite as soon as he has indicated, at the end of 2001/2002. And the recent manoeuverings in the stock market, with acquaintances of Alex gaining a significant shareholding, have even fuelled speculation that Ferguson could ultimately adopt the sort of 'head of state' role occupied by Franz Beckenbauer at Bayer Munich. It's a pleasant thought for some of us.

But whenever the time comes, the hope must be that the manner of the departure is fitting. What do I mean by that? Well, clearly hammering someone 5-0 in the European Cup final would be half-decent – especially if we can get 3-0 up within the first ten minutes to calm the nerves (Barcelona in 1999 was magnificent, but please spare a thought for the collective blood pressure next time boys) – but winning cups is only one part of it. What I mean by a fitting departure is a tidy, orderly and dignified handing over of the reins. We certainly don't want the non-Red nation salivating at the spectacle of a corporate civil war, a company coup d'etat, or whatever. At the end of the day it must be Sir Alex who decides when the time is right, and how the deed will be done. Those of us who recall the ending of the Busby era regret not only the disastrous consequences on United as a football force, but also the ragged ending of the Busby tenure, as Sir Matt reassumed control in the months following the departure of Wilf McGuiness in order to ease United into what turned out to be a temporary position of respectability. It wasn't good, but I never went along with the theory that Matt's continued presence was the problem, and I hope United's greatest living asset remains as a positive force when we are eventually required to welcome a new manager. Recent signs have been encouraging after the nightmare scenario that seemed set to unfold at the end of last season. But I'm getting way too far ahead of myself. Time to look back before thinking of the future.

It's not until you sit down and start thinking about it that you can appreciate the enormity of the changes that have coincided with the Fergie era. And of course there are many of us who take the view that much of the change in United's fortunes is no coincidence at all, but the fruit of the labour of the man who has become arguably United's best ever manager and (in my totally biased, of course, opinion) certainly one of the two greatest football managers ever.

The era has seen football change from social pariah to social fashion. Football used to be played in football grounds. Now it is played in stadia. From the Baseball Ground to Pride Park; from Burnden Park to the Reebok Stadium. From the old Old Trafford with its Stretford End and its Scoreboard End, and its paddocks and its groundside, to the new Old Trafford – North, South, East and West; Lower and Upper; there you go. All in the name of safety, though somehow other clubs' new stands can safely be named in a more traditional, and a more appealing, fashion.

Who back in Fergie's first year had heard of a plc? In those days Sky TV was the in-flight movie and the Premiership was an end of season rugby league play off. A football ground was controlled by policemen and stewards (proper stewards), and the manager didn't need a minder to walk him to and from his seat. Maybe he doesn't need one now, but he gets one all the same.

Back in 1986 Alex Ferguson was appointed manager of Manchester United. And I mean manager. He was given a responsibility for all aspects of the football club – for Manchester United was primarily a football club in those days (it still is, though from time to time you could be mistaken into thinking otherwise). Football managers were overlords – that is why the greatest figures among their number are legendary: Busby, Stein, Shankly, Clough, Cullis, Chapman. They were men of enormous significance, whose stature within a club was threatened only when they came up against a chairman with a huge personality or ego. These days the chairmen (or chief executives, to give some of them their correct modern title) often call the shots. That's why Fergie is unique in the modern game – he survives as an overlord. In a club that has become a corporation he is not merely a senior manager, but an embodiment of its soul. Not many plcs have a soul, and that's why football is different from other business. If those at the top nurtured the soul they would reap the rewards. Instead they seek (it can appear) to deny to soul, to replace it with a 'customer base', but in the end customers are fickle where fans are forever. Nothing is so out-moded as last year's fashion (and football is currently very fashionable); but nothing is so inescapable as the passion for a football club that you are born with, and that it nurtured. Alex Ferguson knows this.

I remember very clearly the morning after a League Cup defeat at Southampton that had led to the dismissal of Ron Atkinson. Ron had given us some hopeful days – a European Cup Winners' Cup semi-final in 1984; a couple of nice Wembleys; some great players, but a fragile team – and his time was running out. Ron was never, it had turned out, going to win us the league. He had been an unlucky manager in some respects (losing Bryan Robson so often, and at such crucial times, to injury), and he'd tried to provide United with a glamour team to play glamour football, for which we were grateful. But things had taken a grim turn. Struggling at the start of the 1986/87 season, United beat Southampton 5-1 at Old Trafford on 13 September, as result greeted with such relief that I witnessed the extraordinary spectacle of half a dozen Reds standing on the parapet of the Trafford Road swing bridge and diving into the Manchester Ship Canal. Now this seemed to say it all. The Ship Canal was (still is) black and bleak. How anyone knew how deep (or shallow) the water was, or what lay inches beneath the surface, I do not know, but these boys went in head first – and came up cheering. It was terrifying to watch, and it must have been a drippy walk home for those lads, but let's remember the cause of this outpouring: Manchester United had merely beaten Southampton at home in a league match.

Within two months we had a new manager. The 4-1 revenge defeat at the Dell on 4 November proved to be the end for Atkinson. Essentially a winner of cups for United, Ron came a cropper in the competition then known as the Littlewoods Cup. With the appointment of Alex Ferguson United eventually won the pools, and by 1999 had brought a new meaning to the term 'Treble Chance'.

Looking back I suppose we were fairly happy with the choice. Back then you didn't think about a foreign coach – most people didn't even know the names of the top foreign coaches – so you always went with whoever had enjoyed a decent run in England or Scotland. The lottery of all this is summed up by the fact that when United had appointed Fergie's predecessor (Ron), the initial choices had been the flavour of that particular period: Bobby Robson (who with hindsight may have done well), Lawrie McMenemy (who turned us down, went to Sunderland, and blew it), and Ron Saunders (ex-City manager, who'd won the league for Villa, but who departed for oblivion soon after). So the pot-luck in 1986 meant that Fergie, in the frame because of some stunning against-all-odds success at Aberdeen, was to be the new man.

If we hoped for an overnight change we never got it. And that's because it was not deliverable, as a damp squib of a 2-0 defeat at Oxford in Fergie's first match showed only too well. At the end of the season we'd won 14, drawn 14 and lost 14 – mediocre summed it up. As fans we were just feeling desperate, hoping against hope that the new man would make the difference. As we now know Fergie began to get to grips with the whole fabric of the football club, as only a true manager can. From top to bottom he got to work. The youth system was overhauled, but it would naturally be years before we saw it come to fruition (and when it did in 1992, the whole world noticed). In the meantime Fergie did it bit by bit, there was no mass clear-out; but slowly players came and went. Some changes caused eyebrows to be raised – why were Albiston and Moran ditched in favour of Anderson and Donaghy? (I'm not sure I understand that, even now, though it clearly seemed a good idea to Fergie at the time.) And United continued to be a fragile force, ranging from brilliant to very poor. A couple of games linger in the memory – not games of particular significance, but games that for this fan represented particular low points in moral.

On 22 April 1989 United were beaten 1-0 away to Charlton Athletic. I didn't go to the game, but I recall hearing the result that afternoon, and was as depressed as I've ever been by a non-critical football result. After three years of Fergie, and despite all the good work going on behind the scenes, we were still soft touches at places like Charlton Athletic. Would things ever turn around? It is revealing to note that after this match United's last four home games of the season were attended by crowds of 30,000 or fewer (though I'm proud to say that I was at each one).

Things got worse before they got better, and United even flirted with the relegation zone twelve months later, before the Ferguson show got on the road with the capture of the 1990 FA Cup. A few months earlier, on 21 January to be precise, United suffered a televised Sunday defeat at Norwich. It was a wretched performance, with defeat always likely – we always seemed to lose at places like that in those days. United's defeat that day was inflicted by an average forward called Robert Fleck, who scored two late goals and milked it. The game sticks in my mind because it led to some mocking at work the following day. If you think United are disliked now, then in those days we were simply laughed at. Fergie has now changed all that – on top of everything else he has achieved, no one laughs at United any more.

We'll perhaps never really know what would have happened to Alex if Mark Robins had not scored United's winner in the FA Cup 3rd Round at Forest in 1990. Everyone connected with the club denies that the axe was waiting, but who knows how United would have responded to the pressures that may have resulted. It's fairly academic now anyway. Once Fergie's United became winners, and once his youth policy had begun to blossom, United became unstoppable. I don't need to list the triumphs; I simply don't have the space. But Alex Ferguson has given me, and thousands like me, a whole series of 'best nights ever', starting in Rotterdam in 1991, continuing at home to Blackburn as the championship was finally won in 1993, and reaching an ultimate (surely) climax in Barcelona in 1999. We have probably lived through United's most perfect period (past or to come), with so many triumphs and the occasional disappointments that have made the victories even sweeter. Alex Ferguson (with the help of a genius called Cantona) has made all this possible.

One of Ferguson's greatest achievements, and certainly the reason why he is so worshipped by the faithful, is that he has genuinely connected with the supporters. Alex Ferguson has become a Manchester United fan, and it shows. Defeat hurts him as much as it hurts us – one consolation for the fans on the occasional dim days. The alleged mind games are no more than Ferguson telling it as it is – or at least as most of us see it. His use of a them-and-us mentality was a key to Aberdeen's breaking of the Glasgow stranglehold on Scottish football. While at Aberdeen he was motivating an underdog, at Old Trafford he's kept the top dog hungry. His own hunger, reflecting that of the fans, drives him on.

So whatever happens next, however long Alex Ferguson remains at or near the helm, he is a legend. As a child of the late Busby era it has always seemed impossible for me to consider that anyone could ever surpass Sir Matt as the greatest ever football manager, but the fact is that I am now able to mention Alex Ferguson in comparison with Busby. Given my allegiance to Busby any suggestion of him having a rival seems almost sacrilegious, but the very fact that I'm even asking the question means that Sir Alex is at least on a par. One club, two such legends in my lifetime; I'm a lucky football fan. As are we all. Back in 1986, or even three years later, who'd have thought it possible? Whatever lies around the corner, I can only conclude by saying 'Thank you, Sir Alex, for everything.'

Days of Awe?

September 2001. The summer had brought its ups and down, and it seemed that Sir Alex Ferguson may not even be around to embark on the new campaign. But things seemed to have settled down as we looked forward to the season ahead.

Towards the end of last season I bemoaned the view that the campaign had been an anti-climax. The league season had tailed off, for sure, into a run of a non-event defeats, but as I look forward to 2001/2002 my hope is that we will again have wrapped up the title by New Year's Day – and if we can thump the nearest pretenders 6-1 along the way then that would be rather nice too. The trouble last year was that, title won, we all hoped for a decent run for our money in the European Cup. (And boy did we shell out some money – tickets for six home group games and a quarter-final alone costing something in the region of £170.) Anyway, the inquests into European elimination were deep and heartfelt, with Roy Keane for one assuring the fans that their concerns were shared in the dressing room.

Tabloid talk of a crisis was nonsense of course, and the championship presentation (so long after the title was in the bag) was a useful reminder that we'd hardly had a disastrous year – though given our aspiration there was clearly room for improvement. As the season drew to a close, however, things went from 'in need of a minor fix' to 'verging on the cataclysmic'. While the team was playing out time in a damp squib defeat at Tottenham it seriously seemed that United and Alex Ferguson could be about to part company. It would have represented the nightmare scenario, but an outcome altogether possible from the way the relationship between United plc and football's greatest manager had been played out over the years (or at least as it seemed to us, the humble fans). This was a truly shocking few weeks. English football went down on its collective knees to pray that our worse fears would come to pass; Liverpool, winners of three competitions (two of them sub-standard) but not winners of *The* Treble, installed themselves as The Next Big Thing. (Beating Birmingham on penalties in the League Cup, and overcoming some Spanish pub team in Europe's Supplementary Cup sort of went to their heads.) So could it really be all over for United? Without a home game still to play there was no opportunity for the fans to send an overwhelming message of support to Ferguson. Best wishes were passed on by any available route, but we were left to depend on the reaction of the club, and to place some hope in Peter Kenyon, who had told the fans earlier in the season that he would 'under-promise, but over-deliver'. Helplessness what was we all felt.

It's hard for simple people like me to understand what goes on behind the walls of the corporate Manchester United. From time to time I read books by clever people like Michael Crick and Mihir Bose and Alex Fynn, books that are about my football team, but that are filled with a cast of characters straight from the Financial Times or the Investors' Chronicle. At least that's how it seems to me, as I'm not bright enough to read either of those publications, and once I've asked Mr Visa to buy my season tickets my main financial aim is simply to pay him back. Some of the blokes in these books could buy my season tickets with their loose change, and maybe that's why they don't understand the effect of a £2 per match increase at renewal time. My point, though, is that football books today are not like the ones that David Meek used to write, and reading them serves only to make me understand how little most of us actually understand about what is really going on. So when I said the fans were hoping that Peter Kenyon could rescue the Ferguson situation, one thing I did understand was that I have no idea who is really pulling the strings, and I have no idea how fair it is to Mr Kenyon to suggest that it's all down to him. Still he is the Chief Executive, which I tend to think of as the boss.

I'll always give credit where credit is due. And when it comes to Manchester United I do always look to give credit. Supporters who are passionate about the club do not carp simply for the sake of it, and when we do we like to 'keep it in the family'. So somebody behind those walls deserves some credit for the way certain things turned out this summer. Having called on Peter Kenyon to show that he could make a positive difference, it only seems right to congratulate the man on the agreement which will not only maintain the relationship between United and its greatest living asset, but which has allowed the whole club to move on, having torn up the whole crisis agenda. United has gone, in a few short weeks, from being a club about to discard the manager that the rest of Europe covets, to being a team with a renewed sense of purpose.

On the field Ruud Van Nistelrooy had arrived to fill Teddy Sheringham's shirt (though in a different role), but we knew that the team needed a couple more injections of world class to provide the lift for the forthcoming campaign. The month of June came and went; Thuram almost came, but went to Juventus; Vieira was probably never likely to come, but it was amusing to see his club so ruffled. As we entered July Kenyon responded to the lack of additional signings – be patient, he insisted, the club would make acquisitions from its shortlist of genuine talent. And sure enough, within a couple of weeks Veron was a United player, we'd signed a promising young goalkeeper in Roy Carroll, and all of a sudden we can hardly wait for the season to start.

Before that there has to be the distant tour, of course, and the media, no longer unable to peddle the crisis story, was reduced to regenerating some now worn and weary tales. The Far East backcloth prompted some sparkling press comment about United fans not coming from Manchester, and more implied criticism of the club's over-emphasis on commercial progression overseas. Lovable Liverpool, on the other hand, were apparently in the same region of the world simply to spread the hand of sporting friendship. Back in Manchester all Reds are immune to this sort of thing by now, indeed after the back page headlines of May it was almost nice to see United receiving some routine and (as we all actually know and understand) ridiculous abuse.

For the fans the real story should always be played out on the pitch, and United's early tour matches underlined the confidence we have in the coming season. Plenty of goals, some good performances, nice signs of settling down by the new boys. Even Fabien up front. All is well with the world for now. The value of signing top quality players is the lift they give to all around them, whether by inspiration or simply an essential element of competition. Cantona and Yorke had a similarly positive effect in previous years, and it was nice to see Yorke himself, Cole and Solskjaer respond to the arrival of Ruud by scoring plenty of goals.

We don't know how the new season will turn out, and over-optimism is hardly in my nature, but you've got to enjoy the moment and right now things look to be progressing very well. I still hope the league is won by Christmas, because I want United to win every game, but I also hope we can slip out of second gear more often in the coming season − because to see this team playing as it can would be an awesome sight. All this and the chance of seeing Peter Schmeichel a couple more times − all aboard for Fergie's finale. Come on you Reds!

The Super-Coach

October 2001. United seemed to be missing Steve McClaren, the coach who had left to manage Middlesbrough. It prompted some reflections on the role.

The recent travails of Steve McClaren at Middlesbrough and Peter Taylor at Leicester City have been much in the news. After all of four matches, both were struggling to kick start their seasons, but while the freshly-appointed McClaren clearly had the benefit of time Taylor seemed to be staring down a barrel. After all, he's had the job for over a year now, and it must be all of nine months since he was regarded as the most likely future England manager, a probable successor to the suave Swede. McClaren and Taylor were, of course, the acting England management team before Sven arrived with his Messiah act, and together they seemed something of a dream ticket. But whereas Taylor has been forced to concentrate on domestic matters (this seems mainly to involve answering questions about the likelihood of him having a job come October), McClaren is still spinning the England and Middlesbrough plates at the same time (albeit with one of them looking a bit wobbly). Mind you, this hasn't stopped McClaren facing an inquisition as to whether he shouldn't just stick to the day job.

It made me realise that being a football manager must, by definition, be harder than running the country. How so? Well simply because football managers either have to concentrate on one job at a time, or deal with a third job in the form of constantly justifying the attempt to juggle the other two. Meanwhile your average member of parliament or cabinet minister seems to have little difficulty in occupying seats on a number of company boards while attending to the small matter of representing you and I. Didn't Kenneth Clarke delay his appearance in the Tory leadership campaign until he'd completed a tobacco-selling mission in the Far East? No one seemed to bat an eye at that bizarre juxtaposition, but Sven had better not get any ideas about undertaking a sales mission for Boddingtons in Burundi. It just wouldn't do, and may even reawaken his adoring public to the now long-forgotten fact that he wasn't born within sound of Bow bells.

McClaren and Taylor are part of the new breed, they are regarded as super-coaches. Super-coaches have a certain aura. They have this appealing mixture of sportiness (they can play football) with intelligence (they sound like they know what they are talking about). Long gone are the days when the coach simply put the fear of God into players, barking at them as they ran up and down the terraces of deserted football grounds, and locking up all the footballs between Monday and Friday in the odd belief that this would encourage the players to want the ball more come Saturday afternoon. The super-coach has read the books and done the exams; he's studied the videos and he uses computer technology to analyse his players' performances; he leaves no page unturned within the manuals, connecting with sports scientists and experts in other sporting fields to maximise his understanding of how to get the best from the players at his disposal. Oh, and the super-coach (unlike the untested TV analyst), does the business – his teams win matches, or are visibly better performers than the collection of players that he inherited. Just witness the calm transformation of Middlesbrough last season once Venables had got to work; seemingly doomed to relegation, he kept them up.

But a super-coach can lose his mystique by taking one very chancy step, by which I mean giving up what he's best at to become what is referred to as a Number One. Just as Brian Kidd couldn't resist the manager's office in the end, McClaren has taken the plunge. Maybe it's because I'm United to the core that I can't see why being manager of Blackburn or Middlesbrough is preferable to being a United super-coach, but I'm prepared to hold my hands up and accept that it's only one of many things I don't understand. I wish though that the super-coach turned manager would follow at least one of Taylor's characteristics – he still turns out looking like the coach he is. I confess to grimacing slightly when I saw McClaren in jacket and tie at Boro's opening games; I think it reminded me of poor old Brian Kidd in that expensive-looking brown overcoat, greeting his new Blackburn crowd along with Jack Walker. As his team struggled to find some decent form Kidd looked forlorn issuing tactical instructions in that big coat. It might work fine for the Fabio Capello's of this world – he's Italian, after all – but Kiddo soon resorted to the tracksuit, though sadly not in time to keep his job.

United's recent trend towards super-coaches like Kidd and McClaren working alongside the managerial Wizard is another of the club's modern-day departures. Their predecessors over many decades had a much lower profile outside the bounds of the Red family, but interestingly they are relatively few in number, as I realised when I sat down and thought about it.

The first United coach I knew as a supporter was the great Jimmy Murphy. Although he was officially Matt Busby's assistant manager Murphy was originally a man of the training pitch. I remember him as a kindly-looking and statesmanlike figure, but only because I was too young to remember the hard-as-nails sergeant-major type who helped Matt nurture the Babes, and who almost single-handedly kept the team going during the dark days of 1958. United's coaching staff also included Wilf McGuiness, something of a young super-coach in his day, and a man who made up for a career lost to injury by gaining sufficient respect on the training field to be a part of the England 1966 World Cup coaching team at the age of just 28. In the same period Jack Crompton, goalkeeper in United's 1948 Cup winning side, was described on all the team photos as United's 'trainer', a term little-used in the modern era; it now tends to refer to a ludicrously overpriced shoe as seen in a twenty-five minute long advert at half time on Sky Sports. As it happens Jack moved on from United to mange Barrow FC (a league team in those days, and later a learning ground for Brian Kidd), though with precious little success – perhaps (like Wilf) an early warning to later coaches-turned-managers.

Jack Crompton used to run on the field carrying a sports bag to treat injured players, usually by soaking them in cold water. In those days, before we had superstar coaches, we didn't have proper physiotherapists either. Lawrie Brown was probably United's first specialist physio, but other coaches – notably Tommy Cavanagh – did the magic sponge duties before it became the exclusive realm of the expert physio.

In the late 1960s the phrase 'tracksuit manager' was often used to describe the new breed of thinking coach – they were the super-coaches of their day. It seemed that most of them were prodigies of West Ham, and they included the likes of Noel Cantwell, John Bond, Malcolm Allison and the duo who took control at United, Frank O'Farrell and Malcolm Musgrove. Ironic then that among the accusations and counter-accusations that flowed in the wake of O'Farrell's downfall was the suggestion that the United manager had remained aloof from the training ground as our old, once great, team crumbled before our eyes.

Tommy Docherty came along and soon brought Tommy Cavanagh in as assistant manager and coach. Cavanagh survived the Doc's downfall to work alongside the studious Dave Sexton – another in the super-coach mould, and a man whose ultimate limitations as manager of Manchester United should not detract from his abilities as a coach. Perhaps Sexton is yet another example of good man but wrong job, and another argument for fine coaches sticking to what they do best.

For sake of completion we should add in the names of Mick Brown, assistant and coach under Ron Atkinson, and Archie Knox, Fergie's first right-hand man. In other words, in the post-Busby era United only had four head coaches (Musgrove, Cavanagh, Brown and Knox) in a twenty-year period. And none of these were household names, household faces. Are the higher profiles of Kidd and McClaren – and the array of jobs they were offered to lure them into the suits and ties of management – reflective of changing times, or indicative of their abilities represented by Fergie's trophy haul?

It is perhaps the latter, as Jimmy Murphy himself was never short of lucrative job offers. The United legend turned down the vast fortunes on offer from Spain, Italy and Brazil because of his love for our club. Sadly the United of his day did not appear to repay his loyalty with appropriate gratitude upon his retirement, so who can blame Kidd and McClaren for taking a chance when the offers came along? None of us, of course. But to those who remember, or to those who have taken the trouble to learn and understand, Jimmy Murphy will always be the foremost super-coach of Manchester United, for so many reasons.

Nobody Does It Better

November 2001. United were giving us a bumpy ride in the league, but retained the ability to perform irresistibly against the odds.

I got a few birthday cards recently (well, it was my birthday, after all) and I spent a little while looking at them – really looking at them, as opposed to just scanning the message and thinking how much nicer that card would have looked with a ten pound note enclosed. And I realised that your birthday cards tell you quite a lot about yourself, or at least a lot about how people see you. When women reach a certain age they start to receive those dull cards with vague pictures of flowers on the front; for men it's a little less clear cut. Men, it is understood, want to see a matey sort of card, a jokey one. So you get the 'Ho! Ho! You're getting on a bit, you old git' card quite a lot, or if people are a little more appreciative of your sensitivities you may just get the picture of the pub crowd, with jolly pints of beer, dart boards and fishing lines. And, yes, I did get one or two like that. But what was interesting (and I may be getting too analytical here, but hang on) was that I'm still getting quite a few cards that wouldn't have been out of place many, many years ago.

I'm talking about all the cards with footballs on, or footballers, sometimes containing the words 'To a Manchester United Supporter on your Birthday'. All they seem to lack is the 'I am 9' badge. But really I thought this was very nice. I don't go fishing and I don't play darts in good old English country pubs, so I don't really need those sorts of images on my birthday cards either. At the end of the day I'm still the same besotted Manchester United supporter I was when I was nine years old, so I'm fairly comfortable with other people recognising the fact. I was just grateful that I didn't get an official Manchester United birthday card with printed signatures on, because I find that those sort of things only serve to underline the fact that no Manchester United player actually gives a stuff whether it's my birthday or not, and is even less likely (ie not likely at all) to wish me any happy returns.

But it's not really about individual players – except in certain special cases. The players may have no wish to become close to individual supporters, but they can and often do develop a strong bond with the 'crowd', recognising the throng almost as an individual entity. Players like David Beckham and Gary Neville typify this, and the fondness of the fans is their reward. Players such as these become our special cases, but in the main it is the Club – or rather the Shirt – that demands our loyalty and our unquestioning dedication. Supporters of Manchester United are not so much loyal to any individual (though clearly the likes of Law, Best, Ferguson, Cantona and Beckham are omitted from this generalisation), and never to any concept of a 'brand'. What we are addicted to (and that is not too strong a term for the longstanding supporters, the hopeless cases like me) is a certain something that distinguishes Manchester United from all other football clubs.

There is a spirit about the way United teams have always gone about things, a true heroism – in the classical sense, with all the flaws that this implies. The team demonstrated this perfectly at White Hart Lane at the end of September. There is no other football team that can be so full of talent, yet which can play so ordinarily as United did in the first half at Tottenham, yet which can still consider itself relatively unlucky to be three goals down against a team that has had only three shots on goal; and there is no other football team that could have reappeared after half-time to dismiss the opposition so beautifully and so clinically. At least, no other football club can do this sort of thing so often that it has become a sort of trademark. That day at Tottenham was in every respect a typical Manchester United day, draining to experience wherever you were, but a day that left you tingling if you have even the slightest appreciation of what this football club is all about. The parallels with my personal favourite-every derby match – at Maine Road in November 1993, when Eric Cantona led the irrepressible second half comeback – were stark. I know, though, that I was not the only United supporter to see the Spurs game as the latest in an even longer tradition of heroic fallibility and fortitude. After all, wasn't Manchester United's greatest-ever league game also played in North London, as the Babes triumphed 5-4 at Highbury, gaining then losing a three goal lead before prevailing in the end? And wasn't Matt Busby's first triumph – the 1948 FA Cup – initiated with a 6-4 victory at Villa Park in the 3rd Round, when United conceded a goal after thirteen seconds, replied to lead 5-1 at half-time, and faltered to a 5-4 advantage before scoring a sixth two minutes from time? Only United do that sort of thing so often; only United no matter what anyone else says.

Geoffrey Green, author of the best history of United, published at the time of the real centenary in 1978, recalled the joy of leaving Villa Park on that winter's day in 1948: "I felt quite limp and emotionally drained. It was still raining, and the water made a gurgling sound as it ran in the street gutters. Yet we were all on fire. At that moment I would have been happy enough to be nailed down in a box and buried ten feet deep." Well I'm not sure about the last bit, but I think that all United supporters have felt that way many times over the years. It's only a game of football, but it is also so much more. And nice, too, to recall the words and style of a journalist like Green – what would he make of the press United get these days, I wonder?

What would he have made, for example, of the treatment dished out to our own David Beckham? Our man was hideously crucified in 1998, and certain sections of the media still found it in them to criticise Beckham's futile fingered response to the vulgar abuse he suffered from pond life in England colours at Euro 2000. Didn't one self-important public figure label Beckham a 'national liability' at that time? As United supporters we understood that no player from any other club would have been treated so obscenely for such a trite indiscretion as the flick at Simeone, and the sub-plot of hounding Beckham off to Italy, if not to Highbury, was not lost on us either. And so there is a nauseous irony to the acclaim afforded to Beckham after he almost single-handedly led England to the next World Cup – we cheered for him, but we did not cheer alongside those who were his enemies (and therefore ours) for so long.

Beckham, you see, is one of those special cases. One of those players we hold dear. He might not send me a birthday card, but he does relate to the crowd – his dad is in there after all. He knows Manchester United are different, and that we have a different way of going about things. It was the United spirit, in the person of David Beckham, that saved England against Greece, but perhaps his greatest miracle was that for a few days everybody – and not just his fellow Reds – loved him to bits.

Keep the Red Flag Flying High

December 2001. United had endured a wretched autumn in the league. Sir Alex Ferguson became the target amid a media feeding frenzy. It was time for the fans to stay loyal, and by the time this article appeared the team was heading back to the top of the table.

And so we come to the last Red News of 2001. It's unbelievable how time flies – it seems only yesterday that we were relishing the prospect of cheering a team enhanced by Veron and Van Nistelrooy towards yet more glory. We'd had the upset of watching a disgruntled Fergie sorting out his future, and we'd feared the effect of losing Steve McClaren, but all seemed set fair after an encouraging pre-season trip to the east. Since then all hell seems to have broken loose. It began with 'Slam, Bam, Thank You Stam', as Jaap departed to the puzzlement of us all; continued with some swashbuckling (and at times semi-suicidal) performances; then took a plunge with the wretched non-showings against Bolton and Liverpool. There was even a supposed revolt by that well known non-rebel, Paul Scholes. At that point I suspect we were all a bit stressed out, and were wondering what was in store for us next.

Now, Manchester United is a sort of family, or at least a very tightly-knit community. Like any family we will have our disagreements, but they merely represent differing views on achieving the same objectives. So while we enjoy some healthy debate among ourselves, we're always pretty circumspect about extending the rows outside the confines of our own four walls. And that's what made the post-Liverpool period so difficult. Because everybody – absolutely everybody – wanted to have a little pop, or at least to invite some opinion on what was 'wrong'. While we've got no problems mulling such things over within 'the family', it becomes tiresome having to respond to some smart-arse who declares that a United 'youth team' defeat in the League Cup represents the end of our last chance of qualifying for Europe next season. Apart from being total nonsense, this sort of comment isn't even witty.

Some things never change. A couple of years ago I wrote a piece in Red News after an autumn thumping at Chelsea. The gist of the article was that we'd have the last laugh – as we'd done in an earlier season when heavy defeats at Newcastle and Southampton had been suffered at the same time of the year. Fans (and players!) of those clubs can treasure their 5-0 videos; our boys are champions. I well recall, too, defending a certain Peter Schmeichel in the pages of this humble fanzine. It was the autumn of 1998, and the great man had slipped up a few times (notably in the last minute in Munich, then committing a howler at Hillsborough). I suggested that come season's end Schmeichel may yet be a champion again, and sure enough no one was laughing at him in the Nou Camp. Two years on he is still an awesome presence. It remains unclear whether United can regroup to similar effect this season – I write after witnessing the inept display at Highbury, made all the worse after the promise of no repeats after Anfield – but a sense of perspective must be retained.

There is, as Ryan Giggs mentioned last season, a pressure on United to keep winning the title, because not winning it brings a pile of ridicule – if we finish second on goal difference a national holiday would probably be declared. The reality though is that this long run will end at sometime, and although it would be nice to make it four in a row this season (a record that would stand unequalled for many, many years), it may not happen. The important thing is that next time we are pipped at the post we bounce back as we did after 1992, 1995 and 1998. If we can't win it every year (and we can't), then the aim must be never to be out of the frame – not to disappear for a dozen years as Liverpool did then their time was up. No one decries clubs such as Real Madrid and Barcelona, Juventus and AC Milan, for not winning their titles every single season. In any country there will be at least one great club that finishes empty handed at the end of the campaign; but great clubs come back for more, and should remain a constant presence on the European stage. This is what United failed to do through the 1970s and 1980s, and it must never happen again, whether we win the championship, or indeed anything, this season or not.

But for the present we have to bite our lips while the press has its field day. It is clearly open season on Alex Ferguson, and he has chosen to treat the newspapers – through silence – with the contempt he feels they deserve. Few of us would disagree with him, but the papers are preparing their revenge. Unable to understand why they cannot be free to discredit our club with impunity, they demand the time and respect of a man whom they openly dislike. If they choose to rehash old interviews in the light of recent events (as they did with mischievous quotations from Ferguson and Mikael Silvestre in recent weeks) why the hell should they be able to take for granted his availability? A recent article in the Guardian (of all places – it is hardly the most hysterical of newspapers) referred to the 'huge gulf in personality' between Ferguson and Wenger – the latter being praised for his openness with the press, or as they put it being 'smart enough to realise the benefits of working with the press rather than against it'. It almost sounds like some sort of protection racket to me. The article disparaged Ferguson for a habit of dismissing the press with the words 'Away and write your shite', but why complain if that is precisely what they do write? Most bizarre of all was the suggestion that the media is generally biased towards United, and that any view to the contrary is merely confirmation of a Red paranoia. Well call me paranoid, but I'm sure I didn't make up the outrageous coverage of United's visit to Brazil in 2000. The most extreme recent example of gratuitous media abuse came with the suggestion that Roy Keane, who made no complaint about a simple red card at Newcastle, had somehow insulted the memory of the victims of the New York terrorist attacks. 'Away and write your shite', indeed.

And the Guardian tells us that the angry editors are plotting revenge on Alex Ferguson by airbrushing Vodafone's logo from photographs of United's matches. Irony is too tame a word to describe their desire to nail Ferguson, matched only by a desire to hear him speak in their presence. It's little wonder the great man has had it up to the eye-balls, but it has less to do with his menacing personality and the insatiable demands of modern media than the fact that Manchester United are involved. After all, you only have to take a trip back to the more gentle media world of the early 1980s and consider the plight of a true gentleman called Dave Sexton. His sacking was partly orchestrated by two former heavyweights of the tabloid football scene who even went on local television to explain why, in their opinion, a decent man should lose his job. Their reason was his lack of communication – that is, his failure to provide enough headlines for them. Although many United fans had no complaint when Sexton left Old Trafford, theirs were football reasons alone; the hacks' grubby campaign showed that even in the days when United were winning nothing we were still the target of the less edifying back pages.

Another more recent example of questionable reporting came after the win over Leicester, when Fabian Barthez used a bit of gamesmanship to outdo the Leicester penalty-taker, Muzzy Izzet. Now, I'm nothing if not scrupulously fair – as I may have mentioned before – so I would have had no objection to a yellow card against a goalkeeper who was clearly monkeying around. But to suggest, as Des Lynam did, clearly outraged, that he'd never seen such antics, made me think of how we were all invited to chuckle along with Grobbelaar as he mucked about to similar effect in a European Cup final many years ago. But it was noticeable that ITV did not show the actual Leicester penalty incident in their post match analysis – it would have shown that the award was a total travesty, and that justice had been done. It would all have been a little too inconvenient.

As for the constant comparisons between the nasty Sir Alex and the urbane Monsieur Wenger, I simply don't know whether to laugh or cry. If around forty United players had been dismissed in the last few seasons, and if the response of the manager in practically every case had been to cry 'too harsh' or 'I didn't see', then I presume he would have become a laughing stock by now. I suspect that the world loves Wenger so much because for the last few seasons he has represented the nation's main hope of denying United a championship. We saw a similar thing with the once lovable Alan Shearer in his Blackburn and early Newcastle days. Once he stopped being the country's main weapon against Manchester United he actually started to receive a little critical press. It makes you wonder how the papers would react to their friend Arsene if he took over Sir Alex's chair one day.

So as 2002 dawns, what lies in store? Is it the end of our road, as so many hope? The answer to the last question is clearly 'No'. Supporting United is an endless journey, it has its high roads and its low roads, but any Reds worth their salt will be on board come what may. Whatever this season brings, be it the Glasgow European Cup final fairytale that is surely too much to expect, or a true damp squib (to put all careless talk of anti-climaxes last season in the shade), we owe it to Alex and the boys to stand firm with them. Within the United family we can ponder the changes in recent months, but when we face the outside world it is worth remembering that it is us against the rest. And that Manchester United will never die.

Goals for Life

January 2002. Something caught my eye at Villa Park ...

I had one of those odd can-I-really-be thinking-this moments at Villa Park for the recent FA Cup match. Whiling away the moments before the teams appeared I found myself contemplating the changing nature of goalpost stanchions, and I began to see them as reflective of some of the wider changes in football in recent years. Clearly I was displaying some sort of subconscious psychological ploy to detach myself from the building tension of the occasion, or perhaps I am simply going dotty, but my mental meanderings were so fascinating that I'd feel selfish if I didn't share them with you here.

You see the Villa Park stanchions, like those everywhere in modern English football, consist of two or three upright poles behind the goal to which the net is attached (and thereby held up) by a tight string. The resulting effect is that the goal net is box-shaped (all 90 degree angles), and because the stanchions do not actually meet the back of the net there is no longer the possibility of balls hitting them and rebounding into play with everyone wondering whether or not a goal has been scored. So you see these new fangled stanchions are pretty cleverly designed – and that's my problem.

Goal nets like these have been a feature of continental grounds for many a year, but they seemed to descend on this country in the mid-1990s in one fell swoop. It was a nifty ploy – before anyone had noticed (and has anyone else actually noticed?) they had replaced proper English stanchions forever. So why is this a shame? Well simply because (as an admittedly sad child who didn't get out enough) I always claimed to be able to identify football grounds by looking at the goalposts (and stanchions) alone. And I'm now feeling nostalgic for some of the old surroundings as things increasingly look the same, the whole world over.

In the 1960s Old Trafford had a funny sort of stanchion. For a start I remember it as being red, but the most distinctive thing about it was that it didn't join the goal quite at the top of the crossbar, but just beneath it. Later it became white, and reached up to the top of the goal frame, but that wasn't the classic Old Trafford stanchion for me. At least we never had those triangular bits sticking out behind the top of each post – I always had those down as a third division sort of stanchion, though we all remember how cool it looked when Trevor Brooking managed to plant a ball right into one of these shapes when playing for England in Budapest.

Some stanchions were fairly close to the posts – the net was therefore not very deep, and a well-struck ball could rebound into play after hitting any part of the back of the net. This used to happen on small, tight grounds where there was little room between the goals and the fence behind. By contrast Wembley had a lovely deep curving stanchion that never changed from my formative years until the new continental-style nets were introduced around the time of Euro '96. What a shame this was – Wembley's grand, deep nets used to gobble up the goals, the beaten keeper had to walk about twenty yards in there to fetch the ball, and there was no chance of a misleading rebound back into play.

For some years the football authorities had been concerned about balls rebounding from stanchions back into play. I always thought this was a bit of an exaggerated problem as I've hardly ever seen it happen in almost forty years of attending games. Everyone quotes the disallowed Clive Allen free-kick at Coventry, when a twenty-yarder hit the back of the net, rebounded off the stanchion back into play, and the bemused official waved play-on. But the fact that this incident is recounted so often proves how seldom this sort of thing actually happened. As United fans, therefore, we were privileged to witness our own stanchion incident, and one that went in favour of our boys. Were you at Boundary Park in December 1974 when a shot by an Oldham forward entered United's net then rebounded back into play? We all had a chuckle as the game went on with the referee thinking the shot had hit the bar, but there wasn't a lot else to cheer about as United lost the second division (oh yes) match 1-0.

Back to Villa Park, where in my reverie I imagined myself as a Mastermind contestant, answering questions on 'first division stanchions 1966-1974'. But what would be my chosen subject in the next round of the competition? Perhaps it would go something like this:

Magnus Magnusson: "Your name please?"
Me: "Tony Smith."
MM: "And your chosen subject tonight?"
Me: "International goalposts 1960-1978"
MM: "Mr Smith, you have thirty seconds on international goalposts 1960-1978, starting from now ... Why did the goalposts at the 1978 World Cup in Argentina have a black band painted round the bottom of them?"
Me: "I dunno, I always wondered that."
MM: "Do you remember those wacky red and white striped goalposts, like barber's poles, that you used to see in fuzzy photos of Latin American football in your old annuals?"
Me: "Yes I do. Blimey, what happened to them?"
MM: "What were the geometric characteristics of the classic Hampden Park goalposts?"
Me: "Wow, they were square – four sided – and really chunky, and they hurt when you ran into them. Not round like some, and not pointy at the front like United's."
MM: "Correct, but do ever feel you ought to get a life?"
Me: "Yes, I suppose I do."

But what sort of life? Given how observant I clearly am on the trivialities of football matters, I thought lately of how neat it would be to have the life of an official UEFA observer. Now I have no idea what the UEFA observer actually does, although clearly he swans around Europe on a UEFA expense account watching (or rather observing) loads of football matches. I think he has to sit down and write an essay about each of his trips, a bit like we used to do after the school holidays. But because he is a UEFA official his essay is called a 'report'. Sometimes when European Cup matches get all hot and bothered UEFA tell us that they need to read the observer's essay before they decide what to do. This is known as 'awaiting the report of the UEFA observer'. Judging by the usual outcome of such matters the UEFA observer's report probably reads something like this:

> "Well I had a really great trip to Kiev. Everyone in the hotel kept calling me 'Sir', which was nice, and they gave me loads of presents. When I got to the match it was really cold, and I wasn't surprised to see the visiting Benfica players wearing plain black gloves. I don't think we have a rule yet saying that all gloves must have the Champions' League logo stitched onto each finger, so I suppose that this was all right. The goalposts were painted plain white, just as we'd told them, and the nets were held up by three poles – none of them old fashioned stanchion things that we have done away with. Anyway there was a bit of scrapping in the game and a few bottles and coins were thrown onto the pitch. The police let their dogs loose into the crowd and one of the dogs ended up choking to death. So no real problems to report there. However there was a bit of naughty goings on after the goal was scored – number 94 for Kiev took off his shirt and twirled it over his head, but he was wearing a scruffy string vest like Rab C. Nesbitt's rather than an Adidas one with a Champions' League logo on the left nipple. I don't think we can be having that, so I suggest we make an example of both teams by fining the clubs severely. Make that £2,570 for Kiev and £3,274 for Benfica (come to think of it I really didn't like their gloves). All the best, and looking forward to Seville a week on Wednesday. PS Expenses claim enclosed."

Do I get the job?

Banana Kicks and Scary Beards

February 2002. United signed a Uruguayan called Forlan to go with Veron from Argentina. South American players had always held a fascination.

With the World Cup coming up, something made me watch again the official film of the 1966 finals in England. Although nothing in football (and therefore life) is ever what it used to be, the movie 'Goal' is one of those things that is highly evocative of a former time and of the way things have moved on. For a start it was shot on colour film, unlike the television coverage of the tournament itself, when the powers that be decided to save a few bob, thereby passing up the chance of preserving part of English football's heritage in a more fitting manner (they repeated the error when it came to United's European Cup final two years later). But it is the colour film of a by-gone age, over-dubbed with fake sound effects and crowd noises, while the narration conveys the drama in the sort of clipped tones that pre-dated even Kenneth Wolstenholme. What the film does brilliantly, for me, is to convey the sense of wonder I used to feel at the first sight of the exotic teams from around the world. While the England players were still to be seen smoking Woodbines like the working lads they were, the Brazilians and Portuguese arrived with their bewitching names (Garincha, Eusebio, ...) and wondrous ball skills; the North Koreans were mysterious and deadly (naturally), and their Italian victims were … well, Italian with cool suits, tailored kits and suicidal unpredictability.

You see, back then the opportunity to see such players was as rare as a Gary Neville goal. Television had not even begun to train its prying eye on the world game, and for English clubs in Europe a visit to Spain or Italy meant the boys were on their own – no camera would catch the crafty opponents at their tricks; defeat was odds-on. Football certainly had its darker side in those days, although we now regard those years as fresher and more innocent than today, with a money-dominated business built around a sport. But what price sport back in 1966 when Pele was assaulted with impunity, booted out of the tournament in the group stage, with his team soon to follow?

Brazil were (still are, really) seen as the nice guys of South America. Every other team from that part of the world was presented to us (in the words of Alf Ramsey) as 'animals'. It's true that many of these teams would have struggled to pass an 'O' level in public relations, but I for one was too young and naïve to understand that the English team was in turn reviled for its arrogance in that part of the world, and consequently I was unable to understand the fascinating role that national psyche has to play in world football. The battles that took place in 1967 and 1968, first between Celtic and Racing Club, then between United and Estudiantes, had me quaking in my boots from a distance of several thousand miles; it was all intimidating stuff, and these opponents seemed like beings from another world. Whatever game they were playing, it wasn't quite our sort of football. But it was probably as much to do with mutual misunderstandings, fuelled by nationalistic prejudices. Things no longer appear that way now the world is a smaller place and familiarity has bred respect rather than contempt. It sort of brings it home to you to realise that Juan Ramon Veron, father of our very own Juan Sebastian, was a member of the seriously dodgy Estudiantes team that, in 1968, ensured United would have to wait 31 more years to claim a World Club Championship.

As I say, it worked both ways. Nobby Stiles, on the after-dinner circuit, tells an amusing tale of his victimisation in Buenos Aires. Stiles (or Steel-ez as they called him) was seen as England's own 'animal', and you have to wonder what the public of South America made of our bespectacled Norbert when, fresh from locking away their wives and children, they set eyes for the first time on Collyhurst's finest as he stepped from the plane. My respect for Nobby Stiles, as a United legend, a fine player and a very nice man, is total, and there is no doubt that he was, like many of his generation, a very tough opponent indeed. But the thing about the Latino hard men was that they actually looked very scary indeed. He may be a cultured and cosmopolitan modern footballer but Sabre Veron clearly possesses the scary gene. Did you see him on his recent visit to Lazio, sitting in the tribunes with the ear-rings in, head freshly shaved and goatee-beard cut to menacing mode? He turned to a neighbour and made a remark, and I expected a subtitle to appear on screen, reading 'Not so fast, Mr Bond!'.

My own special favourite baddies over the years have been the Uruguayans. Uruguay – even the name of the place evoked something far removed from Salford, and when I found out its capital city was called Montevideo I was hooked. How cool was that? The thing about Uruguay, I was to learn, is that it is a tiny place in comparison to the Argentinas and the Brazils. There are only about three million Uruguayans – there are more people in London than that. And given all this, isn't it neat that Uruguay have actually won the World Cup twice, and have made footballers their most notable export? Maybe this explained their approach to international football, which seemed to consist of a gripping combination of sublime talent and vicious cynicism – either way, it was always worth tuning in when Uruguay were playing in the World Cup. For the Uruguayan football team seemed to carry on its shoulders the responsibilities of the entire nation, and seemed to crave respect so much that they'd go out and mug you for it. As recently as the 1986 World Cup in Mexico the Uruguayans snarled across our TV screens in a fashion that was compulsive to observe, but totally counter to their own ambitions. And in the figure of their star player, Enzo Francescoli, they were encapsulated as sublimely talented, yet haunted and brooding, over-burdened by expectation and liable to self-destruct.

But just to prove that things have moved on, and that the world really has become a smaller and more familiar place, we now find a Uruguayan player in the United squad. Ironically, I hope, of course, that Diego Forlan will become in time a true Manchester United player – all flair and glory – but I realise that it would also lay to rest the last vestiges of my personal image of the Uruguayan nation if he turned out not to be possessed by demons. Just as I'm questioning my recollections of Estudiantes now I know Veron's dad was in their team, so I'm wondering if the Uruguay of my imagination could possibly have produced the civilised-looking Forlan. But then I hear that Forlan is not sure to be picked for the World Cup in Japan and Korea because he is in dispute with his FA over something that could never happen over here – something to do with agents, I heard, though I am probably mistaken. Maybe Uruguay is a different world, after all. I mean, an English player would never be out of favour for his national team for such a silly reason, would he? Over here inclusion in World Cup squads has simply been a matter of your football talent and your willingness to visit the faith healer!

If the fascination of World Cups is not what it was, there is at least the opportunity these days to see United players in almost every group. It'll be fun to see Veron face the United lads in the England v Argentina game, but as ever I'll keep keeping my own special eye on the Dick Dastardlys of the Uruguayan team; with or without Diego Forlan, what will they have in store for us this year?.

Eric and the Universe – Discuss

March 2002. It is almost five years since Eric Cantona left Manchester United, but his name is still sung at almost every match.

Eric Cantona is, as we all remember so well, a man of relatively few words, but he had the enviable knack of delivering a memorable phrase with practically every utterance. Even the blandest comment was delivered with such style and panache that we often felt it necessary to contemplate its inner meaning. The catchphrase "It's the way I tell 'em" could have been coined for him. Who needs a dictionary of quotations when you can have a copy of *La Philosophie de Cantona* on your bookshelf? I sometimes wonder if Eric used the long silences to plan his next dramatic proclamation, or whether it is simply true that the less someone speaks, the more reason there is to listen when they do. Come to think of it, Arsene Wenger has had a great deal to say recently, and most of it has been total garbage, so based on a representative sample of the citizens of France my theory seems to hold good. Now there's a bit of scientific hypothesis testing for you.

Among my collected texts on the subject of Eric the King is a biography by Robert Ichah; I found it in a bookshop in France a few years ago, and it includes an appendix containing a fascinating questionnaire, supposedly completed by Eric. The answers to most of the questions make classic additions to the canon of Cantona quotations, but my two favourite responses are these:

> Q: Your dream of happiness?
> A: That the world stops turning after my death.
>
> Q: How would you like to die?
> A: At the end of the world.

Blimey! And this guy did a nifty back-flick as well!

These comments have stayed with me, largely because I couldn't have put it better myself. You've only got to watch a few episodes of Star Trek to wonder what the world will be like in several hundred years time, and once you've let your mind meander down that devastating path it is irritating (to put it mildly) to realise that you'll never be around to find out. Why, for example, does the starship Enterprise not have a football pitch onboard? Could it be that we are all getting worked up, in the early years of the 21st century, about a pastime that will prove to have the lasting endurance of witch-dunking? It is all fairly disquieting, as a passion for football and a sense of perspective do not naturally go hand in hand.

Forgive me if I digress for a moment (it was Eric that started this, after all), but this whole 'universe' thing really does my head in. Never mind the 'fact' that the universe is said to be up to 20 thousand million years old (in fact, don't even pause to think about it, or you'll seriously start to regret it), nor that it is said to be ten-to-the-power-of-ten light years across, nor that there are countless millions of galaxies out there, any one of which is, on its own, far too big to imagine. No, the thing that niggles me is that there are actually people who tell us they might even have an inkling as to what this universe is all about, but when you ask them to explain it – really slowly, you understand – they go on about things like anti-matter and black holes. In other words, they try to explain the probably-inexplicable in terms that are themselves total mysteries. For a start, how can you have a Big Bang unless there is someone around to hear it? (No giggling at the back, Dwight.) Honestly, I feel that these clever sods make even less sense than Arsene Wenger at an FA disciplinary hearing.

Now if one universe isn't bad enough, some would have us believe that there are more of them, and they call them 'parallel universes'. It's even said that these parallel universes may be just millimeters away from our own, but I can reveal that I've looked as far as the bottom of our garden without finding one. The common perception (maybe it's a misconception, but whose fault is that?) of parallel universes is that we are all over there doing our stuff, but in perhaps slightly different ways. Could there be another Manchester United out there somewhere, and are they doing well in the Parallel European Champions' League? Do all the Parallel People really love them, and if so is this because the Parallel plc has announced that it won't yet abandon the ticket price freeze originally announced in Parallel 1981? And do they have an Arsene Wenger out there? Or are they still wondering what happened to him after he 'failed to see' the black hole just in front of the sending off incident, then disappeared into oblivion just as the cry of 'Everyone is just picking on us' floated around the Parallel Highbury? Come to think of it, maybe our Arsene Wenger is actually the Parallel Wenger after all, and the story of him previously managing a club in Japan was only put about because no one would understand an explanation of a black hole.

You know, I think I may be onto something here. Who needs a radio telescope and a million pound research grant when the evidence has been before us all this time? It is now clear to me that the Parallel Premiership may be close to us after all. If you close your left eye and look with your right eye you'll see a slightly different (yet parallel) image to the one you'll see through your left eye when your right eye is shut. The effect is clearly the same as that which occurred in recent matches between Aston Villa and United (in the FA Cup) and between Derby County and United at Pride Park. I had been under the impression that Mr John Gregory (the opposing manager at each of those games) had used his post-match press conference to spout twaddle, but maybe (just maybe) the view from his own seat was not that of the match we had all been watching – maybe he had glimpsed a Parallel FA Cup tie in which Aston Villa had actually merited a two goal lead before unluckily losing to a fortuitous United, and maybe he had seen into a Parallel Pride Park where his team's opening goal had been scored from a position two yards *onside*. You never know.

I suppose the only thing I really know about the universe is that Manchester United are the greatest football club in it, and will remain so until such time as football ceases to matter. If the universe has another 20 thousand million years to go (a thought to depress Eric and myself as we wonder just how things are going to turn out) the chances are that Old Trafford will undergo a few changes in that time, and that Manchester City may even win a major trophy before the cosmic floodlights go out.

Among the many incomprehensible theories about the universe that I've heard on BBC2 are those which say it is based on 'order' or 'chaos'. Now I have no idea whatsoever what those terms may mean to a cosmologist, but in my own little world 'chaos' was last November when the team was tripping up, Fergie was heading for the black hole of retirement, and we all wondered if the dark side of the moon would be a decent destination for a summer holiday. So it's great to know that Fergie is staying on (the football equivalent of God being in his heaven and all being well with his world), and that we have had 'order' restored to our own little part of this particular universe at this split-second in the history of time. Now that is something I do understand. Lovely.

On Our Toes – A Review of 2001/2002

April 2002. Another remarkable season was drawing to a close. Trophies remained a possibility – something that had seemed unlikely a few short months ago. In the event we finished empty-handed.

With the league title sewn up by January, and with United out of the cup competitions, it was relatively easy last April to review the season that was drawing to a successful, but rather low-key, close. I wish, at least as far as the league is concerned, that matters were equally clear cut this time around, but with games still to play against Arsenal and Charlton the outcome remains in the balance, albeit with a fourth title in a row looking increasingly unlikely with games running out. With the prospects of European Cup glory similarly up in the air after our 2-2 semi-final first leg draw with Leverkusen, it's a bit like being asked if you've enjoyed your meal before the dessert has arrived.

"Well, the aperitifs were promising, but the starters made me choke. Thankfully the head chef decided not to clock off early, and the main course was as sumptuous as I'd come to expect. I'd like something memorably sweet for afters, but we'll leave the champagne on ice if the cream turns out to be sour."

The 2001/2002 season has been an eventful one, for sure. After the routine successes of the two seasons that followed our amazing glory-trip of 1999, there were hopes that a spark would light up Old Trafford again this year. The addition of Van Nistelrooy and Veron to a squad that had walked the previous season's championship seemed to be the answer – we'd play with a greater flourish in the league, and pose a genuine threat abroad. But it didn't quite work out like that at first.

It's impossible not to wonder what United could have achieved if the team and its talent had been let of the leash from the start. Instead, the early months were spent experimenting with formations designed to make the team more competitive in the final stages of European competition. And so it was that we went to places like Blackburn and Aston Villa – truly ordinary teams – and came away with unconvincing draws. Results like those, as much as the home points thrown away against the likes of West Ham and Bolton (with the deadly Van Nistelrooy given those days off!), will be significant if a fourth successive title eludes us by a handful of points.

It is something about being Manchester United that makes it impossible to play a containing game. At Arsenal in November we packed the midfield and offered no attacking threat, but the home team simply threaded the ball through the crowd as though it was not there, and they created more one-on-one chances against Barthez than I could bear to watch. It continues to baffle me how a mediocre Bolton team can similarly shut up shop to good (although very dull) effect. Not that any United fans would tolerate a Liverpool approach to achieving success – while United went back to Matt Busby's philosophy of simply scoring one more goal than the opposition, Liverpool remained in contention for honours by looking to concede one fewer goal than the opposition, and even if it wins them matches they can keep it.

One thing that I do not question about the approach taken by Sir Alex Ferguson to the campaign is that he was entitled to play it as he deemed fit. Ferguson has, if nothing else, earned the right to do things his way, and if the fine victory in the European Cup quarter final in La Coruna had anything to do with the lessons of the early part of the season (notably the need to support a lone Van Nistelrooy with a free-roving Giggs rather than an unhappy-looking Scholes), and if United can progress to the European Cup final, then it may all have been worthwhile. We've all cried out for 4-4-2, but in truth we're happy to leave these numbers to the railway engine spotters as long as United are giving it a go. So we hated the approach to the Arsenal away game as much as the result, but we were happy enough to see Giggs roving and Solskjaer playing wide as we went on the rampage at Stamford Bridge in April.

The events of the early part of the campaign now seem so distant that it can be easy to forget their impact on the season's outcome. What do I know from my seat in the stand, but I still believe that the absence of Steve McClaren from the coaching staff was a huge problem as the season began, and that the defensive frailties displayed by the team were in no small part down to this.

And there were ructions, the like of which we had not seen for years. It began with the Stam affair, as a dodgy book release was followed by a dodgy performance against Fulham, a shock transfer to Lazio, then a drug test that was both dodgy and a shock. Before long we had the bewildering news that Paul Scholes – seemingly the most loyal and accommodating of individuals – had declined the invitation to play for United in the League Cup at Arsenal, and with a few (no doubt doctored) quotations from Mikael Silvestre filtering through from France that seemed to display a lack of respect towards the manager, it began to look as though a sense of common purpose had been lost.

There were always brief spells during the glory years of the 1990s when United gave the opposition the opportunity to go a little giddy. Unlike other clubs in their prime United have always had the knack of taking the odd five or six goal thumping, then resuming normal service without breaking stride. A few years ago one particularly gruesome week culminated in a home defeat to a Vialli-inspired Chelsea, but when Chelsea did a similar thing in December 2001, the prospects of recovering the season seemed unlikely. Fergie himself cut a lonely-looking figure as a fair number of the crowd decided to take early leave. Although many have claimed that their departure was indicative of depression rather than disdain, the result was that those who remained gave a rousing display of support for the manager. After all he'd given the fans, it was the correct way for them to respond. Much as I do not wish to return to the subject of Liverpool, it is worth noting that as the season draws to a climax they are still in with a chance of winning their first title in years, but that they have been booed off their own pitch on countless occasions this season. You need class in the stands as well as on the field, and United's loyal fans did well at that Chelsea match.

There was one more nightmare to come, a truly bottom-of-the-barrel defeat at home to West Ham, with Keane in the back four, Van Nistelrooy 'resting', and Dwight Yorke playing and seemingly resting at the same time. After that we stopped messing about, and the remainder of the season has been (mostly) excellent stuff. Starting with the 5-0 defeat of Derby on 12 December, the points tally has been exceptional.

In mid-December, then, we would have settled for the position we now find ourselves in – we have an outside chance of claiming the title in the last week of the season, we have assured Champions' League qualification for next season, and we have seen some thrilling football in the best United tradition, including a couple of 5-3 wins in London and a fantastic FA Cup showing in the third round at Villa Park (what a shame that it all went to waste in the next round at Middlesbrough).

As for Europe, the whole Champions' League thing drags on and on. While the tills are ringing there is clearly no chance of sharpening the format of this competition, but I can't be the only person with a fading memory of early season encounters against the likes of Lille and Olympiakos – what purpose did those games serve other than to wring yet more money from our long-suffering pockets? But here we are in the semi-finals again, having reached the last eight for the sixth successive season – a great achievement by United, showing a level of consistency unmatched in Europe, even if going the whole way has proved slightly trickier.

I must mention a few individuals. Cole, to whom we bade farewell with thanks and respect; Irwin soon to follow. Keane, ever more-awesome. Van Nistelrooy, the best centre-forward to play for United since Denis Law; and Solskjaer – has any United player in recent years ever earned so much affection? Veron has been savaged by some, but I remain hopeful that he will, like Sheringham before him, overcome all that. And Laurent Blanc. For me it has been a pleasure to watch Blanc play; he is a genius of a footballer, world class, it must be great to be able to play football like that. It's not really fair to leave anyone out. Butt has had his best-ever season; Beckham, now beloved of the nation, hit top form along with Giggs and Scholes as the season progressed. And Gary Neville, excellent in central defence as the season was rescued, played his part with Beckham in ensuring that the whole country learned the meaning of the word 'metatarsal'.

So we may win a big trophy or we may not. More important perhaps is the fact that we are in with a shout, because we were well out of contention just a few months ago. Our biggest victory of the season, however, was the news that Sir Alex was postponing his retirement – normal service was resumed from that moment on. Over the course of the season we've been kept on our toes, as well as our metatarsals, but all of a sudden we look like United again. We'll never stray far from the top with the great man at the helm.

Who Do You Support?

August 2002. Looking forward to the media coverage of the new season.

It's been a flag-waving summer, the summer in which the English flag of St George became a firm national symbol. The Union Jack, for so long carried abroad in support of English teams (and falling into disrepute, partly as a consequence), now seems out of place. England is different from Britain, after all, and the English are starting to feel comfortable with their Englishness – even though Englishness remains impossible to define. Now there are clever people who have been analysing this phenomenon for some years, who have dissected the impact of political devolution for Scotland and Wales, and who have pondered the impact on the rump of Britain – also known as England. I'll leave that to the smart folk, the Observer journalists and the talking heads on Channel 4 News; what do I know anyway?

Whether it is a good thing or a bad thing, I know one thing for sure – it has been refreshing in an odd sort of way to listen to the verbal flag-waving by the TV and radio commentators at the World Cup and, closer to home, at the Commonwealth Games. What is so refreshing is not any sense of nationalism or jingoism, it's just that I was struck during the World Cup by how openly biased the commentators felt able to be. Not only were they clearly urging on the English team (as you'd expect), but they were also quite content to take sides in other matches – delighting in the progression of the South Koreans, for example, or bemoaning the way the Germans were able to scrape their way to the final with a series of 1-0 wins as the draw opened up for them.

The commentators weren't above giving out a little personal stick. Clive Tyldesley mocked Oliver Kahn's 'silly sideburns', and Ron Atkinson continued where he'd left off in the Nou Camp with a poke at the not-especially-handsome Jens Jeremies who, according to a classic Ron-ism, wouldn't be found riding the white horse in a Western movie. Now this is all good knock-about stuff, and although I should be ashamed to admit it, I found it hugely entertaining. I know, I perhaps ought to get out more, but at least I own up to it.

This mood of let-your-hair-down-and-sod-the-impartiality has led to the now familiar running of the cameras on the studio pundits as the game is being played out. It began with the Beckham equaliser against Greece, when Lineker and friends went bananas in the studio while Alan Hansen sat on his hands looking a little self-conscious. His demeanour was one familiar to any Red who has sat in the home end at an away game as United have conceded a goal – all around you going mental, you refusing to join in, but being all too aware of the fact that everyone is starting to notice as you try to conjure up an ambiguous expression that says 'Look my English friends I'm only here for the weekend from Latvia, and I really don't quite understand what is going on'.

Anyway, at the World Cup we had Ian Wright seemingly playing to the hidden camera, and Andy Townsend greeting an Irish equaliser against the Germans with appropriate satisfaction, but it got me thinking. Why do we only have this outbreak of honesty when it comes to a World Cup? Why don't we see the real reaction of the pundits for the day-to-day Premiership games, and why don't the commentators just admit that they do prefer one team over another?

Because it is impossible to watch any game of football, or any other sporting contest that you could care to name, without preferring one participant over another. It's just the way it is, isn't it? Have you ever watched any match of any description for more than two minutes without siding with one of those involved? Neither have I. But we are supposed to accept that the match reports we read in the papers, the commentaries we hear on national radio, and the analysis we watch on TV are based on impartiality, objectivity and good faith. Like hell they are.

I'm not making a point about anti-United bias in the media here, well not exclusively, because we know that among the legions of United-haters there are a fair number of Reds in the journalistic ranks, but it would be interesting to hear a no holds barred commentary by certain broadcasters on a United versus Liverpool match. Alan Green, for example, dedicated part of a book (and its serialisation) to the reasons why he dislikes Sir Alex Ferguson. Look, it's a free country, and he can think what he likes, it's just that if I disliked someone that much I'm pretty sure that I wouldn't wish any good fortune upon his football team. But maybe Green is a fairer-minded man than I am.

I just think it would be nice to have an honest statement of where we stand before we read the rantings of a biased journalist or reporter. As I've said, I think bias is a wholly good thing, and I am nothing if not a consistent exponent of the art, so I'm not knocking it. What I am knocking is people slagging off my football team then telling me they are merely occupying the high ground of journalistic integrity – and calling me paranoid when I doubt it.

Let's just keep it honest is all I'm saying, and whatever we do let's not go down the other silly route of local radio, where the rigid regional bias becomes acceptable, even to the point of United fans being expected to wish Manchester City well. This is not the way it should be. Manchester City, for all their faults, at least maintain a corporate correctness in their hostility to United. We really ought to return the fire, but you'll no doubt read Sir Alex's expressions of goodwill towards City in his programme notes this season – the only consolation is that this refusal to treat City as serious rivals really does wind up a lot of their supporters.

So I'm sure things will continue much as they have always done. Last season United finished third and fell in the cups, and something had to be done about it. But many in the media viewed the signing of Rio Ferdinand as a 'bad thing for English football', whereas what they really meant was 'Oh, no, United might now win the league again', which in their eyes is much the same thing. So we'll go on reading between the lines, detecting the hidden agenda and finding ourselves unable to listen to certain radio stations. And if it does turn out to be a 'bad year for English football' at least we Reds will probably have enjoyed it no end.

Time Wasting

September 2002. Idle musings on a holiday theme.

I spent a few days in Amsterdam a little while ago. I missed United's visit for the pre-season tournament by a few days, but I wasn't too disappointed – it's nice to enjoy the short summer break from football-induced anxiety without going looking for more by way of pre-season tournaments. Holidays are for getting away from all that. Some people like to pick up a local newspaper when abroad to get a feel for the real place behind the tourist façade. I can see their point, but sitting there pretending you can read a foreign language is quite sad when you think about it, and if there are people out there who can actually dip into a little Dutch or Flemish then I'd only be inclined to dismiss it as showing off.

My own solution is much simpler. The easiest way to connect with a local community via a medium that is comprehensible and familiar is to browse through the local telephone directory. I'm not sure when I first did this, but sure enough I picked up the Amsterdam version in the hotel room and started to flick through the pages. Now I know what you're thinking, but believe me it wasn't like that at all. In fact my mind drifted inevitably back to Manchester United and I found myself perusing the listings of Van Nistelrooys and Stams. My rationale remains unclear, but I am able to report that although there were very few distant relatives of Ruud in the phone book, there was a much longer list of Stams, and I wondered if they all looked as scary as the Jaapster.

All of which may be fairly childish stuff, but you've got to remember that when I was a child none of us ever went abroad on holiday. Back then Butlin's seemed pretty exotic to me, a false perception that I retained for some years mainly because I never went there either. The endless school summer holidays at that time were mainly spent playing football in a back entry. If you are unfamiliar with the architectural characteristics of northern working class areas, and the terminology used to describe them, you could misunderstand the term, but back entries were (and I guess remain) formidable playgrounds. One of these days Nike will forget about that cage-in-a-boat and shoot a promotional film in one of these places.

The cobbled surface (minus the dog dirt so as not to mess up Figo's trainers) would glisten under a recent shower; the stark and weathered Victorian brick walls would enclose the arena, providing a macho backcloth and a useful surface for rebounds. No doubt Eric Cantona would be the guy in the third house, into whose back yard the ball would occasionally land, prompting that familiar quizzical glare; and maybe a yard close by would be the domain of a strange old man called Arsene, who would confiscate and burst any intruding footballs before telling Edgar Davids' complaining father that he had 'seen nothing at all'. Why not? We see enough of the mythical beach and shanty town breeding grounds of the great Brazilian stars – let us see where Nobby Stiles started off.

Another of my school holiday pastimes was, of course, to hang around the Cliff, brushing shoulders with the likes of Bobby Charlton and George Best. Needless to say some players were friendlier than others, but many local people would simply pop in whilst passing – it was no big deal, and it felt nice just to breath the same Lower Broughton air as the lads. There was always a bit of a gathering, but not on a scale to upset the squad. It wasn't till the mid-1990s that the players needed security staff and iron barriers to protect them from the natives, and within a few years the whole operation had decamped to Carrington, a place so mysterious to young fans these days that the first team can actually attract a crowd of thousands to the strange spectacle of a training session organised for public view at Old Trafford.

Occasionally when out of school I would take myself down to Old Trafford, for no particular reason other than to hang around and just generally be there. There wasn't a lot going on in those days – the old souvenir shop was a walk-through with a couple of people behind a long counter. There was no merchandise to browse around, or to handle and put back. It was simply a question of gazing up at the posters of Willie Morgan, or contemplating (for the millionth time that month) the sew-on badges and car stickers. It was a strange place to be on a typical Tuesday morning – you'd be the only person in the shop and the assistants would glare at you as if to say "well either buy something quickly or get out". It was not an enjoyable, nor a relaxing, retail experience. So you'd walk ever so slowly from the 'in' door on one side to the 'out' door on the other, trying to see everything they had in there, but not daring to pause too long for fear of being asked to hand over some money. As stress goes I'd say it ranked alongside a 92nd minute corner to the opposition when United are leading 1-0.

Now you'll accuse me of making the next bit up, but believe me I haven't the imagination. The souvenir shop was such an attractive diversion not merely for the trivial yet tantalising nature of its wares; the fact was that apart from the shop there wasn't a lot else to do other than to stare at the fairly bleak walls of the ground – there weren't even too many people around to talk to. So I once had the idea that the place should be made a bit more welcoming to kids from Salford who were killing time on their school holidays, and I thought it would be a great idea to build a sort of trophy room that would be open to the public. After all, I reckoned United must have all sorts of odd silverware gathering dust in cupboards, and I wondered if the club even knew of half the things that were cluttered under the stairs. It was many years later that United opened the first museum at Old Trafford, along with all the other facilities that mean the ground is earning money on practically every day of the year, but they could have been coining it a lot sooner if only they'd asked the kid who was scuttling through the souvenir shop.

I have to say though that I hadn't quite thought it through. On the average weekday the modern Megastore probably bears a strong resemblance to the visitors' centre at the United Nations (maybe that word 'United' has confused one or two of them), and maybe the customers retire to their hotel rooms and spend the evening looking for Keanes and Beckhams in the Manchester telephone directory. But not before they've taken the stadium tour.

I've done the tour a couple of times, and although most of it is pretty routine for people who have spent their lives growing up at Old Trafford, I always enjoy popping my head around the inner sanctum that is the United dressing room – its that starry-eyed thing that I hope will never leave me. The last time I did the tour there was an odd exchange between one of the visitors and our guide. As we walked around the perimeter of the pitch the visitor looked at the goalposts and asked the guide how big the goals were. The guide really should have pointed to them and replied "Well, they're that big!", but he missed his chance. Instead, and much to my amazement, he mumbled a bit before admitting that he actually wasn't sure. Ever willing to be helpful, even to someone who is paying good money to carry a camcorder around a football ground without actually knowing the size of the goals, I offered the information that the goals were eight yards wide and eight feet high. I wasn't looking for thanks, and in that respect I was not to be disappointed, but I was a bit taken aback when the visitor (a person at least approaching, if not actually well into, middle-age) asked me what I was on about, and what eight yards meant in metres. I felt like an alien who had just beamed in from the planet '1960s', and in some ways I suppose I probably was.

The stadium tour maybe isn't designed for people too long of tooth, but on balance it probably still beats an evening in with the Amsterdam telephone directory.

Siege Mentality

October 2002. United supporters spend a lot of time being irritated about the media coverage surrounding our club. Once in a while it's necessary to put our point of view. Again.

The entertaining account of Pete McCarthy's journey around Ireland, *McCarthy's Bar*, includes reference to a newspaper report of a farmer who was up before the magistrate on a charge of being drunk and disorderly. Invited to make his plea, the farmer announced that he did not recognise the court, and when asked why not he said it was because it had been painted since the last time he saw it. When the laughter subsided he was sent to prison for two months for contempt. True story or not, it didn't seem fair to me: two months for cracking a very funny joke. There are sitcom writers earning a fortune who can't come up with a line as good as that. But when was there ever any justice?

The rowdier elements of the English media certainly seemed to agree that there was no justice arising from Roy Keane's recent appearance before the disciplinary panel of the Football Association. A mere five match suspension and £150,000 fine for putting his name to a paragraph in a book outraged the tabloids and, so predictable it was unbearable, had the less imaginative radio stations opening up their phone lines for the masses to vent their spleens. To be honest, I can't be bothered analysing the rights and wrongs of Keane's words and deeds; it scarcely seems to matter, because the actions of an individual seem to be judged far too often in the context of the shirt he is wearing. If you wear a Manchester United shirt you need to be whiter than white, and you still need to understand that this won't be enough.

I'll explain what I mean. A month or two ago I remarked in conversation that Manchester City had had three players sent off in successive matches, a fact unknown to the people I was speaking to. However, it's a reasonable bet that had Keane, Beckham and Butt been dismissed in successive matches the United Nations would have convened to draft an emergency Security Council resolution. Similarly United's recent game at Leeds was followed by 'Beckham Shame' headlines that kept the tabloids ticking over for a few days, but which referred to an incident that was trivial in the context of these sort of matches – the Leeds-Arsenal game a couple of weeks later was a real studs-up affair, but post-match interviews and analysis served only to congratulate the preening Mr Wenger.

I am biased, of course, but it is also possible to be fair-minded. Take Arsenal's tally of about two million red cards in the last five seasons. Although their record is often quoted in the media I don't think it is used to beat them over the head. I would suggest (being biased) that Manchester United would have suffered far more sanctions as a result, and that Alex

Ferguson would have been ridiculed had he defended the record in the manner of Wenger. But I would also grant you (being fair-minded) that there has never been a championship-winning team in the history of Association Football (and I mean any championship, anywhere, at any time) that has not had a physical edge or an occasional nasty streak. Is Keane worse than Graeme Souness? Was Cantona worse than Jimmy Case? What about Beckham and Bremner? We all know the answer.

I think it is true to conclude that United have irretrievably lost the media. There is no going back, is there? We now have our Communications Director, working hard for United fans, but it's difficult to see how he can change the press that United receive. Indeed United are now accused of control-freakery in news management. Much of it is probably personal – between the journalists and Alex Ferguson – and therein lies the reason why no amount of fundraising for Unicef, no number of appearances for good causes (such as the Omagh benefit match), no limit to the contribution of United players to the England team will make one iota of difference.

Take England. I was unfortunate enough to hear a whole evening's worth of Ferguson-abuse on BBC Radio 5 in the week leading up to England's friendly with Portugal. A gathering of tabloid writers repeatedly condemned the United manager for the withdrawal of the injured Paul Scholes from the national squad when he had made a needs-must appearance for United against Middlesbrough the same week. This was evidence of the arrogance of United, they declared, a spiteful act by Ferguson intended to humiliate the FA and Eriksson. The presence of Ferdinand (who as we now all know was not totally fit himself) and Butt in the England team, and the contribution of the still-convalescing Beckham during the summer's World Cup was an irrelevance, of course. Staggeringly one journalist went on to say that the absence of Manchester United players had at least opened the door for others, and he went on to describe Alan Smith of Leeds as a delightful young fellow who was a breath of fresh air. (Now I have nothing against Smith playing for England, and his red card against Macedonia was no big deal as far as I was concerned, but please spare me the 'breath of fresh air'.) Anyway, on the day of the Portugal game the BBC TV commentator announced as the teams took the field that this match was not meaningless for those who had deigned to appear (a clear reference to the absence of Scholes), but look what happened the following day. The media largely reported the game as a meaningless (and drab) waste of time while Paul Scholes lay on an operating table. You would have searched the papers in vain the following week for apologies along the lines of 'Ooops, Scholes was injured after all'. In fact the only surprise was that we didn't read the following:

HOW SICK CAN YOU GET?
Manchester United manager Sir Alex Ferguson yesterday hired six Govan heavies to abduct brave England star Paul Scholes. The Ginger Prince was bundled into the back of an untaxed Ford Cortina

and driven to a private clinic run by descendents of Martin Borman. The kraut quacks then performed an unnecessary operation on Scholes's knee using a Black and Decker powerdrill with a rusty bit. At a later press conference Ferguson held aloft a piece of gristle that had obviously been retrieved from the floor of a nearby sausage factory, declaring that the tissue had been removed from next to Scholes's arterial-cruciate-cartilage-ligament-kneecap-thingy, and was the reason why he hadn't played for England. Ferguson then slyly slipped the fatty-tissue into his top pocket for insertion into Rio Ferdinand's ankle and for display at his next rich-excuse press conference. An FA spokesman said reports were awaited from Greater Manchester police of an inquiry into a series of break-ins at the SoggyMeat sausage factory and the PlugInPower Hire Shop. Meanwhile Mr Keith Sad, Liberal Democrat MP for somewhere no one has ever heard of, said he was very cross to hear all of this.

Now from some reporters we don't expect a lot, and in that sense we are seldom disappointed. Take the tabloid man who is determined to rake up every last detail of the United-go-for-Eriksson-as-Ferguson-successor story. It's history, and nothing came of it, so why does it matter? It was apparently fine for the FA to tempt Eriksson away from Lazio (and devastate the Italian club's season in the process), just as it is fine for certain journalists to switch tabloids amid much rancour. But let United do a bit of headhunting and it becomes a treacherous scandal – well it would if the papers had their way.

When it begins to leave a sour taste is when people who should know better get in on the act. Step forward Mr Ron Atkinson of ITV. It is undeniable that despite a period of under-achievement under Atkinson, with just a couple of FA Cups added to the honours roll, many United fans retain a fondness for the man. Not only were there some great moments under his leadership (the 10 wins in a row and a certain night against Barcelona spring instantly to mind), but Atkinson contributed fifty per cent of football's greatest ever commentary in the final minutes of the European Cup final in 1999. But of late, perched on the ITV Premiership panel, he has done his current employer's bidding and has added his voice to the knocking campaign. Most ludicrously he summed up the Keane dismissal at Sunderland by arguing the need for Ferguson to give Keane a dressing down before his team-mates (bizarre in the extreme following events leading up to the World Cup). For a manager whose tenure is remembered for a first-team drink culture and for brushing under the carpet a training ground scrap between Remi Moses and Jesper Olsen, it seems a bit rich that he is now offering Sir Alex Ferguson advice on discipline and man-management.

A Hero – And Some Villains

November 2002. Former United goalkeeper Harry Gregg has published his autobiography.

"I have never been unfeeling, or felt wronged. Danny Blanchflower had me sussed. He once wrote: 'Harry Gregg doesn't fight, he fights back.' This will come as a shock to many, but I never wanted confrontation." – Harry Gregg.

Every once in a while a football book* appears to whet the appetite; the autobiography of a man with a tale to tell. The name of Harry Gregg means different things to different generations. Long-standing supporters will remember him as the Manchester United goalkeeper whose career spanned Munich. If your early days at Old Trafford coincided with Gregg's departure from the club, your first-hand recollections may be of the manager of clubs like Crewe, Swansea and Shrewsbury, who returned to Old Trafford in a coaching role under Dave Sexton. It is to be hoped that Harry Gregg will need no introduction to younger supporters. If you know your history, you know about Harry Gregg.

Whatever your generation it is likely that Harry Gregg is most instantly associated with the Munich disaster of 1958, for he was more than a survivor. He was a hero at the scene, and he has been a dignified bearer of the memory of that tragedy ever since. To many his is the definitive word on Munich and its aftermath, and for that reason alone the publication of his autobiography is a significant event. It is disconcerting therefore to read at the outset that Gregg does not wish to be remembered only as the hero of Munich. Straight away I was conscious that I had opened the book with precisely that perception in my mind. But he is correct, of course. There is so much more to him, and to his life, than that one event, however widely it casts its shadow. Nonetheless, his heroism on that airfield is well-chronicled, and is undoubted.

On that awful day the passengers sensed an accident was about to happen. People changed seats, they loosened their clothing. Gregg lifted his feet onto the back of the seat in front. He put down a juicy novel he was reading, not wishing to have it in his hand when he met his maker. Billy Whelan declared that if he was to die then he was ready. And then the aeroplane attempted take-off for a third time.

After the crash Gregg escapes from the plane and is told by the captain to run from likely explosion. But he goes back into the wreckage time and again. First he finds the baby, then its mother, then his team-mates one by one. Some are wounded – Charlton, Viollet and Blanchflower – others are dead. Some of the injuries are sickening; no doubt he spares us from the worst of the detail, but the horror is clear.

The emergency services at the scene are virtually non-existent. Gregg is taken to hospital on a coal wagon. It is at the hospital that the reality sinks in when, on the tannoy, he hears three words: "Herr Swift dead." Frank Swift, the great former Manchester City goalkeeper, was among the journalists killed at Munich. Given his legendary status in Maine Road history, his death makes the mentality of many modern City supporters all the more staggering. For in 2002, more than ever before, those people (not a small minority) bandy about the word 'Munich' in contempt for all things United. It is beyond all reason and beyond all decency.

We live in an age when compensation is regarded as a statutory right. Where the slightest bump in a car results in a claim for 'whiplash' injury, where you can claim for a fall if you simply weren't looking where you were walking. In 1958 you were on your own. Harry Gregg returned quickly to football, but couldn't understand why he suffered from headaches – it was a little while before anyone noticed that he had fractured his skull in the accident. Responsibility for the crash was never apportioned – recently uncovered documents show that the government was unwilling to upset the German authorities; it was easier to let the pilots take the blame than to ask questions of the airline and the airport authorities. Gregg was given £97 compensation for lost luggage by the BEA airline, rounded up to £100. But when he was subsequently awarded £750 for injury he was given a cheque for £747 to allow for the £3 extra he'd received for his baggage.

Others were treated more outrageously. Compensation, compassion and counselling were in short supply. Some surviving players, unable to resume their careers, were asked to leave their club houses. They carried their bitterness and their sadness to their own graves. All in all, the survivors and the families of those who died felt badly let down by the club. In effect, Gregg says the club has done virtually nothing, and that the memorial match in 1998 generated proceeds from the public, not from United. He acknowledges that senior management was decimated at Munich, and that the club was unable to function as normal, but points to a failure to rectify the situation in the intervening years. One excruciating example came on one occasion when the surviving players planned a reunion dinner at Old Trafford – the club restaurant offered them a reduced rate instead of making the players their guests. Gregg reserves anger, too, for those who have jumped on the bandwagon of Munich, who have exaggerated their role in the events, or who have embellished the facts as he saw them in their writings.

As United supporters we listen to Gregg in awe because of his actions in Munich. We all wonder, when we read tales of horror and tales of bravery, how we would have reacted ourselves. We would all like to think that we would have responded like Harry Gregg, that we would have returned to the wreckage time and again to bring out the wounded. But we fear that we would instead flee from the imminent explosion of aviation fuel. That is why we admire him so much and why (although he does not welcome this) we define him by his bravery.

But the book does place the hero in the context of the man. From a mixed Protestant/RC background in Northern Ireland he has (like Alex Ferguson) no time for religious bigotry. Religion remained important to him, despite the faith-shattering potential of Munich, to the extent that he considered withdrawing from Northern Ireland's 1958 World Cup squad in Sweden because games were to be played on Sundays. In the end the man who had been the world's most expensive goalkeeper when he signed for United for £23,500 in 1957 was voted the best goalkeeper at the World Cup in Sweden.

He was of course a tough and fiery customer (as he remains), never short of an opinion nor disinclined to share it. Angered by the challenge from Bolton's Nat Lofthouse in the 1958 FA Cup final that led to a goal, and defeat for United's makeshift team, Gregg sought revenge for some time afterwards. In the end he mistakenly clattered Lofthouse's team-mate (and Gregg's Northern Ireland colleague) Billy McAdams. Shades of Roy Keane, but the old protagonists Gregg and Lofthouse are now close friends.

For most United supporters under the age of 45 the early 1960s are something of a modern dark age. While the post-war period up to Munich is well-chronicled, the rebuilding phase, which occurred just prior to the advent of widespread television coverage, is less understood. The history books tend to glide over this era, rather than offering the depth of understanding that has emerged about the 1948 Cup winners and the Busby Babes. Harry Gregg provides some welcome insight into the relatively obscure early-1960s period (adding to the recollections of Eamon Dunphy in *A Strange Kind of Glory*) in an industry fighting for modernisation through the abolition of the maximum wage, whilst clouded by the match-fixing scandals of the time. This Manchester United provided the backdrop for Gregg as he built up a ridiculous catalogue of injury, not helped by the most primitive treatment regime imaginable. And there was more tragedy with the loss of his first wife; Gregg, the young father, was on the edge, but he rebuilt his life.

He left United in 1966, but remained in touch with events through football's intricate networks before returning home as a coach when Dave Sexton was manager at Old Trafford. There are some interesting observations on the disquiet behind the scenes at this time, before he was released by the incoming Ron Atkinson following Sexton's dismissal. What becomes apparent is that the club had lost its old spirit by this time. Although this is hardly a revelation to seasoned United supporters, Gregg's description of the deterioration in relationships, and the rise of bitterness and recrimination involving legendary figures such as Busby, Murphy and Charlton does not make happy reading. This is a sad book in so many ways. Harry Gregg also dabbled in the high politics of United, and his part in the attempted take-overs of the club by Robert Maxwell and Michael Knighton make fascinating, and bizarre, reading.

This is a relatively short book. There is probably much more to the Harry Gregg story than has been recounted, and the pre-United years are summarised briefly. But it tells the story of Munich and its aftermath in the words of someone who really matters. There is anger and sadness and regret. If you claim to be a Manchester United supporter it is your duty to read Harry Gregg's account of the defining event in the club's history, and when the time is right you should make sure your children and grandchildren read it too.

* Harry's Game – The Autobiography by Harry Gregg with Roger Anderson. Mainstream Publishing, 2002.

Fergie for England

December 2002. The England cricket team is struggling on its Ashes tour of Australia. But what has this got to do with United?

The departing chairman of the England and Wales Cricket Board, a gentleman called Lord MacLaurin, has reacted to a recent piece of public dissent from Darren Gough. In the light of the England team's humiliation in Australia, MacLaurin was quoted as saying "We don't have the discipline in the England side that Arsenal Football Club have", and he added "Arsene Wenger wouldn't allow anything like that to happen. They give very clear instructions to their players, and we have to move along that way".

Personally I had been under the misconception that the England cricket team was hopeless for the simple reason that you never see kids playing cricket anymore. Not in the streets, not in the schools, not in the parks. You can have all the indoor centres of excellence and 'Kwik Cricket' (or whatever it is called) schemes that you like, but you'll never have a national sport that is healthy and strong unless it is being played by large proportions of the working classes, using dustbins as wickets. It can be no coincidence that England have not won the Ashes in all the years since I last saw an upturned tennis racket being used as a makeshift cricket bat in front of a lamp-post wicket. A game that is confined to centres and schemes will surely go the way of British tennis. I can't be the only former cricket devotee whose interest has drifted away from a sport that has sought to make itself more appealing by having the Lancashire players wear fleecy jumpers with their names and numbers on the back. Maybe they should have gone the whole Arsenal hog and adopted red shirts with white sleeves and a cannon motif on the badge.

I was, though, intrigued by the suggestion that English cricket should call for an Arsene Wenger to resolve some of its problems. Now, all you cynics out there may be slightly bemused by the thought that the cricket team needs to adopt the dubious disciplinary standards of the men from Highbury, but I implore you to think about it a little more carefully. For a start, there are no red cards in cricket, so a Wenger-led cricket team would at least be assured of remaining at full strength for ninety minutes – and let's face it, the current lot are struggling to compete with Australia for an hour and a half as it is. There may be the occasional flying elbow to contend with, and I know this isn't really cricket, but it wouldn't half shake up those snarling, sledging Aussie slip fielders. Their catching may not be as cockily assured if Oleg Luzhny was applying a size ten boot up their backsides while a thin outside edge was hurtling towards them.

You might even think about appointing Wenger as a test match umpire. Brett Lee would charge in, send one down to Nasser Hussein at about 200

---

miles an hour, and watch it crash into the batsman's pads right in front of middle stump. He'd turn round to Umpire Wenger and appeal for an LBW, only to have the impervious umpire reply "I am sorry, but I did not see the incident, and anyway I think it would be harsh to punish this batsman". You can see how this is now starting to sound like a good idea?

One drawback (along with the fact that the wicket-keeper would have a ridiculous pony-tail) would be that the England cricket team would have to include about nine foreigners, mostly Frenchmen. Clearly this would be against the rules, and in any case having the Ashes won by France would probably be less acceptable than losing them to Australia. And isn't French cricket something else altogether, a game that involves standing in one place, unable to move your feet, while trying to prevent a tennis ball from striking you on the back of the leg? If our lot started playing like that someone would surely notice – but, hang on, I think I may just have realised what our players have been up to all winter Down Under. Maybe Wenger is already managing the bloody cricket team after all.

But recent football results suggest that Wenger's magic wand is not all it was cracked up to be in the heady, early weeks of the campaign when the oracles of the tabloid media took part in a lurid, yet predictable, sycophancy festival. It is amazing that United (empire crumbling, greatness remaining only in their own minds) were by mid-December just one point behind Arsenal (best club side ever, and likely to go through the season undefeated) at the top of the table. It was suggested that even Brazil would prove no match for the brilliant Arsenal, a view that with the passing of a few short weeks now sounds risible. I can only think with hindsight that they were actually proposing a game of French cricket on Copacabana beach.

Given that the England cricketers often look like a group of nervous bunnies caught in the glare of some dazzling Australian headlights, it would seem to me that an Alex Ferguson, not an Arsene Wenger, would be more effective in rescuing the team from its current plight. Sir Alex is not, you will be aware, the most softly spoken of chaps when victory or defeat is on the line. I reckon that only a batsman capable of facing a Fergie bashing in an antipodean pavilion should be allowed to go onto the field to face Australia. Let's face it, if you are intimidated by a portly, peroxide spin bowler with sun block painted all over his face you wouldn't last two minutes in a Manchester United dressing room when Fergie is on the rampage. It is difficult to choose between a McGrath bouncer on the helmet or a Fergie tea-pot flying around your head – at least you're holding a bat for self-protection when you're facing McGrath.

Remember Alex Ferguson has already demonstrated his magic touch in one other sporting arena, namely on the racetrack. Rumour has it that at the start of the flat season he gathered his horses together in the stables and produced a sealed envelope from his top pocket. "This envelope," he declared, "contains the name of one of you. It is the name of the horse that I consider is not hungry enough to maintain the required levels of success. But please understand that there are lots of hungry doggies out there, and that you can be replaced." No wonder that Rock of Gibraltar got its backside in gear to such stunning effect. I wonder how it would do opening the bowling?

After Being Famous

*January 2003. Football supporters don't change clubs, but what about players?
Once a Red, always a Red?*

In *As You Like It*, Shakespeare talked of the Seven Ages of Man:

> *All the world's a stage,*
> *And all the men and women merely players,*
> *They have their exits and their entrances;*
> *And one man in his time plays many parts,*
> *His acts being seven ages.*

Association Football was a long way off when those words were penned, but
they still ring strangely true – although today all the world is a football pitch.
I'd say, as well, that there are not seven but Three Ages of Fan.

We spend our early years, the First Age, dreaming of being a Manchester
United player one day. Hour after solitary hour is spent kicking a ball against
the kitchen wall or against a garage door, while an inner voice provides an
inspiring commentary: *"Crerand to Law, and on to Smith ... Oh! It's another
wonderful goal for this brilliant young Manchester United star! The City
players are on their knees yet again. Five-nil. Matt Busby is applauding.
Just listen to the Stretford End roar."* You are in a magical world of your
own, only putting the ball away to practise signing your autograph.

We slip into adulthood, and it dawns on us that we are older than the United
youth team, and eventually older than half the first team. Having missed the
talent-boat, the Second Age of United Fan is therefore spent in the poorer of
the parallel player/fan worlds. Our peers are living our dreams, but we
accept our walk-on roles, our crowd-scenes. When we see a player like
Gary Neville so obviously appreciating his talent, and simply loving being a
United player, we see someone doing it the way we think we would too. At
least, as mere fans, we are not alone – 99 per cent of professionals with
other clubs would probably like to play for United as well.

And then all of a sudden we are too old to be professional footballers
anyway. In the Third Age our childhood heroes reach their sixties, and
people start talking a funny new language. The ground becomes a stadium
and the club becomes a brand. It can be pretty bewildering at times, but we
still retain our natural affinity to the United player – and now to the former
player as well.

Manchester United players have an aura. It doesn't always come from
within, it comes from the club they represent. Today there is a buzz about
being in the same room as a Ruud Van Nistelrooy that is somehow more

exciting that brushing shoulders with a former player. Certain legends are exceptions to this (Law, Best, Cantona, for example), but men who in their day were very good United players tend to reassume mortal characteristics once their playing days are over. No longer superstars, some even revert to being ordinary blokes – often good blokes, and United fans as well.

Being firmly in the Third Age now, I feel able to relate to the phenomenon that is the former-player. He was, after all, one of my heroes once. It's nice when he treads the Old Trafford turf to do the half-time raffle, and it's pleasing when he gets a good reception. Sometimes half the crowd is too young to remember him, and it's sad to think that some old United stars receive a welcome that is muted in comparison with some half-baked celebrity the week before.

Of course being a footballer is not all joy, and for some a club is simply an employer rather than an object of passion. But when players have loved the game and have loved the limelight, it is right that they should be able to bask in a little well-earned glory at the end of their road. If we fantasise about playing for United, we also fantasise about becoming a legend. Legends survive, and are created by their own deeds. But not all former United players are able to do this, for various reasons. How sad it is when a former United player passes up the opportunity to remain a legend because of the circumstances of his leaving, or because he was unable to respect his former public.

My own number one hero, as I've mentioned many a time, is the great Denis Law. Here we have a man who signed for Manchester City twice, and who scored 'that goal' against the United as we were relegated in 1974. But that deed – although it did not condemn United, as is the popular myth – hurt Law as much as relegation hurt the United supporters. Law remained a Red, and an enduring legend. Denis Law represents, in so many ways, what so many of us would like to have become.

And we have Eric Cantona. The only other player to have been called 'the King' at Old Trafford, whose name is still sung at every game, almost six years after he departed. It helped that Eric refused to play for another club, but it needn't have been a problem. Take, for example, Mark Hughes, who played with distinction for Chelsea, Southampton and Blackburn after he left us, winning silverware at two of those clubs. At Chelsea especially he was successful at times against United, but he didn't rub it in. He did his job for them, acted professionally as he had to do, but with dignity too. He didn't go in for ear-cupping and fist-clenching in our faces. We were grateful for that, and now his status as one of the favourite sons of Old Trafford is sealed.

Which brings me on to Paul Ince. I watched a video of the 1992/93 championship season recently; it was a momentous year, and it hardly seems possible that ten years have now passed since we became champions again. Seeing Ince driving United on, and recalling his fine goal at Crystal Palace on the night when we moved to within a stride of the finishing line, you could never have predicted that it would all end in tears. Whatever went on behind the scenes no United fan was pleased to see Ince leave for Internazionale, and many kept an eye on his progress there as we did for Hughes in Barcelona. All it took was a few nice comments from Ince to his former fans in Manchester, and we'd have happily overlooked the transfer to Anfield as we had Law's to City all those years before.

Was it inevitable, because it was Liverpool, that Ince had to fall out with us in order to be accepted by them? I don't know. How significant was Fergie's publicised description of Ince as a big-time Charlie? And was this intended for public consumption anyway? I'm not even sure that I know who is to blame any more, but to me it is a shame that a player who was magnificent for us in the 1990 FA Cup final replay, and who was part of our brilliant 1993 and 1994 team, is now firmly an ex-Liverpool player, and not an ex-United player. His antics after scoring their late equaliser in the 2-2 at Anfield in 1999, clearly hoping he'd denied United a title as the Bayern Munich flags waved across the Kop, were sad to behold. Imagine how Law or Hughes would have behaved in similar circumstances.

So what has brought all of this to my mind? Well to be honest I'm worried about how Peter Schmeichel will eventually figure in the hall of legends. Here we have a man who was clearly our greatest-ever goalkeeper, and the bedrock of so many triumphs. It matters not a jot to us that he may have rubbed up his team-mates, notably Roy Keane, from time to time. A place in the pantheon of United greats awaits him. But is he in danger of messing it up and, worse, does he even care? At the Villa Park FA Cup tie last season, Schmeichel ignored the tribute from the United fans behind his goal – surely a steely determination to win any game you are involved in doesn't mean things should be taken this far? And then there was Maine Road earlier this season. I'm not sure what the Danish is for 'magnanimous' but I suspect it isn't a term that figures high on our former keeper's list of important attributes. Was the fist-clenching a move to gain acceptance from his new public or just a thoughtless act? Either was it was pretty unedifying, considering who he is. Is there still time to fix the damage? I think I still hope so, but it may be his move now.

So I never did fulfil those childhood dreams; few of us ever do. But I still feel luckier than some who were blessed with the necessary talent and the good fortune of opportunity. Because I'd rather never have been a United player than be an ex-United player who has fallen out of love with the club.

On Juventus and Socks

February 2003. Juventus are due in town; their visits are often memorable.

The first time I saw Juventus play was in October 1976, in a UEFA Cup second round tie. Because I am sad like that, I still have my ticket from the match. It is a proper football match ticket – none of your computer printed strips of card containing holograms, or with your name printed on the front. This one is coloured bright pink, and has the signature of the United secretary, Les Olive, on the face, rather like a banknote contains the autograph of some top man from the Bank of England. The ticket was for the Stretford End Paddock, which for those of you too young to remember was a large area of terrace that stretched from the old tunnel on the half-way line right up to the roof behind the corner flag – the corner where you will find the current players' tunnel. In those days the terracing changed from concrete in the lower half to timber in the upper reaches, and it was from such a lofty position that I watched the match.

The ticket marks a bit of a watershed, for imprinted upon it is the price of admission – one pound. It was the first time I'd ever paid a quid to watch a game of football, since United had added a cool 20p to the normal ticket price for this match. At the time I thought this was a bit much, since the tickets had only been uplifted by 10p (to 90p) for the previous round against Ajax. And so there is it, a great big squiggly £ sign staring out of the ticket, as if to say 'This is only the beginning, my gullible captive friend'. And so it was.

Needless to say I also still have the match programme (price 12p), though unusually for me it has been somewhat defaced. You see, I was so upset at the underhand and not-so-underhand antics of the Italian team that I wrote the word 'Animal' under most of the photographs of the Juventus players that adorned the centre pages. I was nothing if not meticulous in my condemnation however, for I spared those members of the Juve squad that had not taken part in the match (Gori, Marchetti and Spinosi), and I also decided that the goalkeeper, Zoff, had not transgressed sufficiently to be worthy of the slur. Zoff always seemed to remain serene, and detached from the carnage around him; no nutty goalkeeper, was he. The guilty ten, the outfield players, were thus given that most typically English insult for dirty foreign players (copyright Alf Ramsey, 1966). They were: Cuccureddu, Gentile, Furino (captain), Morini, Scirea, Causio, Tardelli, Boninsegna, Benetti and Bettega.

That list of names, plus Zoff the keeper, will probably prompt one of two reactions from you. Either you will shrug your shoulders (in which case you are probably under the age of 40), or you will emit a low whistle of appreciation, because there are some legendary names of European and

World Cup football in there. Looking back on it (and on the scary set of mugshots in the programme), our young United team probably emitted a few low whistles of their own that night. It was an evening when the men against boys cliché was quite appropriate. In the event United won the match 1-0, but only in terms of the first leg scoreline. What Juventus had done was to soften up our team to the extent that upon leaving the field that night no one had any doubt as to the probable aggregate outcome following the second leg in the heaving bear-pit of the Stadio Communale, a match in which United were duly mauled, losing 0-3.

Juventus in those days were an impressive sight as they took to the field on their own ground: thin black and white stripes on shirts designed to emphasise physique; their shorts and socks, dazzling white. They were, quite simply, unmistakeably Juventus. (For the record, their shorts were black at Old Trafford because ours were white.) These days they look a pale shadow of their former selves, wearing a kit that has been desecrated by designers with no sense of modern history – in their broad stripes, and with black shorts and socks, they resemble Grimsby Town more than their illustrious and cunning predecessors (well, at least until they kick off). Now I've said it they'll probably go and prove me wrong, but I predict that you won't see a true renaissance in Italian football until Juventus (and for that matter AC Milan too) revert to the cool white shorts and socks.

United, on the other hand, should scrap the current gimmick of wearing white socks for European games, and get back to the proper black (with red and white tops) that were good enough for the Busby Babes. What UEFA needs is a special technical sub-committee to act as a sock-police, with powers to impose punitive-sounding fines in thousands of Swiss francs that equate to about £27.64p, and if that sub-committee needs a chairman, then I'm your man. (And while we're at it, Mr Barthez and Mr Ferdinand, we'll not have you pulling your socks up above your knees.)

All of which isn't perhaps as silly as it sounds. We now on occasion see referees instruct players to tuck their shirts in or pull their socks up (though there may be an age concession in the latter instance, to judge from the hosiery of Laurent Blanc). Maybe that's why Juventus got away with numerous counts of assault in 1976 – they were so smartly turned out that the referee decided to overlook less serious offences such as kicking Coppell and Hill nine feet in the air.

I did, however, think I'd noticed one new rule of association football in the most recent home game against our friends Juventus. You may recall that Ryan Giggs was receiving treatment off the pitch, behind United's goal, and that when he sought permission to return to the field the referee ordered Giggs to trot round the pitch to the half-way line before he let him back on. I was a bit mystified at the time, but who am I to question any ruling by Mr Kim Milton Neilsen? But in the second half of the same game any remaining confidence I had in my knowledge of the rules of the game suffered a further jolt, as Mikael Silvestre, in precisely the same circumstance as Giggs had found himself earlier, was waved back onto the field from behind the goal. Now you are quite welcome to submit your answers on a postcard care-of the editor of Red News, but since we must accept that this esteemed international referee knows his stuff, my theory is as follows. Clearly Mr Neilsen, unimpressed by United's recent tactical formation, was simply stretching his authority a bit with the intention of giving a little help to our out of form number 11. Whereas we all thought he'd ordered Giggs to make his way up the touchline before returning to the pitch from half-way, his actual words to him were probably something along the lines of "You're not coming on this field unless you get back on the left wing where you belong!". If there are any lip-readers among the Red News readership who specialise in Danish accents (and perhaps with some experience of the Schmeichel-Wright lip-reading saga of a few years ago), any light you can cast on this matter would be greatly appreciated.

Red Barrels and Chianti Reds

March 2003: European football wasn't always about the European Cup or the Champions' League. And pre-season matches didn't always involve a stint in the Far East.

The staple diet of English football is the league and the two domestic cup competitions. For the top sides European competitions make up a hefty season. But there have always been experiments with new competitions, as well as occasional one-off tournaments. Manchester United, needless to say, have never been far from the invitations. Most United fans will have uninspiring memories of the Screen Sport Super Cup (1985/86) and the mouthful that was the Mercantile Credit Football League Centenary Trophy (1988), but at least we were spared participation in the pointless Full Members Cup, also known as the Simod Cup and the Zenith Data Systems Cup (1986-1992). We also managed to avoid the futile exercise of the Texaco Cup/Anglo-Scottish Cup, a competition that staggered on under various formats between 1971 and 1981. But we didn't get off completely in those dark days.

The year 1970 was supposed to represent the beginning of a bright new decade. At least it seemed so at the time, and the very sound of that year seemed to have a futuristic ring as we emerged from the 1960s. But 1970 was a grim time for Manchester United. Champions of Europe in 1968, the club was heading down a slippery slope that led to relegation by 1974. As early as 1970 the writing was firmly on the wall. The 1968 team had clearly withered, though it is not true to say that the team had simply aged. Certainly some great players were in the twilight of illustrious careers (Brennan, Foulkes, Crerand, Charlton), but others were hampered by long-standing injuries (Law and Stiles), and there was a group of youngish players who should still have had long United careers ahead of them (Best, Kidd, Sadler, Aston) but who, for various reasons, were unable to form the core of the next great United side. Sir Matt Busby handed over to Wilf McGuinness; it was a messy transition, and we'll perhaps never know the extent to which the upcoming reserves were hindered by the general state of the place.

It was a time of glitzy £100,000 transfer fees (proof at the time that football had gone quite mad), but United's fans stood by as the likes of Gordon Banks, Martin Peters and Geoff Hurst switched clubs with United virtually inactive in the transfer market. Ian Ure arrived from Arsenal in 1969, but was unable to prevent United's defence from becoming a national joke; he lasted just a season and a half. The only other significant signing around this time was Willie Morgan, who did serve with distinction for several seasons.

It was against this backdrop that, in the summer of 1970, United took part in the first Watney Cup competition, a pre-season event that featured two teams from each of the four divisions of the Football League. The participating sides were invited on the basis of goals scored in the previous season.

Now, the Watney Cup has come to be regarded as a bit of an historic oddity, even a source of some amusement, but from my youthful perspective at the time it was actually a competition I wanted to see United win. Because I simply wanted to see United win something, and I wanted to be able to feel that United were still a great team despite all the evidence to the contrary. I suppose many fans will remember the games that took place on a Saturday-Wednesday-Saturday at the start of August that year, but I wonder how many people remember the free Watney Cup newspapers that were given out in local off-licences to publicise the tournament? I got mine from a local corner shop outdoor that had a strong smell of ale and a couple of hand pumps for serving draught – I think I bought a bag of peanuts as an excuse to take a copy of the Watney Cup papers, but despite being something of a hoarder where all things-United are concerned, I no longer seem to have them.

The tournament had a sufficiently high profile for it to be covered on *Match of the Day* and, since we didn't play any of our matches at Old Trafford, it was through that medium that I followed the games, beginning with a 3-2 win at a sunny Reading. On the Wednesday we played in the semi-final, away to Hull City, and a little piece of history was made. The game ended 1-1 after extra-time, but United reached the final by winning a penalty shoot-out. I don't know if this was the first penalty shoot-out that United had been involved in, but as far as I can recall it was the first under competition conditions, and the novelty of it helped disguise the fact that United had made hard work of reaching the final against Derby County. Derby were a very good team at that time, and were on the verge of several fine seasons that saw them win the league a couple of times. United were duly hammered 4-1 in front of a big crowd at the Baseball Ground, a result that was as depressing as it was predictable. I wonder if I threw away my Watney Cup newspapers in disappointment that night?

United were invited to enter the Watney Cup again the following year, but it was a sad sight to see our still-sliding team crash out in the first game at Halifax Town. Our side, including Crerand, Charlton, Law and Best, lost 2-1, and it proved to be a final appearance in a United shirt for Pat Crerand, a player for whom I had a special affection since he scored the first goal I ever saw at Old Trafford – in December 1966.

As things went from bad to worse at our club I had to resort to taking some pride in the fact that United won the Daily Express 5-a-side tournament at Wembley Arena (or the Empire Pool, as it was known then). The slide towards the second division duly continued apace, but not before United embarked on another peculiar tournament adventure in the form of the Anglo-Italian Cup competition towards the end of 1972/73.

The Anglo-Italian Tournament has had a strange history, first emerging in the late 1960s, and then again at various intervals (and with changing formats) up until 1996. United's foray was billed at the time as a means of preparing the squad (and the fans, presumably) for our return to European competition. We had been unable to qualify for Europe since we were unfairly eliminated from the European Cup at the semi-final stage of 1969, but although we were desperate for a return, this wasn't quite what we had in mind.

The United team by now included the great Martin Buchan, signed from Aberdeen towards the end of 1971/72, and a clutch of other Scottish players signed by Tommy Docherty, heralding a tartan craze on the terraces: Alex Forsyth, George Graham, Jim Holton and Lou Macari. In the tournament's complex group phase United were pitted against Fiorentina, Lazio, Bari and Verona, playing each of those teams just once. We began with a pretty forgettable 1-1 draw at home to Fiorentina before travelling to Rome to play Lazio. Lazio were not the famous name then that they have since become, but we soon knew all about them, as our team received a brutal welcome in what was at the time the accepted 'Latin' tradition. It always seemed ironic that Latin was the language of civilisation and of learning; Latin represented a culture of colour, vitality and passion; but in the football sense Latin meant violence and clean sheets (in the sense of goals-against!). Anyway, nil-nil away to Lazio seemed OK to me under the circumstances.

Back at home we beat Bari 3-1 before a crowd of just 14,000, and we finished the group with a 4-1 win at Verona. And that was that, as we failed to qualify for the next stage. I suppose no one was too bothered, and the fact that no one remembers that Newcastle United won the Anglo-Italian Tournament that year just goes to show how little it all mattered in the overall scheme of things. But it would have been nice at the time. And in the event, the Anglo-Italian did not prepare United for a return to Europe either – instead a brief return to the second division was on the horizon. There is one postscript to that particular campaign, however. On 2 May 1973 Bobby Charlton was in the team that beat Verona in front of just 8,000 fans. It was Charlton's last match for United, and he scored two of our goals, and so in a way the tournament does provide one significant footnote to the United story.

Rising from the Dead: A Review of 2002/2003

April 2003: United, on the ropes in the autumn, were closing in on an eighth championship in eleven seasons. We went on to win the league by five points.

It is not easy reviewing a season when there are still two crucial games to play (against Charlton Athletic and Everton), games that will determine whether United have made one of the all time great comebacks to snatch a delicious championship or whether we will fall just short, left to spend the summer ruing some ludicrous dropped points. But in a way this is the best position from which to take an objective look at the season – looking back with the title in the bag can make criticism seem churlish, whereas a review from the empty-handed perspective can take the shine off the achievement of being so close to a title at all.

It seems so long ago that Rio Ferdinand's prolonged transfer was finally sealed, and the team embarked on a campaign perhaps surrounded more by hope than expectation from the terraces. After all, the defence – our weak link as evidenced by the club's willingness to pay so handsomely for the acquisition of Ferdinand – was immediately hit by injuries to Rio himself and to Brown in Hungary, while Gary Neville was still recovering from the broken foot that had kept him away from the World Cup. Instead United turned again to Blanc, and to the relatively inexperienced O'Shea, and although the latter excelled throughout, the team stuttered (and occasionally self-destructed) from August to the end of November.

At home we struggled to score a goal – just one from open play in our first four league games, and that a late effort against a West Bromwich side whose inadequacies would soon become apparent to the whole league. More puzzlingly we began that match with only Van Nistelrooy as a spearhead, but more of 4-5-1 later.

Away from home we fared no better. By the end of November we had been victorious only at Charlton, and we came away from Sunderland, Leeds, Fulham, Manchester City and West Ham with a mere three points in total. This was not a team of obvious championship potential, and to make matters worse the media circus that accompanied Roy Keane following his dismissal at Sunderland, the publication of his book, and his encounters with the disciplinary people from the FA gave United the air of a club in some turmoil. Keane's subsequent lengthy absence for serious hip surgery helped calm the hysteria, but his influence on the pitch was sorely missed.

To make matters worse Arsenal and Liverpool were steaming ahead, and we faced a run of fixtures against these two sides, plus Newcastle, that would either keep us hanging to the leaders' coat-tails (if we achieved the miracle of nine points), or leave us scrapping around among the also-rans.

Needless to say, United, without Keane, Beckham and Ferdinand won all three matches, with notable input from Phil Neville, Fortune and the returning Brown.

As United put a nice little run together, Arsenal (tipped not to lose all season) stumbled slightly, while Liverpool fell flat on their faces. By Christmas we had started to get all giddy again, whereupon our team delivered the reality check of back-to-back defeats at Blackburn and Middlesbrough. But just as we duly readjusted our expectations downwards, the team embarked on a remarkable run of results. There were six straight league victories, plus progress towards the League Cup final and demolitions of Portsmouth and West Ham in the FA Cup. Suddenly all was looking rosy on the home front yet again, though the fans' outlook seemed to be based on fingers-crossed, as opposed to the cock-sure crowing still emanating from the vicinity of Highbury.

And sure enough we received another smack in the face just as we dared to contemplate silverware. Following a depressing home draw against Manchester City (the ultimate game of two halves), we were knocked out of the FA Cup by Arsenal at Old Trafford, with the visitors building on immense good fortune to prevail with some ease, enraging Fergie and ensuring another week of saturation drivel in the tabloids. Then we could only gain a last-gasp equaliser away to Bolton on a day when Manchester City surrendered to Arsenal – it seemed to spell curtains for our late title challenge. The following week Arsenal's lead was extended to eight points as United suffered defeat in the League Cup final to Liverpool, a result built on a lucky first half deflection and second half heroics by their goalkeeper. Some said Liverpool were the better side, but everyone said that their goalie was man of the match – it is hard to reconcile those two points of view.

Anyway, it seemed like our last chance of domestic silverware had passed us by, and so our eyes looked to Europe where United had reached the quarter finals of the Champions' League for the seventh consecutive season – a tremendous achievement that seldom receives due acknowledgement. It had been another long and grinding road, starting out with a qualifying round against that team from Hungary with a long name beginning with 'Z'. United breezed through the two group phases in some comfort, as the plan of supporting Van Nistelrooy with a roving Giggs or Scholes came into its own, and as Veron revelled on the international stage. If the first group phase was a fairly routine stroll, the second saw United's domestic winter revival mirrored abroad, with major successes over Deportivo and Juventus – especially Juventus – warming the heart. After all that we drew Real Madrid in the quarter final. And we were eliminated of course, so missing the chance to compete in an Old Trafford final. There have been too many of these dream final venues in recent years – remember the potential poignancy of a Munich final in 1997, and the promise of a Hampden homecoming for Fergie last year? Maybe we should lobby for the next few finals to be played way off United's romance-radar – they say Transylvania is nice in May. But at least United's elimination at the hands of Real (mainly Raul and Ronaldo) was done in the United way – a totally glorious tie that featured two of the best games of football in Europe this season, with our home leg (won 4-3) sure to be remembered for many a year. When we do it our way – the Matt Busby way – nobody does it better. And it was interesting to see Real widely described as the world's best club team – possibly correctly, of course – when the English tabloids had been suggesting for most of the season that that title belonged to Arsenal on the back of a decent start in the Premiership. Still, I'm sure they all know what they are talking about.

By the time United played Real Madrid the league blips against Manchester City and Bolton had been forgotten. United were now in scintillating form, led by the rampaging Van Nistelrooy. Five straight wins were capped by a 4-0 battering of Liverpool and a 6-2 massacre of Newcastle at St James's. With Newcastle now eliminated from the title race it was between United and Arsenal as we headed to Highbury on a warm Wednesday evening in April. The Gunners' early season self-assurance had been rocked by another stumble in the league and by being bundled out of the Champions' League second group stage without winning a game at home. Fergie made some (fairly accurate) observations about excessive pride preceding a fall, and Arsenal seemed duly niggled. It was a massive match. Defeat for either side could have ended title aspirations; the resulting draw suited United better. Despite both Arsenal goals being of dubious legality – the second being perhaps the most offside goal not disallowed all season – the Arsenal manager complained of injustice owing to the dismissal of his centre-half. But Fergie seemed more than content as he clenched his fists towards the United supporters after the final whistle, and we went home knowing that the Wizard was satisfied.

And so to the run-in. We receive the gift of a Bolton fight back against Arsenal at the Reebok: 2-2 from 0-2. We must win at Spurs the following day, and we do. We have two games left and a five point lead; Arsenal have a game in hand. If the boot was on the other foot I'd have conceded the title now, but because I support Manchester United I remain cautious, and hopeful. No Wenger-like predictions of victory from the United camp. But if we do go on to win it, it will be the loveliest of championships. 1993 was special because of the wait – the next six were special in their own way too – but for sheer against-all-odds courage in climbing a mountain as the preening Arsenal camp looked down and tried to tread on our fingers this could well be the most satisfying of them all. If it happens.

And if it doesn't then we can still have reason to be proud of our team, and to be pleased that United seem to have been reborn in the last few months. If we feared that the bubble may have burst on the day we trooped out of Maine Road for the last time, then we now know better. Fergie is revelling in it again, and Roy Keane – our most honest self-critic – says the spirit is at an all time high. United have won the FA Youth Cup – a significant barometer of the health of the club – and from those ranks John O'Shea has emerged, looking every inch a true Manchester United Player. Things aren't looking bad at all any more.

United Road, Take Me Home

June 2003: An epilogue.

Last month United Road, Sir Matt Busby Way and the other streets around Old Trafford belonged to Italy, as Milan overcame Juventus in a penalty shoot-out at the end of a cagey European Cup final. The real sense of occasion was provided by the supporters of those clubs in the hours before the game, and as they watched events unfold from seats that normally belong to us. In some respects the true drama was in the stands, and was etched on the faces of the Italian fans as the contest reached sudden death on a warm Manchester night. For one side there would be the ecstasy of victory, for the other devastation, but as the penalties began neither side was embracing eventual glory. Instead every face seemed to reveal a dread of possible defeat. The fear appeared all-consuming, and seemed to spread to the legs of some of the world's finest footballers, as the task of beating a goalkeeper from 12 yards out took on immense proportions.

The apparent reluctance of both sides to claim the game in open play, to take a chance on attack, made zero-zero more likely with every passing second. The defending was superb, and the touch of the midfield players was so impressive given the miniscule amounts of space and time available to them. You had to be a very good player to play well in that match, but the technical qualities of the game negated the sporting objective. The penalty shoot-out, for all its intrinsic lack of satisfaction, at least has the effect of removing the shields of the combatants. The penalty taker no longer has ten comrades with whom he can nullify his opposition; instead he must look his opponent directly in the eye and show that he is good enough, or else make that lonely walk back to the centre of the field. And the goalkeeper, he no longer has the protection of his defence – he will at last meet the forward face to face.

In the end the joy belonged to Milan and the despair went to Juventus, and it was impossible not to sense the real disappointment of their coach Lippi as he walked crestfallen around the field, expressionless except for the emptiness in his eyes. Manchester United supporters, having had hopes of a participating role in this European Cup final, were able to empathise with the Juventus section of the crowd, for if you follow football for long enough you experience the crushing of your hopes from time to time, and you become able to recall instantly just how rotten it feels.

At the 1999 European Cup final we were preparing for long journeys home with the unwelcome companion of defeat, and we were just preparing to deal with it when we were sent headlong into the raptures of the ultimate victory. Thus we knew just how fantastic it was this time for the followers of Milan, especially having overcome such intense domestic rivals. Can you imagine how we would feel if United beat Liverpool in Rome? And can you imagine how unbearable it would be if we lost? So the Milan fans, if they are anything like we were four years ago, are probably still glowing from the memories of journeys down their own road to Manchester, a city that will forever hold a special place in their hearts.

Only football is like this. All right, I don't know, maybe there are cricket teams or baseball teams, or what have you, around the world that do this to their supporters. But only football does it across the whole of the world, and only football has done it for so long. Football, so entrenched in its communities that most of its teams are named after places. Football, as Alex Ferguson said, bloody hell!

United Road, then, isn't just a street that runs round the back of Old Trafford, *a place where we belong ... to see United.* If we care about United – if we've been bitten by the bug – then United Road runs in parallel with our lives. Memories of football games, of players, of triumphs and disasters are intertwined with all of life's experiences. United provide so many of our milestones – dates mean championships and cup victories, defeats and relegation, as well as birthdays and anniversaries.

It's a road without end, of course, stretching on and on. Eventually it will be followed by our children and grandchildren. Who knows where it will lead, and what fun they'll have on the way.

ISBN 141200700-3

9 781412 007009